THE STEPPES ARE THE COLOUR OF SEPIA

map on page 30 : Alexandrowsk = Saporozh'je

The Steppes Are the Colour of Sepia

❖

A Mennonite Memoir

Connie Braun

RONSDALE PRESS

THE STEPPES ARE THE COLOUR OF SEPIA
Copyright © 2008 Connie Braun

RONSDALE PRESS
3350 West 21st Avenue
Vancouver, B.C., Canada
v6s 1G7

Typesetting: Julie Cochrane, in Bodoni 11.5 pt on 15
Cover Design: David Drummond
Cover Photo: Ukraine Wheat Field
Paper: FSC-Silva EDI.110 WH (100% recycled)

Ronsdale Press wishes to thank the following for their support of its publishing program: the Canada Council for the Arts, the Government of Canada through the Book Publishing Industry Development Program (BPIDP), and the Province of British Columbia through the Book Publishing Tax Credit Program and the British Columbia Arts Council.

Library and Archives Canada Cataloguing in Publication

Braun, Connie
    The Steppes are the colour of sepia: a Mennonite memoir / Connie Braun.

Includes bibliographical references and index.
ISBN 978-1-55380-063-7

    1. Letkemann family. 2. Mennonites — Ukraine — Social conditions — 20th century. 3. Mennonites — Soviet Union — Social conditions — 20th century.
4. Mennonites — Canada — History — 20th century. 5. Mennonites — Canada — Biography. I. Title.

FC106.M45B73 2008   289.7'71   C2008-904738-9

At Ronsdale Press we are committed to protecting the environment. To this end we are working with Markets Initiative (www.oldgrowthfree.com) and printers to phase out our use of paper produced from ancient forests. This book is one step towards that goal.

Printed in Canada by Marquis Book Printing, Quebec, Canada

In Memory of
Jakob and Maria

To my parents
Peter and Erna,
with love and gratitude

And for Alecia, Erik
and Mathew,
along with my love
to Erv

ACKNOWLEDGEMENTS

❖

To my dad, I lovingly express my appreciation for entrusting me to write his story, and for the freedom to put it together in my own way.

This story could not have become a book without the help of many others. Mary Hark, Helen Schlauwitz, Liz Janzen and Greta Loeppky (the Letkeman women) provided me with invaluable memories, facts and photographs. My late father-in-law, George Braun, transcribed pages of my grandmother's Bible, Dora Dueck transcribed and translated verses of my grandmother's poetry, and Linda Buhler has been a generous source of genealogical information. Through the work of the volunteers at the Mennonite Historical Society in Winnipeg and Abbotsford, a project like this one is possible. A special thanks to Helmut T. Huebert and William Schroeder for the use of their maps, and to Marketa Goetz-Stankiewicz for her help with the German transcription. I have also depended on the work of many historians and writers of Mennonite heritage. I particularly wish to thank Marlene Epp, Bruce Guenther and Elsie K. Neufeld, along with author John Bentley Mays for assisting me in "the beginning."

The professors of Trinity Western University have generously encouraged me to explore and develop ideas concerning the ethics of narrative, the stories of the marginalized, historiography, the phenomenology of memory, and the concept of transcendence. I especially wish to express my thanks to Lynn Szabo for her enduring support. I am also grateful to the readers of this story in its earlier form — as a gift to my dad for his seventy-fifth birthday, March 2006. Finally, my thanks to Ronsdale Press for standing behind this story, and to Ronald Hatch for his kind and patient attention to this work, page by page, from cover to cover.

CONTENTS

❖

AUTHOR'S NOTE

❖

The history of the place I write about is a complex one. Prior to the twentieth century it was simply known as "Russia," and the vast empire encompassed the region known as "the Ukraine," where this story begins.

During the era of 1922–1991, the territory of late Imperial Russia is properly referred to as the Soviet Union, and Ukraine is not merely a region but a union republic. However, the descendants of those who lived under the Czar, and those who remembered the great upheaval of the Revolution and the early years of Soviet Communism, have, in common parlance, referred to this immense land of the steppes as "Russia." Throughout this narrative I retain the speakers' use of the name Russia, but in addressing the historical context I have attempted to make the correct distinctions. The distinction between the use of the phrase "the Ukraine" and Ukraine relates to the period before Ukraine became a Soviet republic and after. This story also encompasses the region of Siberia, and, in the memories and stories of those who experienced suffering under the Stalinist regime, the name Siberia is often associated with "exile."

In 1991, the geographic boundaries of what memory coins "Russia" varied again, and Ukraine gained independence along with other union republics. Today these fifteen countries are sometimes collectively called "the former Soviet Union," of which the Russian Federation is the largest.

In certain places in the story, where the names of cities have been changed, I have placed the original name in brackets.

This story covers a broad geographical landscape and a historically turbulent era, eventually leading to home and to the present day.

Preface

❖

*To feel the present sliding over the
depths of the past, peace is necessary.*

— VIRGINIA WOOLF

It has only been in the last few years that my father's memories have surfaced. They flow to a distant river which is turbulent in spots, nearly impossible to navigate, let alone cross. But along the river bank now and then are stretches of sugar-white beaches, various hollows where willow trees cast deep blue shade over fishing holes, and, further along, near the old quarry, high rocky ledges from where boys whoop as they slice, like blades of pocket-knives, through air and water.

The wide Dnieper River flows over two thousand miles, two-thirds of it through Ukraine. Not far from the village of my father's childhood, an island splices the waters surging towards the Black Sea. These southern lands of the vast Russian plain were once dotted with colonist's villages, situated along count-less small tributaries like blood vessels that pulse into the artery that is the Dnieper. The black earth of this place produces wheat and rye, sunflowers and watermelons. It seems as though the soil of that distant place is under my fingernails as my father tells about living there, and I am struck with this thought: the soil of the steppes and the river are the flesh and blood of our heritage.

But we are not Russian and not Ukrainian. We are descendants of a migratory people, the Mennonites. We are the survivors of dictatorship and war, and are now a Canadian family. In an effort to ascertain my place in history, within both a general context and the intimate family narrative that has thus far been vague, I gather my father's memories into this story that is simple and complex, personal and universal.

Through silence, memory and imagination, I journey into the heart of family, tradition and heritage. My own story is in some ways common these days: the child of immigrants, a first generation Canadian. However, tracing the past has been complicated. Although the Mennonite heritage is one in which ethnicity and religion were interwoven for centuries, the "Russian" Mennonites of this story — as they are called — did not consider themselves citizens of the country they had lived in for more than a century. Moreover, this history was followed by flight and statelessness. And when I ponder that this heritage stems from pacifist convictions that were continually tested in life-and-death situations — a revolution and World War II — I realize that all of these roads are leading to a place of significance. While place is essential to the story, I am not speaking only in terms of a geographical location, but a place along the horizon between two worlds: a place of connectedness by knowing and understanding the past of the present.

Writing this story has not been a straightforward journey. It has been one without clear directions, one in which I had to chart my own way to the true starting point, the first traces of the Mennonite people. But I am not a genealogist, rather a gatherer of stories, and this has been difficult because of the violence of the Soviet regime and the dark side of the German "liberators" in Ukraine, followed by the horrific displacement of the Soviet-German conflict and the ensuing post-war silence. So much was lost, or was too difficult to talk about. The late philosopher Paul Ricoeur acknowledged that before it is even possible to tell the stories of loss, before silence can pass into language, the act of remembering requires "temporal distance." The appropriate amount of time must be allowed to pass. He also stressed that stories empower the marginalized to become agents of history. To borrow a metaphor from Julia Spicher Kasdorf, a writer and poet whose heritage is Mennonite, "the wound becomes a mouth that finally speaks its testimony."[1]

Recently, my father has reached the place, not of remembering, because I do not think he ever truly forgot, but of telling. He narrates for me the era comprising the last of Stalin's purges of the late 1930s, the clash of Hitler and Stalin in Ukraine through to the final days of the war — a time that defined his childhood. These events and experiences are the memories of a traumatic childhood, but the language of trauma is bare, and so those early memories are overlaid with the reflections of a father and adult daughter. Although the rough edges of minimalist nouns and verbs become blunted with time, I don't mean that we softened what was harrowing; I mean that together we sorted through the available stories and filled in some of the spaces between them, crafting the language of narrative.

Along with my father, I owe gratitude to my late grandfather Jakob. The information he gathered in 1947 about the period of Soviet repression was later published (in 1954) by a Mennonite minister in Canada. Unfortunately, Jakob did not reveal much of his interior life, only sparse facts from the perspective of a Mennonite pastor whose church and way of life had been systematically destroyed, and fellow human beings dehumanized under a despotic regime. He recounted the Stalinist persecution that he must have intended to leave as a historical record, but without specific details or exact dates. There are a few possible reasons for this: to protect people still in the Soviet Union, and, because when he wrote, the emotional wounds were simply too deep. From the few pages of the Canadian minister's edited version, I sought to recover Jakob's story.

My grandmother's story was also largely missing. She died when I was too young to know her. Maria's keepsakes were divided among the children, who put them away: a few photographs from life in Siberia and Ukraine, a slim file of documents from the time the family was stateless, Jakob's death certificate dated 1948, along with a few sheets of poetry Maria had written in her twilight years. When my father began to tell his story, his three sisters recovered those artifacts, which served to shape and assist the writing process, an experience that for me became life giving, like that of creating flesh from dust, for narrative and memory ensure the continued temporality of a person.[2]

Through words, along with the imagery of photographs, I have stepped into the lives of Jakob and Maria and their children, if only for a time — a reconfigured human time that is the magic of narrative. The family story I tell is crafted mostly from remembered history. The Canadian poet and author, Anne Michaels, has said, "[h]istory and memory share events; that is, they share time and space. . . . Every moment is two moments."[3] A moment contains the actual event, and, thereafter, while we may never return to the actual event, the remembered moment is derived from it. Conversely, through memory, we attempt to access the trace of the original moment. Whether through history, or in memory, one must seek the truth of the event and of experience. In this attempt, I have added historical research to lend context, and to assist in sequencing personal memories chronologically.

Throughout, I have employed both present and past tenses, the present tense to represent memory and the truth of experience as it was lived by the people involved, the past tense to represent what is known from the historical record. At times, these distinctions of tense become blurred, but essential truths are sharpened.

In this way, it can also be said that history is two histories, that is, the dominant "textbook" history, and the marginalized life story. Again, I turn to Ricoeur, who held that narrative positions history within the realm of *all* participants. Therefore, the story of this family represents the stories of many others, two or more generations, and all such stories inform us about the fullness and truth of history.

The journey of discovery that became the writing of this book has concluded in two ways: with the last page, and with a physical journey to Russia and Ukraine together with my parents and my family in the summer of 2005. The image of rolling steppes gold with sunflowers and wheat is imprinted like a photograph in memories that are now my own. I remember an endless August sky, tall white clouds growing upwards in cotton-candy layers and my first sight of the Dnieper. But the landscape is one of stark contrast; the natural beauty is blighted with signs of the former Stalinist regime's drive for economic progress. At the river, only locals dared swim in the water polluted by industrial waste. The white-and-red striped factory stacks along the banks belched plumes of gray smoke into the air, and the breeze carried it to the villages nearby, just beyond the skyline of crumbling concrete Soviet-era apartment blocks. This setting has become a metaphor of those who came before me — the persistent and resilient. Along the horizon, the shimmering river fused steppes and sky, past and present. And from this vantage point it became clear to me that new life emerges from brokenness and ashes.

Introduction:
Promised Land

❖

Our stories are all stories of searching. We search for a good self to be and for good work to do. We search to love and to be loved. And in a world where it is often hard to believe in much of anything, we search to believe in something holy and beautiful and life transcending. . . .

— FREDERICK BUECHNER

When my father reached his late sixties, he asked me to do something for him. "I'd like you to write this down. It's my story," he said, as he extended his hand, his palm cradling two miniature cassette tapes.

Will I help him put his memories to paper? In his own way, he is reclaiming his history. But he has never been comfortable writing in English with its difficulties of spelling and grammar. When he came to Canada, he worked hard with no time for night school. Dispossessed not only of the land, but also of the language of home-place, followed by refugee life in Europe, he was thrust into other languages before learning English, in which he is now fluent, but without the intimate nuances of the first language. I sense that he is also hoping for a fuller articulation of his story. I said I would try.

While this is the story of one family among all those who have made Canada their home in the aftermath of World War II, it is the story of a Canadian "Mennonite" family. As a story set in Russia, it entails the history of an important era. As a story about Mennonites, it entails the history of a people who have been important contributors to religion and culture since the Protestant Anabaptist break with the Catholic Church in the Reformation.

While one correctly associates the name Mennonite with pacifism or even with German-speaking immigrants, typically, at the mention of the name Mennonite, people often think of the Amish, whose appearance is distinct, marked by bonnets or dark clothes. This book is not about them. While the Amish and the Mennonites stem from the same Anabaptist tree rooted in the Protestant reformation, they have grown into different branches whose religious life and migrations from the old world to the new diverge. The Amish arrived in Canada in the mid–1800s, soon after the ancestors of the Mennonite family I am writing about first migrated to Russia in 1818, although some Mennonites had migrated to Russia beginning in 1789. And even before the Amish, the Swiss Mennonites, who left Reformation Europe for the United States in 1683, arrived in Canada from Pennsylvania around the time of the American Revolution.

There have also been significant migrations of the Mennonites from Russia to Canada, and these migrations constitute the more familiar history of the Russian Mennonites. This book touches only briefly on those. One migration to Canada of Mennonites — who then became known as the *Kanadier* — occurred in the late 1800s — again, at the time the people I write about migrated *to* Russia. Another migration to Canada occurred around the time of the Russian Revolution, and, following that, all during the 1920s until the Bolshevik government cut off the flow of those wishing to leave. These Mennonite immigrants became known as the *Russländer*.[1] However, this book tells the story of those people who remained, even as Mennonite historians declared, "the final curtain fell on the Mennonites in Russia."[2] Their story must also be incorporated into history so that we may broaden our understanding of the past and appreciation of the present textures of society. I have written with this sense of responsibility and deep gratitude.

Those whom I write about arrived in Canada beginning in 1948. Like most post-war immigrants, these Mennonites have raised families and have grandchildren — new generations of fully assimilated Canadians. There are no *visible* markers of identity, as there are in the old-order Mennonite communities, except, perhaps for some, a tell-tale surname, albeit most Mennonite surnames have grown common in every sphere of Canadian society. Their story has been largely overlooked, even by other groups of Mennonites. It arises from the margins of the collective history of Mennonites in Russia. It is also a story from the margins of World War II history. And at the present time, it is a story that belongs among those, only now, emerging from the periphery of the former Soviet Union's history. This story is uniquely situated at the intersection of each of these marginal histories.

My father has asked me to write down his childhood memories. What I have written is the result of listening to him, to his voice, then piecing together, through photographs, documents, research, follow-up conversations, and, at times, my best conjecture, based on those things that happened to one particular Mennonite family in the Soviet Union, prior to, and during, World War II. Because this story involves the history of Russia, and the history of the Mennonites, to more fully understand the context of my father's story, I must reach as far back as possible, when Russia was the land of promise for the early Mennonite people.

To help me begin my project, my father brings me an old chocolate box, shallow and small. It is long emptied of sweets, and instead, holds a meagre assortment of photographs dating from the mid–1940s to the early '50s when my father was already in Canada, still single. Sometime later, I contact my father's youngest sister, Aunt Liz, because he thinks she might have some of their mother's photographs from the early years in Russia, and she invites me over to have a look. She doesn't recall the earliest years of her life, or the refugee years before coming to Canada.

As she pours me a cup of tea, Liz warns me, smiling, that she may know less than I do. "That's okay," I say, but I am hoping for something that may lead us to discovering who our ancestors were, or why they went to Russia in the first place. Before this, the only information I knew was what my father had passed on to me, general information he had been given orally, "We came from Prussia."

My aunt opens the deep drawer of an antique sideboard, and produces her own small boxful of photographs that, with the passage of time, have become images of strangers. But among the small jumble spread over the oak table top, one photo, like a crucial piece of a jigsaw puzzle, catches my eye. It is a small sepia image fixed on its original two-inch square cardboard, so typical of Russian photos in the 1800s.

There can be no doubt about our genealogy. The man in the photo has my father's dark shock of hair, the same narrow face and thin curve of a smile. A stout, somber-looking woman in black dress and black head-scarf sits by his side. "I have no idea who these people are," says Aunt Liz.

He is, I have discovered, Gerhardt Letkemann, the first ancestor, and therefore the first "character" in this story, to be born in Russia, in 1829. He appears "middle-aged" which in those times might only be thirty-something. And because photogra-

Gerhardt and Sarah Letkemann, Russia, circa 1865

phy was in its first few decades — it was unusual for common people to sit for portraits, but growing more popular and affordable for the middle classes by the 1850s — this is likely among the first photographic evidence of my Russian Mennonite heritage, circa 1865. Gerhardt, not a wealthy man by his appearance, poses here with his wife Sarah.

While the stoic faces of this man and wife are embalmed as silent image, a family chronicle lies within. Following the discovery of the photograph of Gerhardt and Sarah, I locate an article in a journal *The Mennonite Historian*, entitled, "The Early Letkemanns," that connects the people in the photograph to the place and to the lives before them.[3]

The [Letkemann] name originated in the northern region of Germany known as Niedersachsen, an area that stretched from the present Dutch German border to West Prussia. . . ." The name, interpreted, means *der kleine Mann*, little man.[4]

The faces in a photograph and the origin of the family name become the first threads of our historical fabric. I can only trace this particular family history back to Prussia, as my father had said, which leads to the conclusion that an ancestor was a later convert to the Mennonites sect, after the group's distinct religious doctrine had been shaped and they had migrated to Prussia from the Netherlands.

❖

The "Mennonite" identity adopted by our Prussian ancestor originated in the Netherlands during the Reformation, following the emergence of the Anabaptists, the Protestant church reform movement sparked by religious, social and political conditions. It began in Zurich, Switzerland in 1525, and blazed throughout Western Europe. The theological origin of the Mennonites is considered to be in the Netherlands, where Menno Simons, a former Catholic priest joined the Anabaptists. Various traditions arose from the movement, of which the Mennonites are one; over time, the number of Menno Simons' followers grew, drawn to the doctrine that he developed from Anabaptism's core tenets.[5]

Translated, Anabaptist means "baptized again." The main belief was the renunciation of child baptism in favour of adult baptism, meant to signify personal faith and membership into the body of believers. Those baptized as infants chose to be re-baptized as adults, and, in the Netherlands, as elsewhere in Europe, these "radical" believers were considered heretics by the Catholic Church, and lived under the constant threat of martyrdom by being burned at the stake, or by drowning — first bound by rope, weighted down with a rock, then thrown into a river. Gruesome stories recounting the earthly demise of these early Anabaptists are compiled in a very thick book entitled *Martyrs Mirror* by Thieleman J. van Braght,[6] which venerates their experiences as saint-like, but not to the point of the Catholic Saints whose lives and deaths are iconically commemorated, or celebrated with a religious calendar.

It was during the 1530s that the northeast regions of Germany and Poland provided relief from the prevailing religious persecution against the Protestant Anabaptist movement. From the Netherlands, Anabaptist people of Flemish, Dutch, Frisian and lower Saxon ancestry migrated to the Danzig lowland, where, under Menno's leadership, their unique spiritual and cultural identity took shape, and they became known as Mennonites, or *Menniste*. The Mennonites spoke *Plattdeutsch* (low German), an unwritten language. They were a mostly agrarian people, hard working, and remembered for draining the swamps of the delta to create a rich farming region in the basin of the Vistula River. They were known for their adherence to a simple lifestyle and their religious principles.

Menno Simons had taught his followers that a faithful church would always be a suffering church.[7] Thus, the believer's reward was in Heaven. Each one's suffering takes on different forms — for the masses over the centuries it has taken the form of starvation, infant mortality, epidemics and war. For believers living under intolerant rulers, suffering would be defined by religious persecution. More expressly, Menno Simons' stream of Anabaptism held that "true" Christians would not swear an oath, take up the sword, or be involved in government. Thus, the Mennonites, pacifist Christian people who practised adult baptism, separated from civil society to form their own communities of conscience, in opposition to political religious authorities. As non-conformists identified by their stance against violence and war, Mennonites would also become known for the steely resolve to live their lives as their world-view required.

❖

Three centuries and generations of lives would pass between the genesis of the Mennonite identity during the Reformation in the early sixteenth century, and the first photographic evidence of my ancestors in Russia, Gerhardt and Sarah (circa 1850). Along this mostly silent span of time, I locate the genealogical origin of this narrative in Peter Letkemann (1756-1796) and his wife Sarah Goosen (1748-1814) — who would become the grandparents of Gerhardt in my photo. Peter Letkemann was listed in a census commissioned by King Frederick II of Prussia, who granted his subjects the freedom of faith and practice, and respect for their pacifist convictions, in exchange for taxation. It appears that Peter was drawn to the Mennonite teaching and converted from Lutheranism, for the name Letkemann is an otherwise unusual surname among these people. I don't know how many children Peter and Sarah had, but three sons' names are also recorded: Heinrich, Peter and Jakob.[8] The 1776 census also states that Peter Letkemann was not a landowner, and his economic situation was not good — *schlechte Vermögensumstände.*[9] There is no way of knowing the exact circumstances or precise reasons surrounding Peter's decision to join the Mennonites, but certainly the fact that he embraced this new identity would have implications reaching through time, until today.

In 1786 during the life of Peter and Sarah's family, King Frederick II died and the state's toleration of Mennonites began to vanish. One outcome was that Mennonites, who were growing in numbers, would no longer be able to purchase land. In the same year, 1786, the Russian Czarina, Catherine the Great, dispatched her envoy Georg von Trapp to the Mennonites of Danzig. She had heard impressive accounts of their agrarian ability and indomitable work ethic — their religious ethic aside — and invited them, among others, to settle the lands north of the Black sea. So begins the tale of the Mennonites within Imperialist Russia.

In response to von Trapp, two men, Jakob Höppner and Johann Bartsch were sent out by their religious community in

Danzig to scout the land and to assess the Czarina's offer of their own colony. These men would become a Moses and an Aaron leading their people. When they arrived on the steppes, they saw that the soil was rich for farming, a river and streams flowing through it, the horizon of the grassy landscape as great as their vision for the future. Catherine the Great signed their terms and conditions of settlement, which called for a closed community and a non-conformist way of life, and a particularly choice tract of land. The first few families left Prussia in 1787, and the next fall, in 1788, wagon after wagon, hundreds of hopeful families, made the trek to Russia. Many would have viewed this as an "exodus," and I have often wondered if the pious among them had visions of the promised land, or a pillar of smoke and fire to guide them.

The land route from Danzig to the Baltic Sea was a rutted wagon trail following the Dvina, then along the Dnieper River which flowed on to the Black Sea. The first settlers arrived in the Chortiza River valley in July 1789. Where the smaller Chortiza River joins with the Dnieper, south of Dnipropetrovs'k, then named Ekaterinoslav, these rugged Mennonite pioneers established their first colony and named it Chortiza.[10] Upon their arrival, however, they discovered that this was not the prime land, belonging to General Ptomekin, for which Höppner and Bartsch negotiated; the piece they had selected for settlement lay further south but skirmishes had broken out with the Turks from whom the land had been seized. The arid tract they were now assigned belonged to General Ptomekin, too, and this was the land, that, after their arduous journey, these Mennonite pilgrims settled. Chortiza became known as "The Old Colony." Under the giant oak tree, once a gathering place for the tribal Cossacks of the Dnieper, the peace-loving Mennonites now gathered for meetings, picnics and worship. They claimed the great tree as a symbol of their new home, a place where their roots could reach deep beneath the steppe.

As previously noted, upon Catherine's invitation to colonize

MIGRATION FROM
THE VISTULA TO
SOUTHERN RUSSIA

- - - To Chortitza (1787-1789)
······ To The Molotschna (1803-1804)
▓ Mennonite Colony

Verst
0   100   200   300
0   100   200   300
Kilometres

WS/95

Helsinki

St. Petersburg

Stockholm

Baltic Sea

Tallinn

Novgorod

Moscow

Riga

Dvina

River

Danzig

Koenigsberg

Orsha

Dubrovno

Mogilev

Thorn

Bug

River

Pripet Marshes

Pripyat River

Dniepr

Gomel

Warsaw

Chernigov

Vistula River

Kiev

Poltava

Khar'kov

Dniester River

Yuzhnyy Bug

River

Kremenchug

Prut River

River

Ekaterinoslav

CHORTITZA

MOLOTSCHNA

Nikolayev

Kherson

Odessa

Berislav

Sea of Azov

Danube

Bucharest

Feodosiya

Belgrade

Sevastopol

River

Black Sea

the region north of the Black Sea — land that would later become Ukraine — the Mennonites were only one group among the groups of Protestants who came. Catholics and Jews also accepted her invitation. The colonists arrived, not only from Prussia, but other northern Germanic regions, to settle in a farming belt along the Dnieper River. And, although the emigrations took place over a long period of time, the first Mennonite settlers came to maintain their traditional Anabaptist beliefs and formed communities separate from Russian society. Later groups followed, prompted by economic reasons, or because of war in their homeland.[11]

Our first ancestral Mennonite, Peter Letkemann died in Prussia in 1796 and in 1803 his widow Sarah planned to migrate to Russia with her three sons, during the new wave of immigration from Germany that began under Czar Alexander I. However, one son died that year, and she, together with her other sons, remained in Prussia. In Russia, with the new influx of immigrants, the Mennonites established another founding (or "mother") colony alongside the Molotschna River.[12] The period of migration lasted over twenty years as Catherine, then Alexander I after her, gained all the territory near the Black Sea, driving off the former Turkish owners. The rich soil of this land simply lay fallow so the Russian aristocrats — not interested in living there or toiling the land — sold tracts to the ambitious Mennonite colonists. As they outgrew their settlements, they purchased more tracts and populated numerous "daughter" colonies.

Hardworking and Bible-believing, the Mennonites were "salt of the earth" people. The metaphor of salt used in Scripture suggests a life-style that influences the culture, but like their forebears, they would have asked themselves, as in Matthew 5:13, "what good is salt if it loses its saltiness?" Thus, among the various groups invited to settle in Russia, these low-German speaking Mennonites valued their separateness, and the homogeneity of their colonies served as salt to preserve their religious and ethnic identity on Russian soil.[13] Whether or not this was positive in pre-revolution Russia is now debated by modern Mennonite historians who note that, consequently, the desire for withdrawal would, in the unknown future, mark these people as enemies of the one great homogenous, classless society known as the "State." Long before this would occur, however, the sons of Peter and Sarah, Heinrich (together with a wife) and Jakob, emigrated from Prussia to Russia in 1818. What prompted these sons of a Mennonite couple to migrate? Their parents had been poor, and, no doubt they, too, were poor. Was land the primary motivation? Or were they devout, drawn by the promise of freedom to practise their faith?

The people of this story descend from Heinrich. In Russia, Heinrich and his wife would raise their own family — in 1829 they would become the parents of Gerhardt (of the photograph), the first ancestor to be born there. Without a family narrative, or names recorded in a family Bible, the irony is that the only "detail" revealed about Heinrich is that his emigration went unrecorded.[14] In a strange twist, recent historians discovered the narrative's trace with the aid of a notorious source.[15] The early migration lists of all colonists would later be carefully researched then meticulously corrected and recorded by the German Reich in its effort to assess the ethnicity of all those living in this land under the German occupation in 1941.[16] With the help of these thorough records, the best information I can now offer of Heinrich's life in Russia is that he and his wife Elisabeth migrated to the Molotschna Colony, then moved to the Chortiza Colony, and settled at Insel Chortiza — the island in the Dnieper River. They had a large family, and one son, Gerhardt, married Sarah Martens — the subjects of my sepia photograph.[17]

By the mid–1800s, the time-period of my photograph, the Mennonites in Russia entered the era referred to as the "golden years." They had formed prosperous communities with businesses, hospitals and schools — entire colonies that became models of success throughout the Russian Empire. Many Mennonites owned large estates, enjoying the aristocratic privileges, even the stylish adornments, of affluence. As for Gerhardt and Sarah, their dark, plain attire suggests that were not among the wealthy. Perhaps they worked on a Mennonite estate, or, at most, owned a small patch of farm. When compared to the lives of the serfs in Czarist Russia, however, their situation would be considered "well-off." Mennonite historians have referred to the Russian Mennonites as a "people-hood." And, in memory, to those whose tradition has grown out of an ethno-religious context into a prosperous community, culture and place often become referenced in biblical terms, a parallel to the "chosen people" and the "land of milk and honey."

In all likelihood Gerhardt and Sarah gathered for Sunday worship at the Mennonite church — "the Old Church" — followed by afternoon picnics under the wide canopy of the solid oak tree in Chortiza, just as their parents, and the Mennonite pioneers before them, had done. Today this oak tree, estimated to be 700 years old, is nearly lifeless; its great trunk is white and dry as bleached bone. Only one persistent branch still bears leaves in spring and drops acorns in summer. The once magnificent oak is a remnant of a former life, as is the faded photograph of Gerhardt and Sarah.

Within this single sepia image lies the story of ancestors who migrated to Russia to find freedom of religion, or to settle on a plot of land they could call their own, or, in any case, to make a good life for themselves and their offspring. As I consider the faces of Gerhardt and Sarah, whose son Jacob would become the father of Jakob Letkemann, my grandfather, an itinerant pastor in the Soviet Union, this photograph also holds a tragic irony. The silent unsmiling mouths seem to hint at the narrative I have yet to recover. So little of a past life in Russia has survived or been preserved, but this photograph spans the old world to the new, and becomes my story's beginning.

PART I

❖

Russia

A Pastor's Record
of Repression

I

❖

Clues from a
Canadian Childhood

Some stones are so heavy,
only silence helps you carry them.

— ANNE MICHAELS

Following World War II, in 1948, at age seventeen, my father
boarded a transport ship, the Cunard Liner, S.S. *Samaria*. It
had been a troop ship, but before that it was an ocean liner,
then a cruise ship. Now it was assigned to the International
Refugee Organization to carry thousands of refugees across the
Atlantic Ocean.[1] The S.S. *Samaria* docked that autumn day,
September 28, in Quebec City, and from there my father caught
the train west for a new life in Canada, leaving behind the
places of his former life whose names had changed to those in
another language, or even ceased to exist on maps. Father's
suitcase was light, but his memories weighed heavily. It has
seemed as if he left most of his memories behind, carrying

Cunard White Star, S.S. *Samaria*

along only the ones that were manageable — the few memories of childhood in Ukraine and the village on the steppes before he was forced to flee in 1943.

Eventually all the darker memories of the war, and of the time before the war, are turned over. Like tilling the soil before a harvest. To everything there is a season, as history confirms. There is a time for war and a time for peace, a time to scatter stones and a time to gather them. This means, I believe, that there is a time to forget, a time for the silencing of traumatic and painful memories. But there also comes a time to remember, and a time to speak, a time to tell the stories of loss, catastrophe, persistence and resilience — the stories of our past and of our heritage.

Our stories are the evidence of our lives. They are also a passport to where we have come from, and stories permit even those of us who have never been there to return to this "elsewhere." I am conscious of the forgotten past, and the words of the writer Frederick Buechner come to mind, "If you forget me, part of who I am will be gone."[2] I desire connection to history and place that as a child eluded me through the displacement of my parents' refugee experience, in particular, my father's, whose silence — but for his few stories — was the remnant of his Russian/Soviet home-place. What driving rains and bitter winds have contoured the fertile landscape of my present life?

❖

Once, on a summer day of my childhood, as we were eating watermelon and *Rollkuchen* (deep fried dough, rolled flat), my father dropped a clue, just a crumb, about his own boyhood. My mother had bought the fruit from the truck in the parking lot outside of Wiebe's Foodliner, in Clearbrook, a community populated by church-going Mennonites. "From Moses Lake," said the sign, which seemed like a good place for Mennonites to buy watermelons. It must have been August. Mother tapped each one listening for the hollow sound of ripeness.

The verdant rind was striped with white, the flesh red and sugary, the slice so much wider than my sticky face. "This is *almost* as good as the ones we had in Ukraine," Father said to Mother, which meant she had picked a good one.

Watermelon and *Rollkuchen*! I ate until my stomach hurt, but my taste buds craved more. Father said our mother's *Rollkuchen* were almost as flakey as the ones his mother used to make from kneaded dough of unrefined flour, skillfully rolled thin, then each piece fried to a crisp in oil pressed from sunflowers. We never had the chance to eat *Oma* Letkemann's *Rollkuchen*, not that I can remember. She passed on at the Tabor Home, her funeral the day before my eighth birthday. We could only imagine how delicious they must have tasted once in Russia, a land of wheat and fields of sunflowers aglow with golden halos. To Canadian-born children, this other place was, and is, at once distant and within. We taste its sweet nostalgia now and then. But there is darkness, too. It lies somewhere behind our eyes.

When I was small, my father told only a few stories about his boyhood and I listened, enthralled, as though I were listening to him tell secrets, for his tales seemed veiled. Father was born in the emerging Communist era, which was a time of danger — of living "in secret" because his father was a pastor. As a child, he grew up in fear of saying "too much," a habit of silence that even now makes disclosure feel unnatural.

But Father did tell us children about washing the horses from the Soviet collective's brigade after a hot dusty day of working in the fields of the "State" farm, of how he would ride these great animals (I imagined them so) into the Dnieper River beyond Rosengart. In his grin I saw how he once looked. I saw how he anticipated racing to the cool water after a long day that started in the dark, grew lighter and hotter with each hour until the sun blazed white and turned boys brown as hazelnuts. Dirt-streaked boys, Peter and his friend Isaac rode to the river on a mare sweat-soaked from working, rivulets sliding down her neck from running. They rode her in chest deep, each hoof-plunge displacing the water in splashes, then they sidled down her back to cool off, equine scent filling their nostrils. "Ah, this feels good, *nay*?"

As Father spoke, a thrill, like horses galloping across the steppe, coursed through my blood. He did not dwell on the work, rather on riding the horses to the river. I imagined the muscled mare that my father, a ten-year-old boy, rode swiftly, squeezing knees tight to horse flesh. In my own ten-year-old eyes my father had been a boy that did exciting things I could not. I only rode my bicycle around our subdivision.

I know now that the plough horses from the collective farm were bony from hunger. And if the boys, inner legs raw from riding bareback all day (for there were no saddles), were caught racing to the river, riding sweating horses into the water, they would be in trouble, most likely beaten by the brigade leader. But at the time of telling, Father did not include those details. He had forgotten that his legs scabbed; he didn't mention that he had to work long hours in the fields even before he was a ten-year-old. Those remembrances are recent and increasingly grow more vivid. He now says, "Riding Nina was like straddling a carpenter's sawhorse."

The early version of the horses and the river were his selective "moments of being" in childhood. As young children my brothers and I were raised to be polite, which also meant that small children didn't speak at the table or ask adults questions — a result of my father's own upbringing that he begins to share openly with me when he is a senior, in the late 1990s — two adults speaking together. In his youth, asking questions, asking for details, would be viewed as prying. This makes sense to me as I contemplate the Communist era. Also, without exception, in my father's youth, in his religious Mennonite culture, children were submissive to their elders.

"And when I was a boy, children came to the table to eat, not to talk," Father says. Mealtimes were not only without the abundance of food, but also without the chatter of youngsters. This view spilled over into our early childhood, although not the poverty, so as a little girl I never asked my father of a time about which he was unable to talk — besides the few tales he told over and over again. I waited for him to speak. When he did, I would listen, closely watching his face for clues hidden in his eyes. I never doubted his stories, but somehow they never fully carried me to the place of his childhood. It seemed that he lacked the details that might bring clarity. His parents, siblings, his friends, his house — the sorts of things so vivid and bright in *my* childhood — remained in shadows. And in his distant colourless world, I never knew if he was ever cold or tired or afraid, for he didn't say.

His stories were adventuresome but at times frightening to me, especially when he told of how men came for *his* father at night in the hopes of capturing him and sending him to a Siberian labour camp, leaving Grandmother destitute with young children to feed. But Grandfather always escaped. My father repeated these escape stories a few times on our Sunday afternoon visits with Uncle Jake's family — our cousins listening, too. As I heard those tales I thought to myself that to live in Russia, one would have to be very brave, braver than I who shivered at the thought of what might have been.

"One night *they* came to the house," my father would say. It was a long narrow house, quite tall under a peaked roof. The family lived in the front; the back was the stable, with only a wall separating these spaces. The attic spanned the length of the house, and here the hay for the livestock was stored, insulating the rooms below from the biting cold.

In the stories, somehow Grandfather always knew ahead of time, and stole away in the darkness before the dreadful shouts and pounding at the door.

Father told us that his mother — our soft-spoken grandmother in the Tabor Home — would not reveal to the men where her husband was. "My husband is not here," she would say boldly as they shouted at her. I imagined the spittle on their angry mouths as they pushed past my grandmother and the children, who stared wide-eyed from the folds of her skirt clenched in their small fists, as if peeking through drawn curtains. The scary men searched the rooms but did not find him. They stomped outside, grabbed the pitchforks standing by the stable entrance, and stormed up to the attic.

"They stabbed at the hay over and over," Father said, making jerking movements with his hands holding a pretend pitchfork. "You could hear the thumping from below." My mind became two little eyes squeezed to slits. I saw dark figures with clouded faces thrusting sharp-pronged pitchforks into loose hay, over and over, in every possible space . . . except for the mound beneath which Grandfather breathlessly lay!

The stories ended with Grandfather outsmarting his pursuers. Then my father would smile broadly, even chuckle to himself, inaudibly. As I think of it, Father *never* said Grandfather lay there, under the straw; rather he implied it, a technique to captivate and hold his now wide-eyed audience. "That was a good story!" we chorused, my brother excitedly rubbing his flat palms back and forth, my body slackening with relief.

Father may not have been born at that time, or perhaps he was very young and only had heard about it. But he remembers the danger at school when the teachers, Communist party "comrades," questioned whether parents prayed at home. This was one lie a preacher's child could tell: "No, we do not pray." Otherwise his parents would vanish. It seemed to me that even the little children had to be very brave.

In the stories, the villains came under the cover of darkness, but this scene was not a storytelling technique employed to make the story better. The night was a mask worn by the authorities: "Black Ravens" so named for the black cars that descended on the colonist villages at two or three in the morning. They were the Soviet Secret Police, called the GPU prior to 1934, later called NKVD, and later notoriously known as the KGB, uniformed men from the cities sent to collect their quota of victims as they lay sleeping in their beds.

"Just for questioning," they said, but the apprehended were always sentenced. A sentence of five years could mean survival. Everyone knew that those who were sentenced to ten years didn't come back, and were never heard from again. It was as if every dropped breadcrumb marking their path through the dark forest had been stolen by malevolent ravens, as in the fairytales of my *Brüder Grimm: Kinder- und Hausmärchen* book, only dreadfully worse, because this was real. In the late '30s, in what was known as "the Stalinist terror" when the purges grew most fierce, trucks drove into villages in broad daylight to round up not one, but many men and boys over the age of fifteen. Sometimes even women and entire families.

I never doubted the truth of my father's "escape" stories about our grandfather. Many accounts among the Russian Mennonite people passed down orally or in personal memoirs tell of such searches during the Stalinist years. Then after Uncle Jake died, Father's storytelling seemed to stop; his older brother was someone with whom he shared memories, the one with whom no explanations for understanding were required. Uncle Jake died in an accident at work when he was fifty-eight. I was sixteen that year, 1978. One image of that era my memory now brings forward is the shelf in our kitchen which held a thick volume by a Russian author: *The Gulag Archipelago* by Aleksandr Solzhenitsyn, published in the West in 1973. Solzhenitsyn reveals what happened to all those who disappeared in those purges, exiled to forced labour in a system of camps like a chain of desert islands across the Soviet Union from where there was no hope of rescue.

Not long ago Aunt Liz shared a story Grandmother had told her. As men jabbed pitchforks into the hay, Grandmother silently prayed they would not discover the small sack of flour she had hidden there: flour she saved ounce by ounce from her quota. During that time of quotas and famine, if the authorities found out about it they would have surely taken it. And she would have been severely punished for accumulating it. It took so little to be sentenced to Siberia for five or ten years of forced labour.

It is possible that these two stories were derived from one terrifying search for Grandfather in the attic; Aunt Liz says she doesn't know. But when I ask my father, he is sure they are isolated episodes; such searches, whether for an innocent person, or for an excuse to make an arrest, were all too frequent.

As I grew older, Father added another story — one that occurred after the German Army retreated from occupied Ukraine. During the retreat, not far away from his village, other villagers were already overtaken by the Soviet troops, loaded into open train cars heading for the Russian interior, then on to work camps in the remotest corners of the country. Those Ukrainians and *Volksdeutsche*, or German speaking inhabitants, who were swiftly evacuated by the retreating German army, like the people of my father's village, escaped mass exile to labour camps by the Soviets. They did not know that the Germans would also subject them to forced labour and other demoralizing conditions in German-occupied Eastern Europe. Even if they could have known this, they would have been more afraid still of recapture by Stalin's Red Army. For the next few years, displaced as refugees, trying to stay ahead of the Soviet front, they would continue to live in uncertainty and fear. With the barest of words my father set the terrible scene during the war's last days — his family lined up in front of a machine gun set up by young Yugoslavian partisans, Russian sympathizers, in charge of the forced march of civilian refugees into Russian-occupied territory in 1945. In this story, Grandfather leaned toward his youngest son standing beside him, my father Peter, and hoarsely whispered, "When they start to shoot, run! Tell . . . what happened to us. . . ."

❖ PEOPLE IN SEPIA

When I was eighteen, following graduation from high school in 1980, I boarded an airplane to Europe for the adventure of travel and language studies, along with a promise to visit relatives in Germany, cousins of my father. They had recently emigrated there from the Soviet Union. With addresses in hand, I took the train to Cologne and from there into the northern hilly region of Westphalia, to be met at the station by a gracious and plainly dressed woman of thirty or so. A head-scarf covered her braid, coiled and pinned. Susie welcomed me into her home among her gaggle of young children. And that December, still in Germany for studies, I joined them at their home for Christmas.

The family lived on a street lined by the houses of relatives, each with many children. It was a hillside neighbourhood that, in winter, looked like an old-fashioned German Christmas card set on the fireplace mantle. Their lives, however, had not been idyllic. They were from Kazakhstan and Kyrgyzstan, unusual sounding places that, at the time, seemed to be of no significance to me.

Mennonite refugees on the Great Trek, 1943 (courtesy Harry Loewen and Pandora Press)

They were *Flüchtlinge*, like my refugee father, who left Russia in 1943 on the great trek during World War II, but they were among the majority swept back into the abyss of Stalin's Soviet slave camps when the dislocated were sent back to their countries of origin under the allied agreement. After Stalin, they still suffered through Khrushchev's Communism, until the more fortunate were "resettled" by Germany beginning in the 1970s. These people were now referred to as *Aussiedler* (resettlers). If I had known of it when I met them, I might have asked my distant relatives of their hardship; but in their hospitality they appeared happy. The teenage children, my age, were increasingly acculturated — we seemed to have much in common. Now I wonder if these families, so fresh from personal trauma, could have spoken about it, when my own family didn't speak about it even after decades in Canada.

And something that stands out now is that one of them, Jasche, my father's cousin, spent his evenings in a closet-size room with a ham radio, transmitting a Bible program, in Russian, over the air waves to the Communist Soviet Union. I did not then fully comprehend the implications of this for the people secretly receiving his broadcast, only that it was forbidden, and covert. The Soviet people were deprived of any religious teaching. But as I momentarily peered in at Jasche bent over the dials, headset on, sounds, almost tangible, were transmitted through invisible strands, penetrating through a curtain of iron.

Along Jasche's road, and on the one below it, lived many more of my father's cousins. It was here, at the home of Heinrich, next-door to Susie and Nikoli on one side, Daniel and Lilli's house on the other, that I noticed a family picture on the wall-unit shelf. It was a family picture of my grandfather and grandmother with their children! In it I recognized my father, two or three years old. What I found most captivating, besides my toddler father, was the faint smile tracing Grandfather's lips. This I had never seen before.

Up to this point, no photos had circulated in our Canadian family, except for the few I saw in an album at Aunt Mary's farmhouse during our visits to the rural Alpine-like valley of Grasmere, B.C. As I expressed my amazement, Heinrich simply gave it to me, my first artifact connecting me to my father's past, this image of silent people in sepia.

When I returned home from Germany, I made copies for my family members and framed one for myself. Nonetheless, for years afterwards, this family's story remained concealed within the photograph. My father did not elaborate beyond his few adventure tales. And I, with my own husband and children, became occupied by my present life. Years would pass before I began to recover the words and stories inside this family photograph. What follows — the unfolding of my father's memories along with more family photographs and other evidence — is the attempt of narrative to seek meaning and order from history's chaos.

2

◈

The Story of Jakob

If there is meaning in life at all, then there must be meaning in suffering. Suffering is an ineradicable part of life, even as fate and death. Without suffering and death, human life cannot be complete.

— VIKTOR E. FRANKL

The photo was taken with black-and-white film, a small rectangle, two-by-three inches, now yellowed with age. I show it to my father who looks intently at it, then comments, "He's younger here than I am now." My father, who at this time in 2002 is seventy-one, gazes for a while at the man, about age fifty-four in the photo, whom he has not seen for over half a century.

Even despite the grainy monochromatic tones in the photo, I can tell that the eyes are clear, steel blue, like my father's, although these are sunken beneath the bones of the brows. Dark hair is razored to stubble, recedes, and bristles gray at the temples. It whitens at last in the moustache above thin lips that curl up ever so slightly into the creases of the unshaven

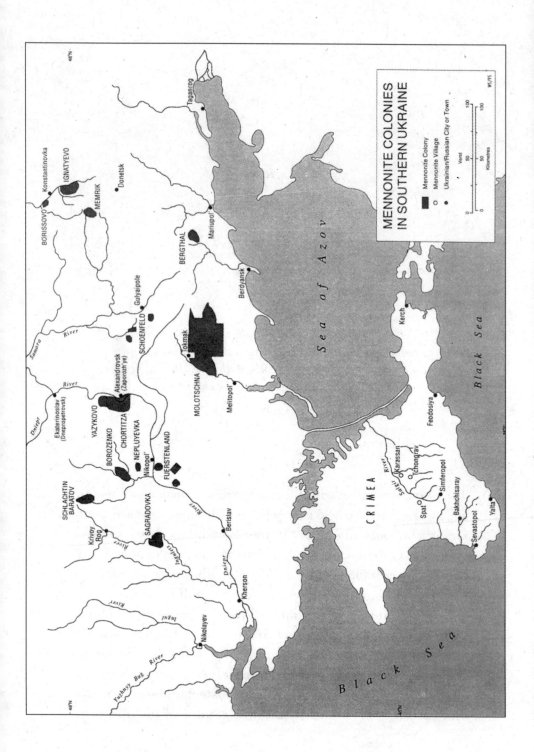

MENNONITE COLONIES
IN SOUTHERN UKRAINE

Mennonite Colony
Mennonite Village
Ukrainian/Russian City or Town

angular face. Despite the weary lines around the mouth and those that run parallel across his forehead, it is the hint of a smile and faint light behind his glassy eyes I love as if I've known him.

I came by the snapshot sorting through photos with Aunt Liz as we sipped tea, and now show my find to Father when we meet for coffee. This must be one of the last images taken of Grandfather, a photo I have never seen before, and it holds a paradox. A familiar

Jakob Letkemann, circa 1945

stranger. I have known so little about him yet, as I inspect the picture, its familiarity is gravity pulling me in.

"He must have already been sick with cancer when this was taken," Father muses, at which point my gaze turns to my handsome father who resembles the stranger, although he is, at this time, almost twenty years older than the subject and is elegantly groomed. A crisp pale blue shirt with front pocket and lightweight wool slacks. Socks that blend nicely. Polished Italian leather shoes.

In contrast, the frayed neckline of Jakob's soiled undershirt peeks from beneath his collared one, likely made from drab, scratchy wool. It is only a head shot taken against a blank background, set a little off-centre. I imagine it was supposed to be the photo used for the emigration papers, and that Grandmother kept it for her self after his papers were no longer necessary.

In this small snapshot, my grandfather appears gaunt, although I'm not certain this should be attributed only to the cancer which had progressed to a terminal state by the time he had seen a doctor. Here is a man aged beyond his years by circumstance, the tumultuous years of hardship and hunger and life-on-the run in Soviet Russia, then during the war that followed. Jakob was a victim of oppression but he was also a survivor; the photo expresses both these qualities.

Along with images, I am hungry for words, recorded and permanent. My father told me that Grandfather wrote an account of his life, sometime in 1947, experiences of survival in Stalinist Russia, after the family found safety in a hilly alpine valley of Austria, in the British zone. Although he sent the writing on ahead to A.A. Toews, one of the leaders of the Mennonite community in Canada, who was gathering such material, we heard that there was a fire in this man's house in Alberta, the flames devouring words until the stories were ashes. Only a few sparse details of Jakob's story survived, and these in an edited collection that Toews had earlier compiled. *Mennonitische Märtyrer* (Mennonite Martyrs) contains short biographies of men he considered martyrs in the religious repression of the Soviet Union during the '20s and '30s.[1] In the brief section devoted to my grandfather, Toews notes that he had written "I could share for hours, even longer, experiences from our brethren in banishment of incarceration, that I have seen myself, experienced, or heard from other eye-witnesses. I have cried until I have no more tears left."

These "martyr" stories of pastors are a kind of tradition in Russian-Mennonite history, a comparison to the martyrdom of their Anabaptist forbears.[2] They are stories about suffering and death. The word martyr means "sufferer for a cause" as well as "testifying for one's beliefs." The word martyr also means "victim." Toews may have meant the former by his title, although to my mind, "Mennonites among the Victims of Stalin" would seem an even more apt title. As for these stories in the book, the accounts are somewhat generalized, as are our family stories. I want something personal and human. I want stories of Jakob.

Born in 1893, my grandfather Jakob was the son of Jacob Letkemann and Helene Loewen, the fifth of their ten children. He was named after his father, set apart by spelling his name with a "k." As farmers, they were not a wealthy family, but neither were they impoverished like so many of the Russian landless. The Mennonite colonies were organized and productive; in order for their growing population to settle and find work, the colony rented or bought tracts of land from the Russian aristocrats. The family lived first in the Mennonite settlement of Olgafeld until 1907, then in Michaelsburg, both in the Fürstenland colony in the region of Ukraine.[3] Jakob's parents created a living on the land rented from Grand Duke Michael Nikolaevitch, the brother of Czar Alexander II. On the summer fallow, they grew potatoes, watermelons and corn for additional income. The work was bone wearying, but there were five sons to help old Jacob in the fields. Helene's five daughters assisted with the list of domestic work, almost endless in the clay-walled farmhouse with a thatched roof.

❖ LOST BOYS

A few years ago a relative visited us, the son of my father's cousin. That cousin had immigrated to Canada as a young child in the 1920s, and now his son showed us a picture of Jacob and Helene with their typically large brood.[4] In the back row, as a young boy, is my grandfather Jakob. His parents were, as most Mennonite couples in Russia, fruitful procreators as if God said to them as he did to Adam and Eve, "Go and multiply."

In the photograph the group is ordered in three rows, parents dressed in black at the centre. All arms fall straight at sides, not one rests around another's shoulders or takes their spouse's hand, only young mothers holding babies reveal touch. Two little girls in matching dresses, Justina and Sarah, primly fold their hands. Appearances were important. But there is a hint of mischief in the eyes of two of the boys in the back row, Jakob and his younger brother Abram, close in age, twelve perhaps.

Looking at these impish faces, captured forever motionless by the camera's shutter, I know what terrible things happened

Jacob and Helene Letkemann's family — their son Jakob is third from left, back row

to these boys after they grew up. On the day this picture was taken, everyone appeared blissful, oblivious to what lay ahead. But in the years to come Abram was exiled along with younger brother Peter. There is no further information given about them — no date of marriage, no date of death — which leads me to surmise they were taken when they were young single men. This photo, in which they still young boys, along with my grandmother's list of names in her Bible, provides the only evidence of their lives. In Russia they simply vanished. Now their memory is entrusted to the keepers of this photograph.

Jakob, at age nineteen in the year 1912, experienced conversion, followed by baptism as an outer expression of inward grace, a complete immersion in water, hands folded in front of his chest. In a small tributary that ran by the village of Michaelsburg and into the Dnieper, the pastor dunked him under the river to wash away his "old nature."[5] Jakob joined the Mennonite Brethren Church, established in 1860 when a group splintered from the original "Mennonite Church" — or "Old Church" — in Russia. The words spoken by the pastor would have been, "Upon confession of your faith I baptize you in the name of the Father, the Son, and the Holy Spirit. Amen." Afterwards, Jakob became a Sunday school teacher and sang in the choir.[6]

In 1912, the old Jacob died, and soon thereafter, in 1914, mother Helene also died, perhaps of a typhus epidemic that swept in and out of the colonies in those days. That was the way of life — much work and an early grave. This followed by an eternal and heavenly rest, or so the pastor might have stated at the funeral where the body lay rigid in an open wooden box, dressed in Sunday best, a sprig of myrtle placed in the lifeless hand. Family members would have solemnly gathered around for the traditional funeral picture, although I found none among our photos, which struck me as odd, as these would have been important.

Following his mother's death in 1914, and still a bachelor at twenty-one, the young Jakob moved across the breadth of the Russian plain with his younger brothers to a Mennonite colony that had opened on the west Siberian steppes. To encourage settlement where the winters were long and the growing season short, young Jakob and other colonists were offered free land in Slavgorod, and a reduced railway fare to the destination near China's border. According to a recent map, I measured out a distance of a thousand kilometres "as the crow flies," but of course the rails threaded through outposts along the way, sewing the long line of Tran-Siberian Railway, a steel seam from steppes to tundra. In the Slavgorod settlement Jakob acquired a tiny speck of land on the great plain of Siberia. It seems comparable to a grain of sand upon an endless shore, but this was a significant spot to him: the address is Saratov No. 89.

◆ WORLD WAR I

Among the earliest photographs are faded cardboard postcards with the name "Jakob Letkemann" handwritten on the flip-side. One shows young men in button-down coats over vests,

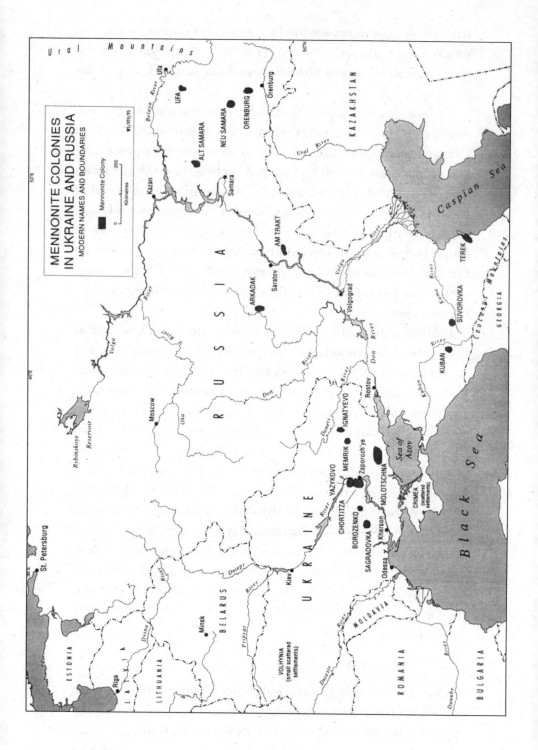

MENNONITE COLONIES
IN UKRAINE AND RUSSIA
MODERN NAMES AND BOUNDARIES

■ Mennonite Colony

trousers tucked into knee-high boots. Visored caps smartly complete the uniform. In another, the men stand against a setting of pointed conifers in front of a steam engine emitting puffs of vapour. One of those in dark uniform is Jakob. In a third postcard Jakob wears the dark uniform, but other men wear white smocks, suggesting, perhaps, that they are doctors or medics.

The settings of the postcards suggest that Jakob worked in a forestry camp, or along a railway line under construction, but in a subsequent document, Jakob used the term *Sanitäter*.[7] Jakob served as *Sanitäter*, a first-aid transporter for the hospital train, stationed out of St. Petersburg. That document states that Jakob served for two years, between 1915 and 1916. Therefore, these images were taken at the time of the Great War that lasted from 1914, when Germany declared war on Russia, until 1918.

Like a rough ocean, Russia churned with unrelenting waves of turmoil during the early part of the twentieth century and the pacifist Mennonites were conscripted to service. One reason the Mennonites first came to Russia was exemption from military service — they had been promised this in perpetuity in their *Priviligium* (terms of settlement). But this proved a tenuous condition; by 1871, under Tsar Alexandr III, a policy was established restricting the colonist's terms with respect to freedom from military service. In response, a group of Mennonites emigrated during the first signs that their *Priviligium* was compromised. As previously noted (in the introduction), these Mennonites resettled in Canada and other places in North America where they became known as *Kanadier*.[8] Back in Russia, by 1874, universal conscription to military service became law. The Anabaptist principle of non-resistance was eroding, so the remaining Mennonites negotiated an agreement with the government in 1890, whereby the young men could serve their military time in forestry camps. (They called this service *Forestei*). The Mennonites even took responsibility for building and maintaining these camps. Now, at the onset of World War I, the

Medical Orderlies, World War I, 1915–1916 — Jakob is seated fourth from the left

alternate service for Mennonites included *Sanitätsdienst* (medical duty) and road building, in addition to forestry duties.

These young men in the medical corps were usually behind the front lines, yet they became caked in mud and blood from the battlefield, the stains on their uniforms and in their memories. They toiled to keep battered and torn bodies from the battlefield alive in the railcars until they reached a hospital. They saved shell-shocked lives. They cleaned and bandaged bloody stumps of missing arms or legs. They closed the staring eyes of dead boys. The sounds of the dying rang in their ears long afterward. The *Sanitäter* also grew familiar with diseases such as typhus, its red rash spreading over the body but leaving unblemished the face, palms of hands, and soles of feet. They did not know it then, but one day, like typhus, a second great war would infect them too. This time they would not be able to perform medical or other service; they would be conscripted to arms. Jakob was released from duty in 1916 and, sometime soon thereafter, proposed marriage to a young Mennonite woman from his village.

❖ MARIA

Her father, Peter Siemens, a farm labourer, was square jawed; his face set off by those familial ice-blue eyes. He was a somewhat stern looking Prussian with cropped hair but a thick white moustache softened his countenance. His wife, Katherina Leidyn, in contrast, was a chestnut-haired woman with a slender, but gentle face that would appear as a genetic sunrise in some of the women in our family.

Katherina Siemens,
Maria's mother

According to Aunt Mary who remembers Katherina, despite her appearance in the photo that suggests otherwise, she was austere. In the two locket-size photos Maria kept of her father and mother, Katherina wears a frayed shawl over her shoulders, her hair is pulled back from her almost smiling face. As I examine the faded brown images, I wonder if there was ever a locket: a locket containing Katherina and Peter's photos, and I wonder if, sometime before Katherina died, she gave it to her daughter. She was Maria Siemens, born on October 29, 1895, in Musew (or Mussiewv), a tiny settlement belonging to a large estate in Dniprope-trovs'k (Dnepropetrovsk), South Russia (later Ukraine).[9] Her grandfather was the

Peter Siemens,
Maria's father

manager of the estate, where, at this time, her father Peter also worked. Maria was the fourth of Peter and Katherina's nine children.[10]

I imagine Maria as a pretty little girl, but not pretty in an overt way. It seemed to me that she once possessed a natural, understated appeal and that when her mouth began to curve into a smile it would be as if she might come into full beauty, like a flower. This girl, who grew to be a pensive woman, must have once smiled at the simple pleasures of her early rural life, watching baby rabbits bounding on the steppes in spring, weaving daisy crowns for her sisters' hair, and singing choruses in the children's choir at Sunday school. Her family moved from the estate when Maria was ten or so, to somewhere in the same southern region as Dnipropetrovs'k, (the name of the place is indecipherable in Maria's Bible). Perhaps it was here, as a young girl, that she first met Jakob, possibly at church.

Maria loved Sunday school and she loved to learn. She hoped someday to become a teacher, but she did not receive the necessary education. The practical reason was that her mother required her help at home. Three of Maria's siblings would die in early adulthood, perhaps of an epidemic illness that snuffed out lives as rapidly as the raiding Machnovite anarchists who would ride into the farms and villages on horseback during the period of civil war.

And this presents another possible reason that Maria was not formally trained. Her young adult years occurred within the turbulent climate of civil war and revolution. The February Revolution of 1917 toppled the tsarist government. In the following month, Nicholas II abdicated the throne and a provisional government took over. In October, the Bolsheviks set off the renowned Revolution and came to power October 25, 1917, threatening imprisonment and forced labour to any and all God-fearing and hardworking citizens, and landowners (*kulaks*), which included the colonists. Sometime during the upheaval, Maria's family moved from the south, where the fighting raged, to Siberia. Maria settled with her parents in the same village where Jakob Letkemann lived, Saratov (*Sartowka*), Slavgorod.[11]

In January 1918, the winter winds howling across the western Siberian steppes of Slavgorod, Maria married Jakob. They prom-

Jakob and Maria (composite photo)

ised to honour their vows, in sickness and in health, in prosperity and adversity, until death. In Russia, the future held much adversity. That summer, in July 1918, Lenin ordered the executions of Czar Nicholas, his wife Alexandra, and their children.

❖ JAKOB AND MARIA

The photograph of Jakob and Maria is a composite: two separate photos fused into one so they look as though they have posed together. As can be seen, he is on the left. His hair is shorn, but still dark. His eyes are large black pools of melancholy. A long slim nose presides over his narrow chin and the straight thin line of his mouth is fringed with a gray moustache. His serious face is unlined but for the creases beside his mouth and the start of crow's feet at his eyes, evidence that he often smiled. He might be in his forties. Maria's dark hair is pulled off her face into a knot. The rims of her pupils are light and I remember that her irises were blue. Her lips, like Jakob's, are thin, beginning to fold into a smile, though not quite; her countenance is solemn, restrained. She, too, is perhaps forty.

The family's history of relocation is recorded in the Bible Maria received as a refugee from the Austrian Bible Society, later in my parent's possession, now in mine. Its testaments smell of age and dust within a cover that no longer cleaves to the spine. Also within is a page labelled *Wichtige Ereignisse* (important events) whereon Maria noted the migrations across the Russian landscape, but offered no explanation. Such details would have been implicit to her. Jakob was not only a fugitive, hiding from Soviet authorities, but also a clever protector of his tribe, seeking refuge and shepherding them to safety, no matter how great the distance. When I inquire of other Mennonite families about frequent moves across the vast Russian horizon among their ancestral stories, their response is usually the same — this is an anomaly. The common situation was to be born, and die, in the same village. Or to be exiled, a journey across the Soviet Union's expanse, and more often than not, without return.

From the time Jakob and Maria married in her parents' home on January 8, 1918, in Silberfeld, a small village in the Siberian colony, they lived as wanderers, though not drifters, finding a home for their family while keeping ahead of district authorities who threatened exile on the orders of officials higher-up. During the first year of their marriage, they moved three times within Siberia — from Silberfeld to Saratov, from Saratov back to Silberfeld. Thereafter they returned to Saratov, where they remained for a period of four years.

It was during the early 1920s that Stalin passed Article 58-10 of the Criminal Code. Religious faith became a criminal offense — a counter-revolutionary act. Aleksandr Solzhenitsyn has described the law this way, "a person was allowed by law to be convinced that he possessed spiritual truth, but was required upon the pain of imprisonment to conceal this fact from everyone else, even his own children."[12] Although Jakob was a pastor, in compliance with the law, he did not speak explicitly about God or quote Scripture to his young children.

Purges occurred randomly, and believers were easy marks for the labour camps. However, while public services were forbidden, private prayer could not be taken away.[13] Jakob and Maria prayed, and while no one outside their home could know about this, in the dawn the tiny siblings sometimes saw their parents speaking to someone invisible, lips moving quickly and wordlessly in the urgent silence of prayer. In the dark, they fell asleep as their parent's breath flowed over shapes of words, in and out, in the hushed rhythm of sentences, like wind through leaves.

Over the next six years, Jakob moved his family between Siberia and Ukraine, back to Siberia, then back to the Ukraine. The dates of the moves and the names of the villages are all that has been recorded of their lives; between these facts are chasms wide and long as time, and as deep as sorrow — that only memories can bridge. But in whose memory after Jakob and Maria are gone? We search for their memories, planted like seeds among our own.

A lifetime later in Canada, in her garden of bright flowers and vegetables, Maria's eldest grandchild, a curious little girl, asked the elderly woman whose eyes were clouded from cataracts, about her only love so long ago.

"What made you fall in love with Grandpa?"

"He was a good and honest man."

Jakob wanted to be a preacher, a high calling that Maria, as a devout Mennonite woman, believed in. Her Jakob. What would she have told her granddaughter about love but that it required commitment, not romance? Marriage was a serious matter; she was his "helpmeet," as Eve was to Adam. This was reflected in the poetry that Maria wrote in her last years in Canada without Jakob. It was how she venerated him, and how she venerated her marriage. Aunt Helen had uncovered them among her keepsakes, and knowing they would be of interest to me, mailed these few poems, thin worn sheets of Maria's words, loops and curves delicately flowing as if embroidered with ink. Transcribed and translated, her poems conveyed her belief that marriage was a covenant until death.

> You two shall now be one,
> Thus God established marriage,
> Surely for the whole of life,
> He said "Let nothing come between you,"
> And so we must be faithful.[14]

They shared only one kiss during their courtship — after they were already betrothed. "We were proper; not like young men and women now-a-days." Grandmother said this in the 1960s.

Maria would not look openly at her fiancé when she felt his gaze fall on her in church. It felt like a shaft of sunlight through the window. They both sang in the choir. And theirs was a simple ceremony of vows, without even a wedding photo being taken. The winter setting would be symbolic of their marriage throughout the bitter circumstances and harsh challenges of the times.

They became one flesh, but were opposites. Jakob was tall and slender. Maria was smaller, though robust. Among his people he was a conversationalist, remembered for his friendliness. His temperament was mellow and gentle, although he was also stern with his children. While it took time for Jakob to reach the outer limit of his patience, when he arrived there, he made his child select the switch, and sometimes sent him or her back to the bush for a thicker one. Maria preferred quietude over conversation. She had no use for idle chatter, preserving her words for exchanges of substance, speaking quietly with other women, mothers alone, widows, women facing hardship, those who stopped by to sit at her bare table and be nourished with hope. Maria reserved her patience for matters such as these. She faced the chores and challenges of life with persistence. She was not an affectionate woman — she did not demonstrate her motherly love through touch. To love her children was to clothe and feed them, to teach them to work, and to pray for them in the night that swallowed day. But both Jakob and Maria sang, and in their music, blended beautifully. Jakob sang tenor, his voice flowing over Maria's alto tones the way a calm brook flows over smooth stones.

Their life together began on the heel of the Bolshevik Revolution and civil war. The strife was greatest in the Ukraine region, during the time Jakob and Maria began married life in Siberia. The older generations of Mennonites know of the infamous bandit, Nestor Machnov, and his band of anarchists who plundered the southern colonies. This area had been German-occupied under the Brest Litovsk treaty of World War I; thus, the farms here were now the target of partisan attacks. For months during 1919, settlements throughout Ukraine were terrorized; hundreds were murdered in the Mennonite colonies. Amid the plunder and rape, raging flames consumed village homes and barns, acrid smoke swirling over the steppes.[15]

While Maria and Jakob, living far away in Siberia, were spared the lawlessness, Jakob's older brother David was murdered in an attack in the Fürstenland colony. Although the raids were not as severe in Fürstenland as they were elsewhere, David and six other men lost their lives one moonless night: some of them killed by gunshot, one by an explosion. In David's case, his skull was smashed with a blunt force from behind.[16]

Then, during the Civil War of 1920 between the White and the newly formed Red Army, troops clashed in the villages of the southern steppes. Produce and livestock belonging to the *Kleinwirte* (small farm owners) were requisitioned, first by one army, then the other, until nearly everyone starved. But when the Red Army gained control of the area, new dangers began to take hold. The nation was to be reconstructed under the direction of Vladimir Lenin. Farms were forcibly collectivized. *Kulaks* (land owners) "disappeared," loaded like cattle in open train cars headed for labour camps in the northern tundra. Although survival was difficult enough in the Ukraine region at this time, the drought of 1921 worsened the situation. Famine ensued. Epidemics followed.[17] In 1922, the Union of the Soviet Socialist Republics was established within the territory of the former Russian empire.

◈ THE LITTLE ONES SUCH AS THESE

In Siberia, Jakob and Maria faced their own personal tragedies. All that my grandmother has preserved of this period is a list of births and deaths in her worn Bible. On another of the almost transparent yellowed pages, under the heading *Kinder* (Children) in the German gothic script known as Fraktur is a verse: *Lasst die Kindlein zu mir kommen, and wehret ihnen nicht, denn solcher ist das Reich Gottes. Marc 10, 14* (Let the little children come to me, and do not hinder them, for the kingdom belongs to such as these — Mark 10:14). Beneath this Maria has entered the following:

Jakob, October 8, 1918–August 10, 1919
Jacob (Jake), January 17, 1920
Peter, March 16, 1921–May 18, 1922
David, April 10–April 20, 1923

In Maria's day, a married woman bore the expectation that her body would produce children. Her first baby was born nine months after her marriage, and she would be expected to bear as many children as she might possibly conceive, despite the loss of life: her child's — for the infant mortality rate was high — or even her own.

Following tradition, Maria named her first son after her husband, and when this little one died, sometime during her second pregnancy that produced another son, she named the second-born son Jacob as well, but the name spelled with a "c." This baby boy survived even the years of famine that devoured entire regions of what once was Imperial Russia. Of the four sons born to the couple in Siberia, only the second Jacob (Jake) lived on as my father's oldest brother.

I wonder about the rhythm of those days and months marked out as the baby grew in the womb along with the couple's hope, their elation at becoming a family succeeded by the funeral of their child on a day after the thaw when, ironically, the earth was in bloom. Does "letting the little children come to Jesus" mean also this? I wonder how much loss the heart can bear. Melancholy had always cloaked Maria, so my father has said. I wonder if it first wrapped around the young woman, not in the post partum of birth but in the grief of parting through death.

There was so much sadness in Siberia. How did she carry on after burying her three little boys there? Years later, Grandmother provides only the name, the dates, her barely legible handwriting fragile as a spider's web, the only historical evidence, for there are no photographs of these infants. To Maria, nonetheless, her newborns would have remained known, her maternal bond strong although the babies were present only for a brief season. Each name and measurement of time represents the one she enfolded in her arms, first to nurse, then to mourn. The dates that bookend their brief lives are pregnant with untold stories, each birth prefaced by a man and wife's desire, set in rustic scenes of sensory details: a child's lusty cry, gnawing hunger, muscle-burning toil, Siberian gales, and in the night, Jakob's warm embraces. Or so I imagine.

Throughout Soviet Russia it was a terrible famine brought on by drought and crop failure, made worse by a government implementing a centralized economy. My father told me that people everywhere starved; there were even rumours that, in the Volga region, peasants ate the flesh of their dead children.[18] He read this in Solzhenitsyn's 1974 book, *The Gulag Archipelago*, the one that I mentioned sat on our bookshelf. The Russian author was in exile in the West, bearing witness about the extent of the famine and a corrupt regime.

Even without Solzhenitsyn's account, the older Mennonites

remember how they starved and family members died. From those who revered God, however, I have never come across a report about anyone eating human flesh. I have only seen pictures of that time in books published by North American Mennonite historians; in one, a photo depicts emaciated bodies with a caption that reads, "During the winter, sights like the above could be seen at railway stations." It also says, "During that time there were no Mennonites, at least very few among them."[19] This clarification means that the likelihood of homeless Mennonites begging along the tracks would have been slim due to their strong sense of community. There are certainly personal accounts of starvation within Mennonite villages.

In the Ukraine region, the Bolshevik government insisted that the grain be shipped to Russia and other Soviet states where people were also starving, or abroad for export, or fed to the collective's animals. The peasants here ate grass, clumps of sod and grew sick with worms.[20] They ate dogs and cats, or the carcass of a horse or pig that had starved, and boiled the hides to eat those, too. Others dug for acorns under the snow, then ate the flowers from acacia trees in spring. They swept out empty village granaries and silos to salvage whatever kernels of grain or corn might be left.[21] People sorted through animal droppings, picking out kernels of grain to clean and boil.[22]

In Soviet Russia's shipyards where the grain awaited export, the outraged workers protested, but the central government remained deaf to the nation's hunger pangs. A mountain of grain rotted in the port as Red Army soldiers guarded it from striking workers.[23] When the *New York Times* reported on Russia's grain shortage, Soviet officials denied the famine. In fact, the regime outlawed the use of the word "famine." The Russian Orthodox Church implored the West to help.

Western agencies noticed that the majority of the starving population consisted of national minorities such as Germans and Tartars.[24] Was this party policy restraining consumption meant for export? Or attempted genocide?

Foreign aid arrived during the second year of the famine, in

1922. In the southern colonies of Ukraine, the American Relief Administration, together with representatives from the Red Cross and Save the Children Fund, set up soup kitchens. Each day people formed lines, great lengths of human chain links. In the Zaporozhye area, Canadian and American Mennonite representatives set up canteens, one in the Chortiza colony. The Mennonite aid-givers were among the Mennonites who had left in the late 1880s, the *Kanadier*, who still had relatives living in the former Russian empire. Their relief effort began what is today, the Mennonite Central Committee, a world renowned disaster relief organization. This Mennonite organization would later, following World War II, assume the role of locating and assisting refugees.[25]

Nonetheless, because of widespread malnourishment, epidemics of typhus and cholera flourished, and millions of children throughout Russia and Ukraine were orphaned. Mennonites from Canada and the United States faithfully continued to send packages of food to their Mennonite relatives in an attempt to help them fend off the ravages of the famine. Jakob wrote in *Mennonite Martyrs* that he and Maria were recipients of help through "friends from Canada."

I cannot find anything more than a mention of the famine in the publication of *Martyrs* by A.A. Toews. Pages were lost in the fire, I know, perhaps pages written about this period of life in the Slavgorod colony along the Volga. History declares that the famine was particularly severe in the Volga region. Maybe this was not discussed in *Martyrs* in a specific way because this suffering was not exclusive to Mennonites, or any believer, for that matter. Did Jakob and others resign themselves to view the famine as simply another condition of life's suffering? We know now that it was preventable, even planned by a corrupt regime. Jakob did write the following about life at that time: "the things my eyes have seen, and my ears have heard, cannot be written down." Maybe, as Jakob concedes, there were just no words to describe it.

As noted, the Mennonites had always built their lives on the model of community, sharing among themselves what they could, even as we have seen, receiving help from family members from Canada. And within Russia, Mennonites also practised community by looking out for one another's children, caring for the orphans. Jakob experienced this in his own family, caring for his younger brothers when his parents died, and in the time to come, he and Maria would take in an orphaned girl. Should their parents die, a Mennonite child would not be left uncared for. "Mother Russia's" children, on the other hand, were without a similar network of care and became known in Russian as the *bezprizornye* — the uncared for: the unwanted.[26]

The following is what history tells us happened to these abandoned little ones: they flocked to railway stations and freight yards seeking shelter and food, like starving birds to garbage dumps. The International Save the Children's Fund learned that hundreds of Russia's children froze to death in train cars during the nights: tiny boxcar hobos.[27]

Perhaps even more horrifying is that when the snow in the fields melted in spring, mounds of corpses and skeletons appeared, awaiting mass burial. Among the wild dogs and wolves prowling among the decay were bands of children, orphaned, abandoned, some as young as three years old.[28] When the Soviet state did not respond to the plight of its children, the International Committee of the Red Cross set up a special relief body for Russia. As the director travelled across the land to make a report, he took shocking photographs of skeletal children begging in streets.[29] Other organizations even printed postcards distributing them abroad to raise funds for the famine, graphic cardboard images of emaciated children or of corpses piled high. Human woodpiles in front of cemeteries.[30]

If Jakob had travelled the rail lines or walked city streets during this time, he saw the starving bodies strewn along the tracks near the stations, lining the gutters, asleep or dead in front of shops. Did the sight of it simply defy speech? Were tears the only language possible? And before Jakob would even set his pen to paper, there would be a great deal more anguish to endure.

And what about the Russian orphans — the *bezprizornye?* When the West became aware of them, the Soviet state rounded them up. They later re-emerged as guards in the camps of the Gulag Archipelago.[31] In all likelihood, exiled Mennonites eventually encountered them here.

❖

Although by 1922 the drought conditions in the Ukraine region were improving and so had the harvest, there was still a severe shortage of food. Unaware of the imminent dangers that lay ahead, Jakob and Maria and their little son Jake, moved back to the Fürstenland colony, to familiar Michaelsburg where a place was available, likely due to another family's departure. Here they were closer to extended family: Maria's parents, who had also moved back, and Jakob's older siblings.

In a nearby village situated along the Rogachik River, another of the Dnieper's tributaries, there was a "Brethren" Church. In addition to an elder or preacher, the Brethren also appointed itinerant preachers to travel wherever Mennonite believers were scattered, and so this church voted to receive Jakob as one of their travelling preachers. Jakob began his vocation in the Olgafelder Mennonite Brethren Fellowship. It was a well-constructed church built in 1911 by a wealthy machine factory owner. The plain building, with its sloped roof, not domed, was large enough to hold four hundred people. Its windows were set in wood. Inside was a choir loft where Maria might sing, although it was a long distance to walk along the dusty road from Michaelsburg each Sunday.

In the year 1923, this area, known as Ukraine, officially became part of the Soviet Union. And here, the following year, on May 21, 1924, young Maria (Mary) was born to Jakob and Maria. Mary was an inquisitive girl whose face opened easily to laughter, the sound pealing like a Sunday bell. Of course, the Mennonite churches did not have bells, and those of every church throughout the land were falling silent.

I imagine Mary as a child, running boisterously about the house and yard like a brook overflowing in the spring thaw, for this is how I remember my aunt as a younger woman. She was formerly a kindergarten worker, growing quieter in her later years, hers and my father's voices dropping as they began to share difficult memories.

A year later, on December 28, 1925, Gerhardt was born, a tow-headed brother, who took after his mother's side. Gerhardt was a handsome child, although at times his temper flared like a struck match. He grew solid across his shoulders, built for hard work out-of-doors. He always tried to keep up with Jake, five years older, also serious, whom he admired. The brothers grew as saplings side-by-side under an open sky, pruned by discipline and physical labour, to become strong-limbed boys.

The children's names and birth dates were added to Grandmother's list, taking their place along the time-line of world events. Soviet Russia was behind in the world economy; Lenin died in January 1924, and Josef Dzhugashvili succeeded him. He named himself Stalin — "man of steel." Over the next years Stalin continued with the forced collectivization of all farms to gather labour for his great industrial projects and "five-year" plans.

From 1923 to 1929, the space of time in which the children were born, was a period of emigration. On June 22, 1923, among those of various ethnicities, well over twenty thousand Mennonites emigrated to Canada and South America — about one quarter of the Mennonite population in the Soviet Union.[32] Germany also accepted German immigrants. As for those living in the Fürstenland colony during 1926, the majority of the group immigrated to Canada. But not Jakob and Maria. Either Jakob did not have the means for migration abroad, or his vocation as a pastor compelled him to stay behind in this land where God's children suffered. And certainly pastors were poor. The church in Olgafeld was closed. Jakob and Maria decided to return to Siberia, and the fourteen families who remained in the settlement faced collectivization.[33] In 1926 Jakob and Maria moved back to the Slavgorod colony, to Kleefeld, and Jakob accepted a preaching assignment in a Mennonite Brethren fellowship there.

Olgafeld became Olgovka. Today it is part of a place called Georgievka,[34] and all that remains of this past life is the remnant of orchards, scattered, near-lifeless trees but for the random cluster of blighted fruit hanging from gnarled branches that persevere like a memory. When I asked my father why the family did not leave in any of the early emigrations, he said he, too, had once asked his father. He explained to me, "In the early years of Communism, after the revolution and first war, my father thought things would settle down — that conditions had to improve. Of course they never did."

❖

In Kleefeld, Siberia, the family acquired a large house with connecting barn, typical of farm buildings designed to withstand the long and unforgiving winters. The Mennonites brought this design from Danzig to Russia when they settled the steppes of Chortiza, duplicating it throughout the other colonies. It is a grainy picture of a house built from clay white-washed bricks. The roof slopes steeply so that the snow will slide off the tiles in winter. Not a straw roof, for this is Siberia. The roof's end-gables are wood-sided with two side-by-side wooden-paned windows. It is a one-storey house, and at the front are three windows on either side of the door. At the far end of the house is the attached barn. Slender birches stand in a row, lining the road that runs past; limbs now bare, their leaves have thickly carpeted the road. Figures almost too small to make out also stand there: Jakob, Maria holding a baby, a teenage girl, another couple and their child. In the background, sitting on the wagon hitched to the horse, is a boy. Is it Jake? Beside him are two younger children

Jakob, Maria, their family and friends before their typical
Mennonite house in Kleefeld, Siberia

with only blank spots for faces (they must be Mary and Gerhardt). In autumn, Jakob and Maria butchered a cow and a pig; they left the meat hanging outside, frozen all winter alongside the icicles.

Aunt Mary has a few memories of her earliest years of life in Siberia. She still remembers how, in a blizzard, Pa would tie a rope to a pole, uncoil the rope and step blindly forward towards the barn. Later, when he finished his work there, he pulled his way back to the house. She recalls winter Sundays going to church in Kleefeld. It seems that Stalin's anti-religion laws were not strictly enforced at this time, in this place. Collectivization had not occurred here. Not yet. Jakob preached at the Gnadenheim Fellowship. Mary's memory of going to church in winter is sensory: a frosty sleigh ride across snow-covered fields, a fur pelt across her lap to keep her warm, not a store-bought one, rather one from an animal that someone had trapped and skinned.

Mary also remembers Mienke, the eighteen-year-old orphan

girl Jakob and Maria took into their home, one of three sisters whose parents had died as they travelled through the Siberian village. The children regarded Wilhelmina (Mienke) as an older sister who helped their Mama with the endless farm and household chores, and minded the children when Maria was occupied with the newest arrival.

August 19, 1927, Maria gave birth to Tina. The child appears in a family picture that I estimate was taken in 1928. Aunt Mary has sent this photo to me where, in it, she is four years old, a "big" sister to Tina. I have never seen this photograph before. Tina is perched on Jakob's lap, her dimpled hand clasping his thumb. Jakob and Maria are a young family, a couple with two little boys and two little girls, along with Mienke, a teenager.

Jakob and Maria and children, 1927

Among the assortment of photographs that have yielded glimpses into our family's past, I select another photo from Aunt Liz's box as we sip tea together. It is one of a funeral, but whose, neither of us knows. Since I do not know who the child is, I will not reproduce it but simply describe it:

In an open coffin ringed with green boughs lies a beautiful child, as if peacefully asleep. The photo must have been taken from the slant roof of the house or barn — a view from above, as if from the perspective of an angel coming to carry the child to Heaven. Around the casket are the mourners, women in *platoks* (head-scarves), men reverently without hats, other children. At first, I wonder if this is Tina, for there are no notations on the back, but the man and woman closest to the casket are not Jakob and Maria. They are likely relatives; I think I recognize them from another photograph. (Maria's brother and his wife?) The child's tiny face is framed by the white blanket, so lovingly tucked around the little body.

Liz says it is a mystery to her why her mother kept this picture so I try to account for it. Perhaps not having her own photo of Tina, Maria found that keeping another one of a child in a coffin was a way to let Tina go, a way also for Maria to preserve all her silent memories of her little girl, even of her death. Was it scarlet fever? Typhus? In those days sickness was the common thief of little children. Which child to take was arbitrary. Mary remembers that her little sister had a fever, and after church one day, the fever grew worse. Tina died in winter, January 16, 1929.

The following spring June 3, 1929, Lene (Helen), was born. She was a fair-haired girl, quiet and lovely, with blue eyes like a cloudless late spring sky. Was this pregnancy a whisper of hope to Jakob and Maria in the depths of winter's hush? But Helen's birth coincided with the pending storm of Stalin's continued plans for industrialization. In 1929, Kleefeld was one of four villages that were combined to form one large collective farm under Stalin's directive.[35] In Mennonite communities, as elsewhere, teachers were dismissed, replaced by Communist teachers and a new curriculum. Instruction in the Russian language was now mandatory. Young men everywhere were conscripted to military service or simply taken away. More churches were closed; pastors, accused of preaching against the regime, were placed on lists, arrested and exiled. Any remark from any sermon, a verse recited, could be construed as "anti-government." Jakob, an itinerant preacher, was not black-listed at this time, but he knew he was not safe.

❖

In October 1929, word spread among the Mennonites that some had obtained exit visas in Moscow and had been able to emigrate. Thousands of Mennonites from all over the Soviet Union crowded into Moscow together with Lutheran, Catholic and Baptist colonists, as well as Greek Orthodox Russians and Russian Jews. All of them desperately hoped to leave.[36] Of the over thirteen thousand Mennonite colonists who applied for emigration, only six thousand were successful.[37] Among them were Jakob's cousin, Liese Loewen, who settled in British Columbia, and a nephew, another Jakob Letkemann, who settled in Manitoba. In the terrible years to come, these families were to play a vital role in the future of Jakob and Maria's family.

Communist authorities acted quickly to dam the human flood in Moscow, closing off all further possibility of emigration. Worse, those unable to obtain visas before the government's crackdown were sent back to their homes, identified and marked as subversive for their interest in leaving. Now they faced banishment as traitors, entire families sentenced to the labour camps of the Gulag and into the silence of history, to die there of hunger and disease under the harshest conditions.[38]

A number of people from Jakob and Maria's neighbourhood in the Slavgorod region, and from the surrounding Amur region, attempted to obtain exit visas. When they were unsuccessful, they devised an alternative plan, looking to the Mennonite villages of the Amur colony for an escape route to China. Chinese traders often smuggled goods across the river, and the year before a number of people had used the route to exit the Soviet Union. The wide Amur River, just south of the Mennonite settlements, cut a natural boundary between Soviet Siberia and Manchuria; in winter's freeze it was possible to walk across at night, slipping past Russian patrols. In the daytime, beyond the river, a blue mountain range, the Lesser Khingan Range (Xio Higgang) lay on the horizon.[39]

All that Jakob mentioned of this daring plan, printed in *Mennonite Martyrs* was that "the trip was difficult so we changed our minds." From this one sentence I envision the scenarios that might have played out for the family.

Jakob and Maria agree to make their escape in winter when the river thickens to a standstill, and when baby Lene is at least six months old. The young family makes their way from Kleefeld to the Amur settlements and waits there, cramped but grateful, among trusted friends that Jakob knows from his itinerant preaching route. They hope for the perfect conditions of a night crossing when the moon will be shrouded, the silver ice black. With each passing day the risk, along with villager's suspicions, increases.

Jakob tests the ice one night: solid, but the river is wide, and in the moonlight it glistens, the guards will surely see their silhouettes. If he and Maria have a good chance of making the journey, what about young Jake and Mary, Gerhardt and the baby? And how will they gather the necessary provisions along the way in China? Could they endure losing another child to sickness, or to hunger and cold in the hostile mountain pass of an unknown country? In the end, they decide against fleeing to China. The borders are rigorously patrolled. Of their two daunting choices, attempted escape seems more dangerous. Hardship is an integral part of their worldview and so they return to Kleefeld.

Patience in tribulation, oh wait on the Lord,
Though help is far off, God is not far,
Oh wait in faith, you are loved by the Lord,
Though your eyes are downcast from weeping.[40]

On a Sunday in January 1930, Jakob preaches, choosing his text from Philippians 2: 10–11. ". . . at the name of Jesus every knee shall bow, in heaven and on earth and under the earth. . . ." Three GPU members (secret police) sit quietly among the pews; the words are embers burning in their ears. Before Jakob concludes, they leave quietly. They plan to return sometime later, after a few weeks, when Jakob will think that the danger has passed.

Hoarfrost coats the window the night of February 11. Thick with snow, the winter air muffles noises and Maria's breath against the glass dissolves a tiny porthole through which she peers out. A group of men have encircled their house. Maria awaits the dreadful pounding at the door. . . . She can answer honestly when they demand to know where he is. She does not know. Earlier, Jakob had vanished like a spirit into the darkness.

❖

In the summer of 1930, in the Slavgorod colony, there is a mass arrest that includes preachers, choir directors, and anyone connected with religion or church. The two hundred prisoners — men, women, and families with children, bewildered and terrified — are tightly packed into waiting train cars on that summer day. But the train does not leave; the cars sit idly for hours under the glare of the scorching sun. The people inside cry out, "Water! Please give us water!" Finally, like a snake in hot dust, the long train pulls away from the siding. It rolls slowly down the tracks in mournful screeches, wheels against rail, steel against steel, heading . . . where? No one knows.

This train may be bound for the forests where families must fell trees in places so desolate that they must build their own shelters with their bare hands when they arrive. Food is only a small piece of bread. Another destination could be the *Weiss-meer Kanal* (White Sea Canal), one of the most important projects of the Gulag. It is to be 227 kilometres in length, a shipping lane from the White Sea to the Baltic; Stalin orders thirty-seven kilometres to be dug out by slave labour, cubit by cubit with spades and picks. So many cubits a day for a kilo of bread. Those too weak to work receive nothing.[41]

Jakob has written the account in *Martyrs*. He states there that he heard the cries of the people; he must have been hiding close by, close enough for those awful sounds to echo in his mind so many years later.

Jakob would have been grateful to escape, but I imagine how, at night, he wrestles with a force, like Jacob in the book of Genesis who, at Jabbok, wrestles with the stranger — a stranger that is really an angel — until daybreak. All night long, the Jacob in the Bible begs for God's blessing. Finally, the angel dislocates his hip. In Russia, although he has escaped capture, if he does not remain emotionally strong, the anguished cries of the people might cripple this Jakob, too. Many times Jakob has almost been caught, but he has grown adept at slipping from sight. He has travelled between the villages so often and knows how to read the spreading rumours as if a barometer. Arrests in a neighbouring colony means the GPU will arrive soon.

I believe my grandfather was an intelligent, quick-thinking, honest individual, but I must be careful not to attribute his survival only to skillfulness; he survived because he was fortunate. Others, too, were clever, but not fortunate. I must also add that, to suggest one survives because one is "blessed" is not to say that the blessing is earned. That is a contradiction: by definition grace is "unmerited." "Life itself is grace," writes the author Frederick Buechner.[42] Jakob's life was filled with grace. As I look up the meaning of the word grace, I find that it includes a temporary exemption or a reprieve. And I come across this terse definition: "Grace period — a period of time beyond a due date. . . ." It seems that death was always looming.

The family photo of my grandfather's family, in which Jakob and his brothers are still young boys, comes to mind. During this time in the early 1930s, Jakob's brothers, Abram and Peter, were arrested. They were likely dead soon thereafter. And while I have no family photos that show Maria's siblings, Maria has listed each member in the family Bible. Beside the name of her oldest brother, Peter, and her youngest brother, David, Maria wrote the word *Verband* from the word *Verbannung*, a word that, like a pallbearer, carries the heaviness of death, but is without closure, like the word, "missing." *Verbannung* means banishment. *Verband* means exiled, past tense. It sounds final. Certain death.

Recently, I found out that David did return to his home after a five-year sentence in the camps, but his health was severely weakened and he died not long after his return. Sometime before his arrest, David's first wife had died of sickness, and he had remarried a Russian woman. Following David's death, his parents, the elder Peter and Katherina Siemens, took their grandson Daniel into their custody to live with them.[43]

And, after more investigation, my father and I discovered that Maria's brother, also named Daniel, was arrested and sentenced by the authorities during the '30s, accused of conspiring to topple the government. Charges of conspiracy were often a groundless but effective means to replenish Stalin's slave labour camps. Brother Daniel was held, with the other accused, in an undisclosed prison. There, he witnessed the beating of another man. A gunnysack, inside it, a wagon axle wrapped in paper. The interrogators swung this against the captive's back, groin, stomach — dull thuds against the kidney and muted sound of iron against bone — until the man's body turned to pulp beneath his purple skin. The prisoner hemorrhaged internally. Three days later, blood flowing from his nose and mouth, he died.[44]

Although Jakob and Maria had decided against fleeing to China the year before, other villagers made the escape as late as December 1930. They left from the Amur colony which bordered China, albeit terrified because the GPU were already suspicious. By 1930 people living near the border had been ordered to leave the area.[45] Those who dared escape to China were among the last to try. At minus fifty degrees Celsius, the crisp night air carried the sound of the sleigh runners. From midnight until the sun began its crimson ascent, a caravan of sleighs slowly made their way across to the Chinese shore. Years later, these refugees reached the city of Harbin, and from there, they emigrated to the United States as late as 1934.

As a six-year-old, Aunt Mary remembers with fondness the small farm in Siberia. It was to her "a large and beautiful farm that we had to desert." She also recalls that even close relatives could no longer permit the pastor and his family in their homes, fearing that the authorities would find out. At the age of six, Mary could not have understood the risk of their flight. To be caught would mean exile. Nor would anyone have comprehended that in another decade, most of those left behind in the former colonies-turned-collectives, would simply be swept into the Gulag system. But I am getting ahead of the story.

With Mienke and their four children — Jake, Mary, Gerhardt and Helen — Jakob and Maria moved from Siberia back to Ukraine, to the Fürstenland colony, to the village of Michaelsburg that they referred to as their "beloved old nest." The family left Siberia by train, the little ones sitting under the wooden slats in the train car, concealed by their parents' and Mienke's legs. The authorities knew that the pastor and his wife had young children. The children played quietly for hours in the dim space under the seats, hiding there, as Mary says, to divert attention from a young family travelling.

My father, Peter, was born in Michaelsburg, Fürstenland

colony, Ukraine, on March 13, 1931. He prefaces his own tale with historical facts and figures: under Stalin's "economic plan" ten million people died. Some figures cite fifteen million people. It is incomprehensible that multitudes died of starvation or disappeared, unjustly branded enemies of the state, co-religionists, intellectuals and writers, farmers — people, as Jakob might describe, "blameless in a crooked and depraved generation, shining like stars in the universe. . . ."[46]

❖ HOME PLACE: THE UKRAINE , 1931–1941

The family picture mentioned earlier that I received in Germany, I now discover was taken in Michaelsburg a few years after my father's birth. The photo shows my father at about two years of age, with typically shaved head, posed between Jakob's knees. He is as tall as his father's waist, since Jakob sits on a stool. Their feet and legs have faded from the photograph and it is as though I have come by this photo just in time, before the years erase their images completely. Jakob wears a cap and a white peasant shirt embroidered down the front, the hem, the stand-up collar and on the cuffs. A faint smile traces Jakob's lips. On the left is eight-year-old Gerhardt on nearly invisible legs, his tunic tied with a cord at his waist. Despite my father's baby face, it is Gerhardt's face, although I have never known him, which touches me in a maternal way. His is the face of my son Erik, at that age — even Aunt Mary has pointed this out. Among the family members, at the centre of the photo, big brother Jake in his striped belted tunic, trying to keep a straight face, is standing tall as a tree. Beside him, to his right, is Mary with brunette ringlets, wearing a dark dress, and next to her is their mother, who is seated. A young woman still, Maria wears a stoic expression and the casual print dress of a farm wife. At her outside elbow stands blonde Helen with a pixie haircut.

Like a quilt spread along the south bank of the Little Konka River that runs into the nearby Dnieper, Michaelsburg is composed of ordered rectangles among lines of orchards, a village

Jakob Letkemann family, Ukraine, circa 1933

of forty or so farmyards patterned on fertile soil. Here, fragrant spring blossoms give way to dangling cherries, peaches, apricots and plums under the summer sky, followed by pendulous apples and pears. But this tranquil bed of farmland belies the nightmarish times.

When Peter is born, Maria, Jakob and the children live briefly with Maria's parents; there is always just enough room under their roof, even with *Grosspa* Siemens, Maria's grandfather, living there too in the little shed out back. *Grosspa* plucks stray weeds from the small garden, or sits on a wooden bench and whittles.

This extended family is important in the lives of the young family. In the future, however, when Jakob and Maria must move again, visits become infrequent, if at all. All travel requires permission. Even so, with all the work to be done, there is hardly time for visiting. And with Jakob's preaching assignments, Maria often finds herself alone to rear the children. Will she ever grow used to Jakob's long absences? She is a Mennonite woman — enduring — as her Anabaptist forebears of long-ago Danzig, who believed that God rewarded suffering. She resolves to hold this in the perspective of her faith, to some-day exchange this life for an eternal one on the far bank, across the River Jordan, in the "promised land." Barely audible strains of *"An Jordans Ufer stehe ich"* float across the darkness, wash-ing over the children in their beds as they drift off to sleep.

There was another famine throughout Russia in 1932 to 1933. According to Jakob's written account, "all farmers were to surrender the harvest to the economic plan, sparing none of the grain for their hunger." Indeed, information gathered since the late 1980s has begun to identify the famine of 1932–33 in Ukraine as the Ukrainian Famine-Genocide. As I write this, the issue is a hotly contested topic. Historians, scholars, and politicians have not agreed on the use of the term "genocide," including Aleksandr Solzhenitsyn, who has said that the idea of *Holodomor*, genocide by famine, cannot be "proven."[47] For genocide to have occurred it must have been planned. Yet it can be proven that collectivization was planned, and that the con-fiscation of land from their owners was brutal, resulting in exile and death. The Canadian parliament has passed a bill (June 2008) legally to recognize the 1931–32 famine as genocide.[48]

During this period, the people experience a constant yearn-ing for food, and a dry season has left the crops dying of thirst. As well, the people long for encouragement. Jakob receives a directive from the church to go and visit the exiled people in Narem, Siberia. The elders have received reports that people are starving in the desolate camps, working endlessly cutting trees for a ration of bread. In other camps they mine coal. They hardly sleep. Many die. In various villages, the "churches," now "house fellowships" which are small groups that discreetly meet for fellowship, have organized to collect money and food. Jakob undertakes the trip with another delegate, but waits until Jan-uary when the ground freezes. Otherwise travel is almost im-possible; the swamps swallow people whole. For those in the camps who are severely weakened by hunger and disease, the difficult terrain of the swampland and the debilitating cold mean a successful escape is unlikely.

Jakob has the necessary identification papers to make the trip, papers that state he has permission to travel. He receives his papers from a trusted friend, a man working at the local office of a collective nearby, who stamps them with an official stamp. Before Jakob leaves, Maria sews money into his underwear, stitch by stitch; she carefully secures it knowing that his safety depends on her skill with a needle and thread.

The railway line spans the horizon, heading northeast almost indefinitely. Day becomes night, night becomes day; the only way to tell where you are going is by the changing vegetation. The snow-covered fields turn to forest, bare deciduous trees, the mountain ash and birch mingling with pines. After a long while only conifers appear, their green uniforms under thick coats of snow.

At one remote stop, a man boards the train and sits down across from Jakob, smoking. This is the first thing Jakob, a non-smoker, notices. That the man is shabbily dressed is not suspicious. No one makes conversation. In this land, strangers never talk to one another, not even to pass the time. Jakob falls asleep. There is not much else to do in the monotony but to doze on the wood benches if you can. The friend Jakob is travelling with is asleep also, but not the stranger.

Eventually Jakob awakens. The stranger is gone, along with one suitcase of food! Jakob pats his chest, an immediate, involuntary reflex like the twitching leg of a dog when scratched on the belly, and Jakob knows by the empty folds in his shirt and coat that his ticket and travel papers are also gone. Only the money sewn into his underwear remains. Jakob puzzles over the stranger on the train: a sly thief pretending to smoke, who, instead, must have blown smoldering narcotics into their nostrils, dulling their minds until blackness washed over them? This is what Jakob surmises. Or could it have been sheer exhaustion, strong as a sedative, which provided an opportunity for a common thief?

At last they arrive safely in the Slavgorod Colony, at the familiar villages of years ago. The congregants of the Kleefeld church collect an offering and gather provisions so that Jakob and his companion may purchase another ticket on to the *Taiga-Sibirj*, the taiga forests of Siberia. These people also have loved ones in the camps. Before Jakob and his companion depart from the platform they are detained by local GPU members and taken to an office where they are interrogated, meaning punched, slapped, kicked, and peppered with the same questions, over and over, "Where are you going? Who sent you? What is your purpose? Where are your papers?" What does Jakob answer?

"I am continuing on to Narem to look for my brother." This isn't exactly a lie, for the Brethren, according to their name, call one another "brother." "The papers were stolen," Jakob has written in *Marytrs*.

I don't know how long they are held; Jakob doesn't say. But the weary men can eventually go. Not, however, before the interrogators take some of the money from the offering, whatever is left over after new tickets are purchased. It will cost Jakob and his friend something in order to travel on without papers.

At the last outpost, the most difficult part of the journey begins. With some of the money hidden in his underwear for this purpose, Jakob purchases a horse and sled; he does not rent them or hire a driver, for who wants to drive them into the horrible Siberian cold? Nor does Jakob want a hired hand to report their plans to authorities. The icy breath of Russia blows through their threadbare coats.

On the seventh day they arrive at the barracks. Jakob is shocked at the sight of the sick and starving exiles, living corpses whose eyes grow dim like lanterns without oil. And after they distribute what they have brought, which is so little, but in ways, so much — a word from home, "your wife sends her devoted love," or a memorized portion of the Bible, "the Scripture offers this hope . . ." — the two weary men start on their journey back. And again along the way they are interrogated, followed, kept under surveillance, suspicion appended to them like shadows.

Jakob's long absences are the way of life for his small children. When a man approaches their yard the little ones wonder, "Why does this haggard beggar come here? Doesn't he know Mama has no bread?" His protruding bones poke almost through his skin, and his clothes hang like sacks, but if they look past his scruffy beard and unkempt hair, they will notice his eyes are silver blue. When Maria sees him open the gate she breathes these words, "*Gott sei Dank!*" (Thanks be to God).

The book of *Mennonite Martyrs* contains the following gripping line, written by Jakob: "I have gone through the experience of incarceration, through river, in Siberia all the way to Narem." But in the book, there is no record of his imprisonment, nothing within his brief biography, and I wonder if the "river" he mentions is a literal one, or if it is a metaphor. Jakob does cite the prison experiences of others.

Jakob wrote about a young woman named Neta whose entire family was exiled in 1932. In the forest camp, both her parents and two of her siblings died of starvation. Soon after, she and another orphan attempted escape — their only route being through the swampland. Jakob comments on what Neta must have seen of the others who had preceded her in attempted escapes: the top of heads, one here, one there, shockingly visible to Neta and her companion as they trudged through the muck. Although exhausted, the women continued, for if they stopped, even for a moment, they, too, might have disappeared into the mire. "*God have mercy*," Jakob wrote, as though years afterward he was horrified at the conditions that, throughout the time of his own survival, were numbing. And Neta? "Afterwards," Jakob concluded, "Neta was recaptured, but no one knows if she survived."[49]

The final sentence of Jakob's account, placed there by an editor, says that there are more stories to be found elsewhere.

Where are these personal narratives? Perhaps these are the stories destroyed by fire long ago in Canada.[50] If a generation's stories are extinguished, their voices, like candles, snuffed out, we forget to remember the ones, who, before us, suffered unjustly. They disappear into the mire of atrocity.

My cousins relay an oral story passed on to them from either their father Jake sometime before he died, or more recently by Aunt Mary. It is a story of Jakob's conversation with another prisoner about faith.

"Jakob," says a starving prisoner, "how can you believe in God in a place like this?"

Jakob responds, "If I die an unbeliever, I have nothing to gain. If I die believing in God, I have everything to gain, so I choose to hope in something better than this."

His words sound similar to those of Blaise Pascal's, who wagered that "if you gain, you gain all" and "if you lose, you lose nothing." The difference is that Jakob could never have posited such a state of nothing-ness after all this worldly suffering.

❖ THE FUGITIVE

All preachers must renounce their vocation and their religion. Either that, or register with the Communist Party as a "cult practitioner." Once registered as such, the preacher has all his rights as a citizen rescinded, and that means the right to eat. The GPU arrives at Jakob and Maria's house. While two men take Jakob aside, two others lead his wife and small children out to the field as he watches. "Look at them, Jakob. Is your God worth it?" Jakob is tormented by the very thought of his family suffering, and yet, has God not always provided?

At this moment one of them tells Maria, "Unless Jakob renounces God, you and the children will go without bread." Maria silently thinks that to go without bread is not new to her, but if Jakob signs, what then? Either way, she is terrified of her children starving to death. Jakob will not deny his belief in God, so he and his family are denied bread cards. And Jakob is unemployable in the village. The family is destitute. This is the price of faithfulness.

Throughout the region, Jakob's name is openly posted. This effectively means that he is a "wanted" man. But Jakob is resourceful, selling sunflower oil to support his family and to aid his work as an itinerant preacher. He travels the dusty roads and foot paths from village to village, or rides the rail lines between Ukraine and Siberia, or sometimes the Rostov Baku rail-line winding from Ukraine through the craggy Caucasus Mountains down to Crimea. Wherever Jakob travels, he stops at Mennonite settlements along the way. Everyone has relatives scattered about. While Jakob is hungry for food, they are hungry for news: a fair barter for all. They even purchase his sunflower oil.

At his lowest point, Jakob walks past a cemetery, and, for one moment, envies the buried ones. He has seen a lifetime of suffering across this young Union of Soviet Socialist Republics, the people in exile, many living in hunger. In this life of suffering, all walk like skeletons. He prays for strength and patience, perhaps in the language of faith that my grandmother would later use in her poetry:

> Patience in tribulation, the Cross is your need,
> The soul grows weary, the heart becomes soft,
> In the Cross, age finds meaning in death,
> As we journey through tribulation to Heaven.[51]

The criminal code will not tolerate the religious conversion of children by parents: at school all children are indoctrinated with Communism by teachers. A razor-thin line lies between Jakob and Maria's safety and that of their family's. The authorities would sever families, parents from children, because of faith. Jakob and Maria are cautious. Although they have told the children stories, only much later will the children realize that these tales are from the Old Testament — stories of a talking snake, a whale, and a boy who slays a giant with a slingshot. Such stories help the parents instill in their small ones moral integrity — the values of honesty, obedience and bravery. Occasionally the siblings sing the chorus, *Gott ist die Liebe* (God is love) in round-song with their parents. However, Jakob and Maria do not speak to them about salvation, the very thing Jakob and Maria believe their faithfulness promises. To speak of this to the children is a violation of the criminal code. To "convert" them to the Christian faith would make the children an "enemy of the people."

My father recalls the simple prayers of his childhood. In his earliest memory these were purely rituals to him. As tiny Peter learns to speak, he learns also to pray. As he grows older, each night he dutifully prays for forgiveness. The little boy confesses his specific sins, "Today I told a lie; please forgive me." Or, "Today I stole a fallen apple from under the neighbour's tree; I'm sorry but I was so hungry." It is customary to first ask his parents for forgiveness for wrongdoing, then the Lord: *Lieber Heiland, mach mich fromm, dass ich in den Himmel komm.* All the children recite the German bedtime rhyme in the same cadence as this English one, "Now I lay me down to sleep, I pray the Lord, my soul to keep, and should I die before I wake, I pray the Lord, my soul to take." At the hand-hewn table, before a slice of bread, they utter this simple prayer, *Komm Herr Jesus, sei unser Gast, and segne was Du uns bescheret hast.* Its English equivalent is "Come Lord Jesus, be our guest, and let this food to us be blessed." Choruses and prayers by rote are as nursery songs and rhymes. Maybe someday, when the children are older, they will discern spiritual truth for themselves, in accordance "with the law."

All the while, the faith of their parents is tested at the deepest level. In the lamplight before kneeling together on the earthen floor, Jakob and Maria pull thick curtains across the wood-framed windows, for the windows are eyes, both out of, and into their home. The Bible is outlawed . . . but scriptures offer spiritual hope: "Blessed are those who are persecuted, for theirs is the Kingdom of Heaven" (Matthew 5:10). Were the teachings from the Bible to be interpreted literally? "But I tell you this; do not resist an evil person. If someone strikes you on the right cheek, turn to him the other also" (Matthew 5:39).

On December 24, 1935, the Mennonites, persistent in their faith, gathered despite the danger, but in keeping with the law there were no children present to celebrate this holy eve. There was a tree, lit with candles. The church was packed, over capacity, and the air, warmed by the heat of bodies, was redolent with pine and wax scent. It was such a beautiful sight, this evergreen — a symbol of life — commemorating the birth of a baby. The adult choir practised hymns and the song *Stille Nacht* (Silent Night), and the young single women with plaited hair, old enough to attend church, recited the nativity passage from Luke Chapter 2: "And so it came to pass that in those days a decree went out from Caesar Augustus that all the world should be taxed. . . ."

Taxation . . . levies . . . a people under the government. Yes, this story resonated. Of course, the pastor must not allude to political or religious oppression. "And the Angel said to them, 'Fear not: for behold I bring you good tiding of great joy which shall be to all people. . . .'" Fear not. But the program was interrupted by murmuring in the congregation, and all heads craned towards the back. The village chief arrived to announce that the GPU wanted Jakob Letkemann. After the service, Jakob stole away to the neighbouring Russian villages and then to Nikopol, the city close by, where Jewish friends took him in.

Days later: three sharp knocks at the door. Maria knew it was Jakob; he sometimes came at night to bring her bread, or potatoes, or perhaps cloth from the city. Maria was a good seamstress. But Maria never knew from one time to the next when, or even if, he would come.

Another time, one winter evening — or this could be part of the 1935 Christmas episode, for all of Jakob's flights seem to flow together in family memory — a group of men appeared at the door. They came to take Jakob to the local office for questioning. This time he was there, and he went quietly. The image reflected in Maria's eyes was of Jakob on the back of the sleigh, against the frozen luminescent steppes. Besides her beating heart, the only other sound was the horses' crunching footfalls on the snow, fading until Jakob disappeared from sight.

Somehow Jakob did not arrive with the sled for his interrogation. During the ride, he rolled off the back and dropped, unnoticed, into the darkening vastness. He burrowed under the snow and lay there until he felt safe enough to make his way home, to retrieve a sack of clothes and some bread, stashed away in the event of necessity.

❖

Here is another story of Jacob's escapes, this one occurring when my father was still very young, perhaps four years old, and I wonder if this is a missing piece, a fragment of a larger story, as if memories born from trauma are thrown against the mind's bone wall to shatter. Could this be part of the story about the attic that my father told in my childhood? *Was his father hiding there* when his mother received a visit from the local officials? Usually a trusted villager sent a warning ahead about which person the authorities in the city would be coming for, so possibly, Jakob fled beforehand.

After a knock at the door the official shouted: "Your husband owes outstanding taxes!" Of course Maria had no rubles to pay. With excessive quotas, one barely managed. It was an excuse to evict them, or to scare Maria into denouncing Jakob. "If you inform against your husband, we will forgive what you owe." The Communist regime used blackmail to incite one person to inform on another, children on parents, husband against wife, wife against husband . . . and if fear could not tear apart the fabric of family, exile would.

When Maria refused to inform on Jakob, the men ransacked the house for clothes, bedding, what little Maria had to clothe, feed and keep her children warm. They stripped the cupboards, and took what was there to the local people who would certainly have use for them. Maria's father attended the sale to purchase back her sewing machine. She would need it to mend clothes or sew garments in exchange for bread. And Maria persuaded a neighbour to purchase her hand-sewn goose-down duvets so that she could later buy them back. But even their beds had been sold. (Jakob later wrote that everything sold for thirty rubles. Did it remind him of another story about a wanted travelling preacher and thirty pieces of silver?) Maria and the children, with no place of their own, stayed with her parents. After a while, Maria went on to the next home: to her sister Liese who also lived in Michaelsburg. Liese and her husband David took them in until enough time passed and Jakob could safely return. For her own safety, and for the children's, Maria never knew where Jakob was.

I find out that this is where the story of the sachet of flour comes in. It was here, in Liese and David's barn, that Maria hid it. David, who worked in the village office, was already under suspicion because of his house guests. Office workers always heard about whom the authorities were looking for, and David became increasingly uncomfortable. When he discovered the bag of flour Maria stashed away, he asked his sister-in-law and her children to leave. All over, people were being arrested for hiding food.[52]

The flour incident was censored from the family stories, but the part about Mrs. Unruh, the kind woman who sheltered them, was never omitted. Grandmother preserved the story, naming her trusted friend; my father told me about her. Apparently the same thing had happened to Mrs. Unruh, the authorities had stripped her house of all its goods. Alone, without a husband, she and her children had very little to live on, but they had a hovel in which to dwell, and she possessed mercy and courage enough to take in another desperate mother and her five hungry children. Once, when the cupboards were bare, the two women discovered a loaf of bread on the doorstep . . .

Jakob? Soon after, he returned to Michaelsburg to collect his family from Mrs. Unruh, with many thanks for her help. The years ahead, from 1936 to 1938 would become known in history as the "Great Purge."

3

◈

Childhood's Time

Why is it that my town still enchants
me so? Is it because my memory is
entangled with my childhood?

— ELIE WIESEL

◈ SAKHALIN, 1936

The little Ukrainian settlement had once been part of a large estate that had been collectivized. It was named after the island off Pacific Russia, near Japan, where Stalin condemned prisoners to harsh labour. When Jakob was given work as a herdsman in the village Sakhalin, the overseer of the collective at Rosengart, three kilometres away, granted Jakob permission to settle in a vacant brick hut. It was this overseer, a Mennonite man in a position of authority, who had been providing Jakob with travel and identity papers. Although it was a lonely place with only six Ukrainian families, none of whom knew them, the sole "German" family, Sakhalin was a refuge for a time.

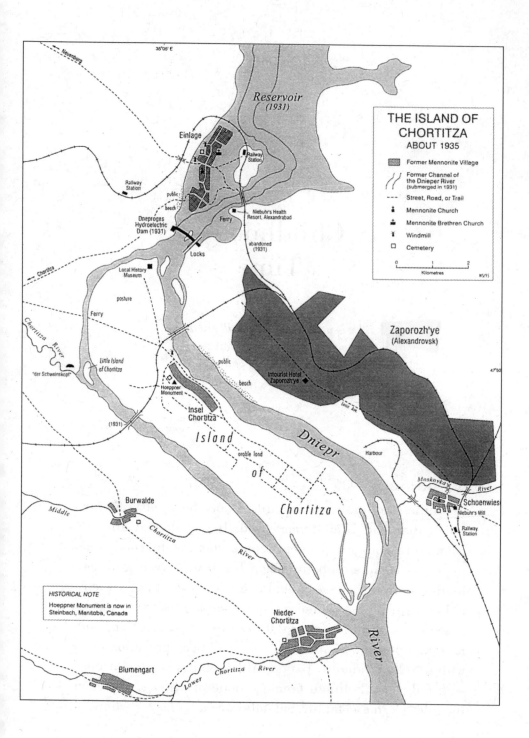

THE ISLAND OF
CHORTITZA
ABOUT 1935

Former Mennonite Village

Former Channel of
the Dnieper River
(submerged in 1931)

Street, Road, or Trail

Mennonite Church

Mennonite Brethren Church

Windmill

Cemetery

0   1   2
Kilometres   WS/15

35°05' E

Neuenburg

Reservoir
(1931)

Einlage

Railway
Station

Railway
Station

public
beach

Dneproges
Hydroelectric
Dam (1931)

Ferry

Niebuhr's Health
Resort, Alexandrabad

Locks

abandoned
(1931)

Local History
Museum

Chortitza

pasture

Ferry

Chortitza River

Little Island
of Chortitza

'der Schweinskopf'

Hoeppner
Monument

public

Insel
Chortitza

beach

Intourist Hotel
Zaporozh'ye

Zaporozh'ye
(Alexandrovsk)

47°50

(1931)

Island

arable land

of

Dniepr

Harbour

Lenin Ave.

Moskovka   River

Chortitza

Schoenwiese

Niebuhr's Mill

Railway
Station

Burwalde

Middle

Chortitza

River

HISTORICAL NOTE

Hoeppner Monument is now in
Steinbach, Manitoba, Canada

Nieder-
Chortitza

River

Blumengart

Lower   Chortitza   River

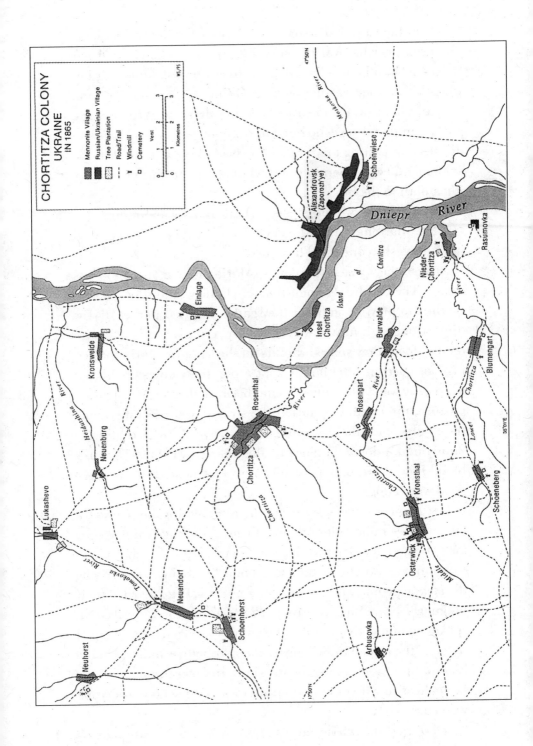

CHORTITZA COLONY
UKRAINE
IN 1865

Mennonite Village
Russian/Ukrainian Village
Tree Plantation
Road/Trail
Windmill
Cemetery

Vent

Kilometres

WS/95

Dniepr River

Alexandrovsk
(Zaporozh'ye)

Schoenwiese

Moskovka River

Rasumovka

Nieder-
Chortitza

of

Chortitza

Chortitza River

Insel
Chortitza
Island

Burwalde

Blumengart

Einlage

Rosengart

River

Kronsweide

Rosenthal

River

Schoeneberg

Heidelbach River

Neuenburg

Chortitza

Lower Chortitza

Kronsthal

Osterwick

Middle

Lukashevo

Chortitza

Tomakovka River

Neuendorf

Schoenhorst

Arbusovka

Neuhorst

Out in the yard, Peter sometimes noticed the next door lady, Shamrei, peering over the stick fence. When she clucked her tongue at him he used to stick out his own pink tongue at her when his mother was not looking. On more than one occasion Shamrei bent over and flipped up her dress, wagging her fat, pale behind at Peter, who burst into a fit of giggles. And Shamrei did the same thing to Maria, who always kept to herself in the settlement, even when in the yard hanging out wash or sweeping a path to the hut.

"That colonist woman has airs, and so fussy about dirt!"

"*Ach*, that Shamrei," Maria clucked her tongue and pursed her lips as she continued her work.

At first, there was no garden, so Maria planted one. Food was scarce. The children's stomachs were hollow. And there was little time to play. In summer they gathered dried patties of cow dung along with tumbleweeds to store and use for fuel in winter. For food, they snared rabbits on the steppes. Maria roasted pigeons. Because the family kept a pig, the youngsters picked weeds, pig weed they called it, and because there was no private pasture, the children plucked the stray grass bunching along the roadside for the cow tethered in the yard. In Sakhalin the family had a dog, a large white dog that growled as if a wolf's blood flowed through her veins. Nero was mean, but she was a good watch dog.

Herding cows was work generally reserved for the poorest, a job least desirable, but work nonetheless. Although quite young, Peter helped, too. He was not old enough to go to school where Russian was taught in the classroom, but living here among the steppe people who were not Mennonites, Peter learned their language, branching out from *Plattdeutsch* (or *Plautdietsch*) spoken at home. In fall, the older children walked over the open fields to the school in Rosengart where other German-speaking Mennonites lived among the Russians and Ukrainians working the collective. Of course, when there was no school, everyone worked.

It became the whole family's job to watch the animals as

they wandered the boundless steppes in summer to graze — long hot days spent among the tall grasses, an acacia tree here or there casting a spot of shade. Jakob looked after the horses together with Jake, a strapping teenager considered a man. Mary and Gerhardt attended the cows, while Helen and Peter minded the heifers calmly nuzzling spring-born calves.

The aromatic steppes spread beyond the village, unhindered by fences, grasses mingling with blue and purple wildflowers in spring, sprinkled with lilies-of-the-valley, crocuses, and wild daffodils. Alongside the sleepy calves, Helen and Peter wandered and amused themselves, as little ones do, often gathering bouquets to brighten Maria's humble table, or for her to dry and take to the bazaar in nearby Zaporozhye, the city by the large dam, twelve kilometres away.[1]

On a summer day when Peter is four years old, Maria says to him, "If you like, and if you walk like a big boy even when you are tired, I'll take you along with me to market." Peter is so happy he promises to cooperate, and oh, he can hardly sleep the night before when he must go to bed earlier than usual for the big day tomorrow.

They leave early. The air is still slightly cool and the steppes are moist with dew.

At the outdoor market in Zaporozhye, the *babushka* selling eggs has stacked them into one large pyramid. The old man selling peaches piles the fiery coloured balls in this manner too, taking the fruit from the top to sell; no one touches the peaches but him! A lady sells bouquets of flowers like the ones Mama sometimes brings, and the women who live in the city buy them for their kitchen tables. Peter thinks the vendor has flowers of every colour on earth! The butcher has pig feet and snouts, chicken feet, and thick yellow slabs of lard. The fish counter displays huge fish from the Dnieper. Sold separately for soup, their detached heads, big as cabbages, have thick lipped, gaping mouths, and bulging eyes that stare blankly at Peter.

At mid-morning Maria says, "It's time to go, and now I have

one more surprise for you." The sun is glowing white, the air is hot and dry; Maria brings Peter to the nearby sandy shore of the Dnieper, to a beach where they can swim. "*Mama, guck mal* (look) . . . all the *Tanten* (ladies) are swimming in their underwear!" shouts the little boy pointing. Maria undresses him and he stands there almost bare, in his underpants. The women and children swim in one area, the men in another. Under the brilliant sky, the river is lazy and sparkles as though someone has sprinkled sugar crystals on its surface. And the beach is so white, it looks as if it is made from sugar.

But what Peter will always remember about this wonderful day is his first taste of ice-cream. "Vanilla, between two cookies like an ice-cream sandwich. I can still taste it," my father says.

◈

The sun rises early and the work of herding the animals begins at first light. A piece of dark bread, half the size of Peter's palm, and a cup of hot *Prips* (a drink from roasted grains), all that Maria has to give, will not be enough to keep away the hunger pangs during the work day that ends in darkness. Bread without butter is poverty — especially dark bread! (To this day my father savours crusty white rolls with a dollop of butter, a personal luxury.) But on the steppes, Peter sometimes finds a bird's egg, unattended. So as not to crack it, he coats it with dirt and spit, before placing it in the late-afternoon camp-fire to cook. At other times, Peter meanders to the collective's potato fields, and when no one is looking, snatches a few like cookies from a cookie jar. These too, he brings back to put in the camp-fire on the steppe to roast for a snack. How delicious.

While herding in the fields one day, five-year-old Peter and seven-year-old Helen grow distracted by the wild flowers and cicadas. By mid-day, the hours stretch long as the horizon. The calves begin to stray close to the border of the village, not Sakhalin, but another small one. Two older fellows from the other village are also herding cows nearby. They approach. A little girl and her smaller brother would be no match for these tall boys, big like Jake, and young Peter just *knows*, anxiety like a large stone dropping to the bottom of his stomach, that these are two are coming to take the calves.

But today Jake is not far away and once in a while he casts a glance at his little siblings. He, too, notices the strangers. With saucer eyes, Peter watches Jake amble closer, suddenly breaking into a sprint, waving his club, the one he uses for the stubborn animals. The two herdsmen see him and decide to abandon the robbery. They turn and run. But Jake aims and throws the club hard. It hits one of the would-be thieves behind the knee, who yelps and falls, while the other scrambles off like a mongrel caught near a hen-house.

Peter's lower lip quivers. He understands the significance of this event even without Jake scolding him harshly, his eyes flashing. Jake exclaims: "If they had taken those calves, it would be off to Siberia for all of us!" No doubt missing calves would mean disaster. Peter rapidly blinks away the tears clinging to his lashes. Jake must not think he is too small to watch the calves properly. He can! Thereafter, Peter and Helen always keep closer watch.

Each day the family herds cattle; at dusk they walk the herd home, their hooves tethered to long mauve shadows, moving slowly across the darkening fields back to the corrals. Then again, even before the rising sun pushes up the pink morning, they lead their assigned cattle out to the steppes. Day after day.

On one particular spring afternoon, a light breeze ripples the fields into a sage-coloured sea. Like a tiny boat under sail, a man approaches from the distance. Nearing, his form grows, until he looms over Peter. In Russian he asks, "Can you tell me where Jakob Letkemann lives?"

My father reflects, "I must have looked like a little Ukrainian peasant.

"You can speak German to me," Peter says wrinkling his nose to squint up at the man standing against the sun.

The nearest settlement is very small. It shouldn't be difficult for the man to find who he is looking for, even if the child won't say. In this area, a German-speaking boy could likely be Jakob and Maria's. And a child so small would not be far from home. As the stranger walks on, the little *Bengel* (rascal) stands, hands on hip, shifting one hand to visor his eyes as he watches the man shrink into the distance.

The traveller eventually found Jakob and Maria and told them about the amusing little "German" boy he had encountered on the steppe. The parents glanced at one another and shared the thought, "Who could that be but our Peter?"

And though all was well — for the man was an old friend to Jakob and Maria but unknown to Peter — when the family gathered at the end of the day, Jakob and Maria sharply reminded Peter, as if he might one day forget, "*Never* let a stranger know where we live." It was a standard reminder to each one of them.

They might have said to Peter, instead, "Never draw attention to yourself." This was an aphorism they also lived by.

❖ ROSENGART (NOVOSLOBODKA), 1937–1940

After the family had lived in Sakhalin for a short while, Jakob acquired permission to move into the large collective nearby. It was already, by this time, a well-established collective. Perhaps this is the reason that its workers were less prone to random arrests compared to the people living in many of the other villages dotting Ukraine. Rosengart was originally settled by sixteen Mennonite families in 1824, one of the Old Colony's last settlements.[2] It lay five kilometres away from Chortiza. By 1918, each of the village farms had sixty-five *dessjatimen*, the equivalent to approximately 162 acres. In those days there were thirteen landless (tenant) families hired on to work. As the population increased, families split the land into smaller parcels, passed it on to a son, or sold it. In 1928 Rosengart was collectivized and each house was allotted approximately one acre of land. Since then, only one man and wife had disappeared from the model state farm, and this was in 1931.[3] Inhabitants said the couple had complained about the village's collectivization.

This former Mennonite village had been turned into a showpiece to foreign dignitaries who came to view the success of Communism. During the early 1920s at the World Exhibition in Paris, the design for Rosengart won a prize. Nearby lay Dnieprostroi, the new dam across the Dnieper. People at the World Fair did not know that the cement for the dam was to be mixed by the feet of Gulag prisoners. It was inaugurated in 1932, and reached its production capacity in 1939. It was the world's largest dam until the Hoover Dam in America was completed.

Close to the new hydroelectric facilities near Zaporozhye, Rosengart was surely the Marxist ideal. The women who milked the cows wore crisp white aprons and colourful *platoks* covering their heads. The cattle and horses were prize-winning animals. There were seven orchards, three vineyards and nine vegetable gardens. There was also a feed mill, a blacksmith's forge and a carpentry shop. The collective boasted thirty wagons, four grass-cutters, one shear plough, thirteen multiple-shear ploughs and eight machines for sowing grain.[4] It was impressive to see the men working in the fields with machines, cultivating the surrounding land into a golden sea of wheat, barley and sunflowers. Foreigners who came to view it exclaimed that Communism was good for the people!

There was a village school made of brick with a clay tile roof, built in 1909. There was also a library with Russian books but no German ones — from the time when the Mennonites had lived there earlier. Although the railway tracks ran past the village there was no train station here; the closest one was some little distance away at Dnieprostroi. And there was no church in Rosengart; in the old days the Mennonite residents were members of the Chortiza church.[5] Besides, now Sunday was a work day.

In 1937, it was here that Jakob believed his family would be safest. Stalin's purges continued, and the Mennonites were particularly suspect, considered subversive because of their German-ness. The Mennonites believed they were viewed as enemies because of the help they received from abroad during the famine.[6] Certainly, the Mennonites' resistance to Communist youth programs, in particular, drew the attention of the authorities. The Mennonites did not want their children exposed to atheist teaching, or to swear their allegiance to the Party, as required. Nevertheless, here, in the mix of German, Ukrainian, and Russian workers, Jakob's family could blend in. Jakob would work with the animals and on the machines. Maria would hoe in the tomato fields, or the cucumber, carrot and cabbage patches.

There was no house for them, but the family received a patch of dirt at the crest of the steppe before it sloped gently down a long and gradual hill into the settlement. Theirs was the last street in Rosengart, on the *Böweland* (low-German word for upland), although it was not higher by much. Below their street were the show barns for the cattle and for the dairy. Here, too, were the threshing barn and the first and second brigade clubhouses. At the opposite corner, where the middle road and the first street met, in a shallow bowl of land, sat the schoolhouse. The first road continued past the school, up a long hill, beside the cemetery and crossed over the train tracks. It was a cobblestone road built by the Mennonites who first established Rosengart. To enter the village from Chortiza, or from Zaporozhye, one came by the cobblestone road.

Before the family moved into Rosengart, Jakob, together with Jake, spent hours, after their work in the fields when the sky remained light longer, preparing the home-site, chopping trees from stands of slim birch behind the village. From these slender trunks, four to five inches in diameter, they fashioned the rafters. At day's end, their shoulders sagging, father and son fell into step, the tired rhythm of their footfalls forming wordless conversation from the *Böweland* of Rosengart, for the three kilometre distance over the steppes back to Sakhalin.

The rest of the family also helped on Saturdays. Jakob staked out the dimensions of the house with twine. Maria stood by envisioning the rooms through imaginary clay walls: one main room where the family would visit and eat, and, where, afterwards the couple slept; another room behind this where the children slept and for the oven, the oven's breath to warm the slumbering children during winter; and behind the outer wall, the summer kitchen. The bricks for the house were made of clay mixed with straw. Trampling the straw into the ooze was a job suitable for Peter. The older boys poured this into a wooden form that measured one-and-a-half feet long by one foot wide, and eight inches thick. After the mud dried, everyone stacked the bricks for Jakob to lay. These walls, he thought, would shield his family from the short summer's intense heat, and shelter them during the long cold season that began in late September and lasted until the snow disappeared in spring.

To coat the interior walls, Maria, Mary, and Helen mixed cow manure with water, smearing this plaster over the bricks and rubbing until the walls were smooth. Then an application of paint — lime, water and flour. Every Saturday's housekeeping chore thereafter was to cover dirtied areas with this white mixture. Also on Saturday, Maria swept the dirt floor, first smeared with manure and dried; afterwards, white sand sprinkled over to make it look nice. It stank, but it looked nice. And, along with the other Mennonite women, she swept the walkways and dirt yards. Rosengart, like the other villages founded by the Mennonites, was lovely. Even before it was taken over and collectivized, it was tidy in comparison to the surrounding Ukrainian villages. Just like the other uniform brick houses in Rosengart, theirs too, had windows in the end gables. They looked like eyes peeking cautiously beneath sloping straw hats.

This was the family home with a warm oven and a wooden table to gather around, although there was never enough food to fill their stomachs. Nevertheless, they did not starve. Each household received nine kilograms of flour, 200 grams of butter, and 400 grams of oil per month — if these were available after the quota.

Beneath the kitchen was a root cellar where Maria stored her garden's potatoes, carrots, beets, cabbage and onions and apples for the coming winter. Maria pickled almost everything, even watermelon, and she preserved or dried the produce against the time when the ground no longer pushed forth something to eat. She cooked fruit soup (*Moos*) with cherries, apricots and plums from her few trees. From her garden came dill, tomatoes, potatoes, carrots, onions, beets and cabbage. Picked, washed and chopped with help from her girls, Maria then simmered the vegetables into a tasty *Borscht*. And if the cow produced enough, Maria kept a pail of milk to sour in the summer kitchen. Jakob also built a large clay oven in the yard for her to bake bread on long plates during summer days. That is, if ingredients were available. At the back of the house was a small barn for the cow, pig and hen. Here, too, the bee-hive.

And in the frozen winter, insulated somewhat by the straw roof, a bucket in the barn served as the toilet. The children made sure to go before bed; a trip there in the middle of the night would sting their buttocks and they would shiver long afterwards beside their siblings under the down covers, the sound of chattering teeth filling the darkness. In warmer weather they used the outhouse, pinching their noses against the smell that drew bluebottles and horseflies, clenching their mouths tight against the buzzing black swarm bumping against the walls.

There was an endless amount of work to do at home after their labour on the collective. And much of the household productivity was taken as quota. In Rosengart, each household had a quota of milk from their cow to deliver to the collective, and half of their produce or meat from their own butchering, along with the milk. Even if the cow was dry, there was a quota to fill. The inhabitants devised a system. When the family cow was dry, Maria obtained milk from the neighbour, and when their cow didn't produce milk, they came to her. They worked together in this way so each neighbour could fill his or her quota. Everyone was also levied a little of what was left over from the quota for their own use, and if there was enough to spare, Maria took something to market to buy other staples or supplies.

It seems an irony to me that they lived in the same manner as their forebears did, close to the earth, toiling daily, but now under a system and society that claimed to be the most advanced in history — one that, instead of liberating the people, oppressed them to an unbelievable degree.

The purge that began in 1937, when the family moved to Rosengart, lasted to 1939. Even young children knew what it meant when the sound of a motor broke the darkness. There were no cars in the village; it was always a black car from the city. It came at night to catch people sleeping in their beds — but Jakob always heard it, the way a dog hears the high pitches a human cannot. In their beds, the children shivered until after the distant car engine died away; then they could slip back down the narrow black well of sleep. But sometimes trucks arrived in the villages in broad daylight with guards on top. Millions of people everywhere were arrested, the human resources to implement another "Five Year Plan." During that time, even in the model collective, four men disappeared, three in 1938, and one in 1939. One more man also disappeared in 1940.[7]

❖

As children generally do, the children of the collective acclimatized to their circumstances. Peter's memories take shape, grow firm like modelled clay, not yet dried or shattered. His happiest memories of home will remain intact, and when he is a grown man, they will pull him back. Place is the anchor of memory.

The Middle Chortiza River, actually a slender stream, winds its way through the settlement the way a small garter snake slips through blades of grass. Its serpentine formation necessitates four small, wooden crossings so that the cobble street may run straight. From the bridges, Peter tosses in pebbles, his pockets always bulging with them. Or sometimes it is sticks, which he watches as they bob swiftly downstream like miniature barges on the pretend Dnieper. Black, curly Mops, barking excitedly, races along the grassy bank to fetch them. Nearby, at the water's edge, Maria rinses her laundry on wash day. Sometimes in summer Peter swims here, but the undertow is swift, and once pulled him under. The swimming hole is further along the river at the far end of the village. On his way there, the dry dusty road puffs clouds as he runs, barefoot, along it.

In August, the leaves and vines are verdant wind chimes as the breeze sweeps through, carrying a fruity scent. In among the leaves are apples, the green-skinned kind, heavy and tart with flavour. But there are guards with front-loading shotguns they stuff with salt to fire at birds, or apple thieves. A blast of salt spray in the backside will sting like angry hornets.

Peter loiters by the feed mill, then the blacksmith's forge and the carpentry shop. The sounds of tools and machines ring like songs in his head. And the sheds are potent with the smells of sweet grain and burlap, axle grease, leather, heat and sweat.

Sunday is a work day. Everyone may rest on Saturday, but on Saturday, the Mennonite women tend their own little gardens, clean their houses, sweep their yards. With no day to worship on anymore, Saturday does not replace the day of rest for Mennonites for whom, it seems, cleanliness is next to godliness. Sometimes on Saturday afternoon big sister Mary takes Peter and Helen to pick wildflowers on the steppes. Then Maria composes small arrangements in a symphony of colour. On rainy Saturdays Jakob crafts shoes with a wooden sole, a leather piece covering the front of the foot. For winter wear, Maria quilts leg warmers to slip on. All of these items Maria can sell at the bazaar.

On the day Maria walks the twelve kilometres to Zaporozhye, to the city market to sell her wares, Helen and Peter remain at the foot of the road. They watch as she grows smaller until at last she disappears, bearing the weight of milk pails on a yoke. With one pail hanging from either side she resembles a walking weigh scale. Brother and sister play away the hours — conjuring toys from rocks and sticks, and in summer, from cucumbers — until at last their Mama returns. Their imagination brings the toys to life. Cows, horses and dogs. Soft bodies of over-ripe cucumbers with sticks poking out for legs. They mimic what they know, herding cucumber "cows" in the dirt.

If Ma has rubles from trading, once Peter and Helen get a little older, seven or eight, the two walk the five kilometers, in the opposite direction of Zaporozhye, to the Old Colony, to a bakery in Chortiza-Rosenthal where they line up to buy the allotted two kilos of bread per person. The lineup is always so long! An hour or more, and often there is no bread by the time Peter and Helen reach the front. When this happens, they go home empty-handed, wake up earlier the next morning, and walk all the way back to stand in line, until their legs ache again. But Peter has a better idea. If they cut in, they will shorten the time. If they sneak in more than once — more bread! They collect six kilos once, one loaf each above the allotment, before the store clerk catches on. The siblings sprint down the main road through Chortiza-Rosenthal, Helen running with the bread loaves to her chest, precious as dolls, her braids yellow streamers behind her, and Peter squeezing his loaves tightly in his armpits.

These few years seem the best ones. Unlike their watchdog Nero, who is mostly chained to the tree, the affectionate Mops is a companion to Peter. At home when the family is all together at the end of the day, Mops entertains everyone by howling accompaniment to Jakob and Maria's singing.

A rooster crows heartily each morning to wake the family. He is regal, crowned with a red comb, a strutting, dandy bird, with a brown chest, shiny black neck, and shimmering green tail feathers that he permits the children to stroke. When he is not preening in front of the chickens, he trails after Peter and Helen playing in the yard. Does he think he is a cat? He certainly is as tame as one; the children grow to regard the rooster as a pet. He delights them with his proud *ku-ka-rye-ku*.

And on the warm summer evenings, over the cicadas' chorus, the nightingales' songs ring out from the thickets behind the house.

On that first Christmas in Rosengart, my father was seven. It is the Christmas that stands out in his mind above most others, because, on that one, his mother somehow scraped together a paltry but precious supply of eggs, butter, sugar and flour to bake cookies. On Christmas Eve, Maria set out plates bearing a few candies from her trading in Zaporozhye and a home-baked cookie or two for each of the children. It was a Christmas miracle. I remember such plates that my mother set out for us on Christmas Eve, part of our family tradition throughout my childhood. Our plates, my brothers and mine, spilled over with foil-wrapped Santas, peanuts, mandarin oranges, and candy-canes. My own memory makes the world of Father's childhood seem terribly far away. "There wasn't much," he says and wonders aloud how his parents managed.

Most memories of this early time, before my father was ten years old in Rosengart, have long lain dormant, but as my father remembers one, it tugs another to awakening, such as this one involving his father and that rooster. It is springtime. It is the morning when the cock didn't crow.

The rooster won't crow all that day, or the next morning. Or the next. He no longer struts about the yard: he takes only a few lethargic steps. Peter notices that the bird's lovely feathers have lost their brilliance. The rooster is fading! Peter points this out to Helen, who sees it too, and when Jakob comes home from the fields, they rush to tell him, begging him to fix their pet, "Papa, please! Make him better!" as if Jakob can fix everything, which he generally does, out of necessity — but a dying rooster? Doubtful, Jakob reluctantly agrees to try, and instructs his children to fetch his *Rasiermesser* (shaving knife/razor), and to catch his patient. Helen retrieves the razor, and Peter collects the bird as Jakob sharpens the shaving-now-surgical instrument against the stiff leather strap. Peter carries the rooster into the kitchen, to the table, which transforms into the operating table. At Jakob's strict instructions Peter holds it firmly, wings tucked. A flapping rooster will not do. With a hand clamped around the beak, Jakob lifts the wattle and makes an incision in its *Kropf* (crop), below the throat, in what appears to be the proud chest, which is really the bulge at the end of the esophagus, and as he probes the sack-like organ with his fingers, he finds and extracts the short nail the rooster swallowed. He stitches up the bird with Maria's needle and thread.

"A few days later, the rooster was crowing again and we had our pet back." Thinking about it now, my father seems quite pleased.

I wonder if the memory of the rooster connects my father to this next memory of the winter when he was seven, perhaps the same winter as that first Christmas in Rosengart when Maria baked the cookies. I think that these memories, like the rooster, are stitched together because of Jakob and his shaving knife. I envision Jakob as country veterinarian and general practitioner, the barber, too — even the family dentist, if he has a set of pliers!

My father remembers that in winter he used to get boils due to malnutrition and the lack of vitamins A and E in their winter diet. He remembers how red and painful these were, smoldering volcanoes on thighs and buttocks, or under the arm or on the back — before eruption. In particular, he remembers one, the size of a small egg, on the inside of his left arm.

Peter knows it must be drained but he whimpers at the thought. Swish, swish, swish, goes the *Rasiermesser* against Pa's black strap. Lightly, the hot sharp blade slices the offending boil, just a thumb-width across. This is not as bad as Peter has imagined it would be. Afterwards, Jacob swabs the site with iodine and wraps a clean rag around Peter's arm to protect the incision from infection. It will leave only a small pink crescent.

And maybe that's the reason this small incident hasn't faded altogether. There it is: a curved faint smudge on the inside of my father's left arm. To this day, over six decades later. Left behind like Jakob's finger print as my father and I dust the past for more evidence of his presence.

As for my father's early school days, a few memories of first grade remain.

Peter started school in 1938, walking down the hill with Helen as the early morning mist rose from the river. They were taught Russian in the sparse two-room schoolhouse warmed by the pot-belly stove; the younger children were in one room, the older grades in the other. Mary and Gerhardt, fourteen and thirteen, walked to nearby Osterwick for school. And on weekends, Mary and Gerhardt, along with their classmates killed gophers that tunnelled through the fields, then nailed their skins to boards and brought them to school on Monday — a kind of collective pest control.

The older students, beginning at age fourteen, were to join the *Komsomol (Kommunisticheskiy Soyuz Molodiozhi)* — the All Union Leninist Young Communist League, the youth wing of the Communist Party. My father recalls that Jake, by then eighteen, refused to join, "He didn't want to be a *Komsomol*; so he kept out of trouble, always working hard in the fields. He didn't draw any attention to himself." Those who joined were ensured good jobs, promotions, and a future of higher education. "Privileges." No one in the Letkemann family was ever more than an agricultural worker.

In Rosengart, Peter and Helen's teacher, first and second grade, was a German man, Herr Seibel, who, unlike Jakob and Maria, believed in Communism. At school, the teachers encouraged the children to join the Pioneers, but to be in the Pioneers one must denounce God and swear allegiance to Stalin. Jakob and Maria forbade it.

In summer 1939, when school let out, Peter worked in the fields with the rest of the family. He rose early and went to the "Second Brigade" to ready the horse. Afterwards, it was his job to ride her, hitched to the wooden cultivator with the heavy wheel in front. Sometimes it was a cultivator with a single cutting blade, and at other times an implement with two or three shears, depending on the width required between rows, whether for corn or beans or potatoes. A teenage boy, sometimes Gerhardt, or else a man, walked behind the boy on the horse, holding the handles of the cultivator, applying the pressure required for the depth of the rows.

Peter was to rein the horse in a straight line, but in the heat he did not always pay attention; still tired from such an early start, he dozed and the horse strayed leaving a jog in the row. A clod of dirt exploded against Peter's scalp, thrown by Gerhardt to wake him, a dry cascade filling his ear and crumbling down his back. That wasn't so bad. At the handles of the cultivator, some of the other older boys cracked the long whip, not caring if it stung Peter's bare skin. The work must get done. When it was lunch, it was Peter's duty to give the horse her water and oats. With her big stained teeth she nipped at Peter. Nina was a mean old nag — the brigade's skinny brown mare with a sharp back-bone. The first few days were always the worst. Against bristly horse hide, Peter's thighs rubbed raw, skin red and throbbing until the crust formed. With scabs like patches, Peter walked bowlegged, but after the scabs fell away, his skin toughened to leather to withstand the season riding on Nina's boney swayback in endless straight rows that cradled the seeds.

At summer's end, on August 23, 1939, in Moscow, far from Rosengart, Stalin met with the German foreign minister Von Ribbentrop to sign a Nazi-Soviet non-aggression pact. Hitler had assured the German people his army would not have to fight a war with Russia, the neighbour to Poland. Following that meeting, on September 1, 1939, as Peter entered the second grade, Hitler marched into Poland. Such matters did not concern eight-year-olds, at least not boys on a collective farm far from the front. At recess they chased their ball made of rolled-up rags, or better yet, got a pig's bladder from the butcher, blown up so taut it bounced. Jubilant boys running across the steppes in the final moments of childhood that would soon be taken from them. As they passed by the feed mill or the blacksmith's, they noticed the men clustered together, more than usual, two or more, here and there, engaged in "men's talk." There were no radios, forbidden by the regime, but there was "news."

"Hitler . . ."

". . . Germany."

Like pups, little boys snatched bones of gossip and ran off when growled at. Morsels spoken in lowered tones pulled them close again.

"War . . ."

"The front is coming closer."

PART II

❖

World War II

A Boy's Recollection
of Survival

4

❖

1941 to 1943:
A Time of Survival

*Alas, my memory / Does not want to leave me /
And in it, live beings / Each with its own pain, /
Each with its own dying, / Its own trepidation.*

— CZESLAW MILOSZ

In the USSR, it was known as the Great Patriotic War. Although in North America the western front is given prominence in the public mind, the Soviet-German clash actually dominated the Second World War and now ranks as the greatest armed conflict ever fought on a single front. It lasted four long years, and the cost in lives is horrifying. The military category alone accounted for over two-thirds of the total world military deaths for the entire war. Military and civilian, the number of dead came to five-and-a-half million Germans and twenty million Soviets. However, presently, researchers in the former Soviet Union have now projected even greater losses of Soviet people during this time — twenty-six or twenty-seven million,[1] their blood on the hands of both Hitler and Stalin.

Beginning on June 22, 1941, the German forces attacked the Soviet Union in what Hitler named "Operation Barbarossa." His troops, together with Finnish, Hungarian, Italian and Romanian support, advanced 2000 kilometres into Soviet territory. A few years later, the Soviet forces countermarched 2500 kilometres to Berlin.

When war broke out in the Soviet Union, the colonists of German descent, who for more than a century had lived in this land, together with their Ukrainian neighbours who yearned for independence, were regarded as enemies. The Mennonites, as conscientious objectors to war, were no exception. In the past they had provided non-combatant service, but such status would not be recognized now. Instead, they were taken, not to perform alternative service, but to labour camps, imprisonment and death.

In the years leading up to 1941, men throughout the Soviet Union, and particularly in Ukraine, were taken away. Jakob, Jake and Gerhardt in Rosengart had, thus far, been spared, although my father tells me that, after the German forces occupied the area, they discovered Soviet lists at the regional administrative office. On them were names of people for capture, typical NKVD requisitions; both his father and brother Jake were listed. They were safe for the present, but their time would come. As the war progressed, Germany — or the Axis powers for that matter — would not recognize conscientious objectors.[2]

Prior to the German invasion, preparations for war were already enforced upon older students by the Communist regime. Sixteen-year-old Mary and fifteen-year-old Gerhardt were required to practise shooting rifles during target practice as part of their curriculum in the school year of 1940 to 1941. And then, in the spring and early summer of 1941, like tunnelling ants, Russian soldiers swarmed the area. At this time, Jake, Mary and Gerhardt, along with Jakob, were among those in Rosengart taken from home, into the *Trudarmee* (work army) to dig trenches. In June 1941, those from Rosengart included seventy-three men, ninety women, and 182 teenagers.[3]

Civilians from the various villages were assembled for work detail and ordered to dig anti-tank ditches with spades and other hand tools. They were instructed to slope the ditches on the one side, so the approaching German tanks could drive in, and to dig vertical for a number of feet on the other so they could not rumble out. Later it was discovered that the ditches were poorly designed; the Red Army Generals had not considered that the *Panzer* would be larger than their Soviet tanks.

At night, filthy and exhausted from her work on the trenches, and separated from her family, Mary was frightened. She cried quietly before succumbing to sleep under the stars, the cool breeze over the steppe her only sheet. She recalls, "In the same encampment were two boys, older than I, from my village. They heard me cry. I should calm down, they told me; in a few days we will escape."

I have read other personal accounts of this time, and when the diggers describe leaving the trenches and making their way back to their families, they use the word "escape."[4] Speaking with the knowledge of hindsight, I can see that they mean escape from the deportations and subsequent Soviet exile, or execution that was in store for them when the work was done. A few years ago, Aunt Mary told me something else about this time, something also disturbing. "Early one morning when I awoke, I saw a few of the girls from our brigade stumble back into the camp. . . . During the night the soldiers in charge of us had dragged them off." I know she means the soldiers raped them, but she avoids using the word, for the act is unspeakable. The ugly word cannot encapsulate the experience of violation, and it's as if saying it might re-victimize those girls, or — as it often did in those days — stigmatize them: mark them as damaged.

In August, in response to the ethnic Germans in Ukraine, Stalin's *Politburo* decided to expel them all.[5] Rumours of deportation abounded, ". . . whole villages east of the Dnieper have been sent further eastward. Even the cattle!" To escape this deportation, Mary, together with her companions, made her way back to Rosengart through fields, avoiding the roads. What of her village — her mother, Peter and Helen?

It would be another seven days from the time Mary returned to Rosengart, before Jakob, Jake and Gerhardt also made their way back. Somehow each family member managed to return before they, too, were deported further into the interior, and there, vanish altogether. Of the seventy-three men who were taken from Rosengart to dig trenches, only twenty-four returned. All the women returned, but two of the teenagers remained missing.[6]

Countless throughout Ukraine did not return to their homes. In a desperate military evacuation, those along the east side of the Dnieper River were swept away into the chasm of the Gulag by the receding wave of Soviet troops. Today historians say there is insufficient evidence to guess the number of all those imprisoned or executed.[7]

❖ THE SOVIET EVACUATION

Like the terrifying storms that flashed and boomed with great force over the steppes in summer, the *Wehrmacht* swiftly advanced. On August 16, the retreating Red Army began the evacuations of Zaporozhye, as well as the nearby Chortiza settlement. Thousands of refugees poured over the bridge that crossed the Dnieper near the hydro-electric dam. The crossing was clogged with wagons heavy with crates or sacks of supplies. Elderly grandparents, young children, and women all trudged along together; the stream of humanity was a slow trickle instead of a rush.[8] Rosengart was among the last of the Chortiza villages to be evacuated. Inhabitants took their milk cows, and as they departed they often wondered, "If the Germans occupy Russia, could they be worse than Stalin and the constant threat of exile?"

Afterward, the main street lay as a discarded ribbon. No one travelled along it. Windows in empty houses mirrored deserted yards, and no horses or wagons were left. The Germans were so near that the few remaining people could hear the machine guns rapidly tapping out rounds. If not for bullets cracking the air, the collective was eerily still. When Soviet troops discovered Jakob and his family, the officer ordered them to leave that day, or be shot. Jakob did not want to leave, but there was little choice.

As a last effort, he decided to hide Jake in the cellar. With few words and silence heavy with meaning, Jakob locked the cellar door. The younger children could not know this, but Jake was waiting, hidden in the darkness of the root cellar, under the house. He planned to surrender to the Germans rather than face the Red Army. It was a matter of rescue from Stalin — and from certain death.

The shade of summer sky deepens in the late afternoon. The noise of artillery has ceased and a light wind carries the silence. When the officer returns to the yard, he exhales sharply. "Let's go! Now!" he commands Jakob.

"Then I need your help for a moment. Please." Jakob points to the scraggly chicken in the yard. Two young soldiers accompanying the officer comply. They fashion a rough cage of sorts from pieces of wood, nails and binder twine left in the shed. As they do so, they eye Gerhardt helping his father hitch the wagon to the milk cow. Maria turns to collect provisions of *Zwieback* (double roasted buns) and *Schinkenspeck* (smoked pork) from the kitchen, just over the cool cellar where Jake crouches below. Then she closes the door, places the food onto the cart. The milk cow bellows.

Jakob slaps the boney cow. The wooden cart creaks and the beast strains under the burden, which is nothing compared to the weight that Jakob and Maria carry, as heavy, it seems, as a load of stones as they leave their yard — and leave their son behind. The young Russian soldiers escort the family along the upper road to the corner and then turn back to rejoin their unit. The Germans will arrive sometime soon. As the evening begins to fall, the family walks on slowly behind the cow, down the hill, past the brigade sheds, past the school, and past the fields of *sudanka*, tall grass that must be cut for the silage, but now there is no one left to do it. The air is sweet with its scent.

They proceed along the cobblestone road that bends upwards towards the tracks, but part way along the rise of the land the cow puts her tail in the air. She spurts a stream of green manure. The sack of potatoes tumbles off the cart and the cooking pot clangs onto the road. Everyone scurries behind, stooping to pick up rolling potatoes and the pot.

When my father tells the story today, a city man, not a country boy as he once was, he shakes his head with a smile at the thought of the ornery cow hitched for the first time to a cart. "Her tail up like a flag," he says, "her beige rump turning the colour of swamp." In memory, there is no more unknown danger as there was that day when he was ten. Now he can laugh about the cow.

On the way up the hill, the cow veers off the road into the *sudanka* looking to eat the sweet grass. She stops in the field near the cemetery, where the neighbour Braun's little boy, who drowned in the swimming hole, is buried.

The sun is descending and Jakob decides the family will stay here. They set about raising the stalks high around them to conceal the cart and the resting cow. They gather more grass and leafy branches from a tangle of poplar trees for camouflage. The family sits beneath, without Jake, in the purpling nightfall. They are only a few kilometres from home, but with no lanterns glowing from the windows, the village houses are merely vague shapes, hard to distinguish. Gunshots puncture the darkness. They lie close to one another in their bed of grass, but do not sleep. Above, stars glitter like broken glass.

The account of this fateful night is difficult to untangle.

Maria and Jakob whisper for a while, then Jakob says, so that the children hear, "Peter and Helen, go with Ma. Follow the road beside the field, *but stay off it*. Keep out of sight." They are to walk further, past the field, to the outskirts of the settlement, to the house of another Jakob Letkemann, a nephew.[9] "See if they are still there, take shelter in the house, and *wait for us.*" No one will notice them there, and Jakob is certain the German troops will arrive by morning.

With Peter and Helen at each hand, Maria approaches the house on the fringe of the village. She peers through the windows into murkiness, raps softly, whispers urgently, "Is anyone here? This is *Tante* Maria. . . ." In a moment, the nephew opens the door, "Quickly," he beckons her from the shadows.

The long hours pass slowly. The sounds of trains and combat nearby keep Maria awake in the night as her small ones sleep fitfully, tucked tightly against her sides, warmed by her body.

When I ask Aunt Mary about the night, she remembers lying all night in the field with Jakob and Gerhardt along with the cow and their few and only belongings. It is too risky to go with the cow to the house tonight. The shooting draws closer. The temperature falls. Jakob instructs Mary and Gerhardt to dig beneath the grass into the earth. They curl into the steppe's embrace, not for comfort, but for protection from stray bullets that whine through the air like deadly mosquitoes. The clatter of military trains rolling by to the nearest station fills the remaining sleepless hours. The ground shakes.

At dawn, the sun climbs over the horizon and shines on a herd of *Panzer* tanks rolling across the plain. These mechanical beasts send tremors, as if thousands of hooves trample the steppes. As the three lie in pockets among the high grass, Jakob hears German voices shouting over the din. He stands up, holds his arms above his head, so someone will see him. Gerhardt and Mary do the same, and the three walk nervously, hands still held high, towards an approaching German soldier. His rifle is raised and pointed at them.

"*Halt!*" The astonished soldier with the crooked black cross on his uniform shouts for them to stand still, to tell him where they are from and what they are doing in the middle of the field. To his great surprise, Jakob responds in German, *"Wir sind Deutsche"* (we are Germans). And he explains, "We live here."

Soon after, Jakob, Gerhardt and Mary arrive with the cow and cart at the relatives' house where Maria and the younger ones wait. At ten in the morning the earth rumbles; the walls of the house tremble. A column of yellow dust snakes towards the farm. The truck leading the armoured vehicles stops as it passes these peasants standing in the yard. Other people begin to line the road into the village.

"What the hell is this?" the company commander and driver wonder aloud; they thought these farms were abandoned. He steps out and speaks to Jakob, and when Jakob answers in perfect German, he is even more surprised. Germans? Here? But he seems pleased, too. Before they drive off, the commander gives the children, Peter and Helen, candies. Then the family races up the hill towards home, towards Jake.

The German troops soon set up in the surrounding area, and from the island of Chortiza in the Dnieper they bombarded Zaporozhye with artillery fire. On August 20, as the German forces took the city, the Soviets, in their final retreat, blew up the generators of the huge Dnieper hydroelectric power works.[10] The bridge, clogged with civilians caught in the war's cross hairs, was blasted apart.

The Soviet retreat has been described as one of the largest evacuations in history. Stalin ordered the dismantling and removal of approximately fifteen hundred factories. He deported more than ten million people to the Urals and Central Asia — over one-third of the people were from Ukraine — all for slave labour in mines and forests and God-forsaken places.[11] And his army destroyed everything in its wake. Every one of Ukraine's fifty-four blast furnaces was demolished. In the Donets River basin, most mines were flooded; the Soviets set fire to everything they could not transport, leaving behind only scorched earth. Even Kiev suffered more damage *structurally* from the retreating Soviets than from the advancing Germans. Under the pretext of preparing bomb shelters, the NKVD planted mines throughout the city centre. As the Germans approached, the Soviet Army detonated the bombs. Fire engulfed one square kilometre of the city's loveliest neighbourhoods and architecture, leaving days as dark as sunless winter afternoons, with ash falling like black snow.[12]

All throughout the region, the remaining citizens were relieved, even joyful, when the German troops arrived. Their boyish faces, and for some — like the Mennonites and other colonists — their familiar German language presented hope. "*Gott mit uns*" was inscribed on their belt buckles. Surely if "God was with us" life now would improve. At the outskirts of their small towns, Ukrainians set up welcome signs adorned with flower garlands and the announcement: "We greet the German Army as Liberators from Bolshevism. *Heil Hitler*."[13] Villagers lined the roadsides with bouquets of flowers or bread and water, and held out handfuls of salt in customary gestures of goodwill.

❖ THE GERMAN OCCUPATION

The troops arrived first. The Nazi officers who set up governance over the region did not arrive in Rosengart for several more days, and consequently there was chaos in the initial days of the occupation. Horses ran loose, beautiful horses belonging to the Soviet troops when their riders had been shot dead off their backs. People who left with the Soviet Army days earlier were overtaken by German forces, and now they returned, along with those from elsewhere; mostly just women and children returned, German and Ukrainian.

What amazed everyone was the sight of the surrendering Soviet soldiers. There were hundreds and hundreds of them, mere lads it seemed, eager to find out if they could return to their hometowns.

My father describes too, how the villagers, remembering the

German occupiers of the First World War, and their proper behaviour, trusted the Germans. Rosengart's inhabitants returned to their houses.

Jakob assumed that the *kolkhozniks*, (those who had been collectivized), now "liberated," would be free to farm the village for themselves. He rounded up six of the abandoned horses roaming about, including a Russian officer's stallion, white as a Siberian blizzard, and just as fierce. The horses needed to be fed so Jakob instructed Peter and Mary to bring wheat sheaves from the fields beyond their house. Mary was terrified and Peter was unsure what to do; surely the dense thickets of mountain ash, birch, and poplar at the settlement's edge concealed hiding Russian soldiers. When his children protested, Jakob responded, "With the Germans everywhere, no soldier would dare give away his hiding place; you'll be safe." And so they went, obediently, Mary whimpering with fright, her little brother nervously trailing.

Jakob was not usually unbending when he saw fear in another's eyes. An incident remains in my father's mind.

Peter and his father enter their barn in the morning to begin chores. There, in the straw, lies a young Russian soldier. Jakob and Peter are startled, but the young soldier is more shaken. His face is ashen. Trembling, he begs Jakob, "Please keep quiet, don't report me. . . ." Standing behind his Pa, Peter holds his breath. Jakob remains still for a moment, his legs are wooden. But his heart is flesh; he takes Peter's hand and they turn away, allowing the soldier to flee.

Jakob did not report what he had seen. My father now speculates about the frightened young Soviet. "Perhaps he joined the resistance, who knows? Or perhaps the fellow was caught by the Germans and killed."

During those first few days of processing the war prisoners, the occupying Germans did not have their own translators. Jakob, who spoke Russian and fluent German, received a visit from two soldiers. Will he interpret for the captured and surrendered Russian soldiers? Jakob complied, and young Peter went along to a makeshift office: a table to write on and a folding-chair in an open field.

The Germans asked questions, "Unit and Rank?" "Ukrainian or Russian?" "Jewish?" Long afterwards, my father's memory adheres to the question, "Jewish?"

The processing of war prisoners continued throughout the morning. Then there was a break. Those identified and docu-mented were now transported elsewhere. Still waiting was a Russian officer, eyes cold and hard as metal; and when he thought the German soldier was out of earshot, his lips moved to speak, barely a sound, "If you interpret for the Germans, I will seek you, and kill you — you and your boy." Jakob heard him. Without a word, he turned from the officer, collected Peter, and left. They didn't come back.

Under the Germans, just as under Communism, a simple statement about a neighbour could endanger a life. Almost daily the German soldiers asked, "Are there any Communists in this village?" They asked the children all the while holding out chocolate. My father remembers, "I knew one family from Rosengart whose sons were in the Russian army; if I pointed them out, it would not go well for them. The German officers boasted openly what they would do to Communists."

When I ask about the actions of the German officers, Father thinks for a moment. "There were rumours about the officers of the occupational government . . . . We heard things. We heard that in a neighbouring village, where a Mennonite husband and wife had adopted two children, half Jewish children, the Germans took them away from the couple. I heard my parents' voices, raised and upset at the news, '. . . how terrible! . . . . *Why?*' I guess someone in that village must have mentioned these children when asked, 'Are there any Jews here?'"

Throughout 1941, massacres took place by the Germans in Ukraine's major cities. On September 19, the Germans arrived in Kiev and took the capital. Heinrich Himmler ordered his SS units to target the Jews of Kiev. It was the largest Nazi massacre of Jews in Soviet territory — at Baba Yar, a ravine in the western outskirts of the city.[14] Then, on October 24, Kharkov, not far away, fell. On October 13 and 14 in Dnipropetrovs'k, at least ten thousand Jews were murdered, most likely non-Jewish spouses and children of intermarriage as well.[15] Genocide — a word so heavy, it crushes all language

◆

There is one photo from this time that has a certain piquancy, for my father explains that it was taken by a German soldier, and it suggests a developing camaraderie between the German soldiers and the village boys. There are four boys in the photo, and I think Peter is on the far right. They stand in a row at the side of the railroad tracks that run along the lower corner of the photo. Geographically, these tracks are at the edge of Rosengart. Behind the boys on the horizon is a long flat building made of brick. Thin telegraph lines run through the photograph; a pole in the middle holds them up in the open sky. The boys' shadows are longer than their bodies. They are wearing long pants and heavy tunics; two boys hold caps, but otherwise the boys wear none. The sun must be low in the afternoon sky and behind the photographer snapping the picture. If you look closely you see a long thin shadow cast into the photo; the soldier's body forms a faint "t" arms bent at the elbows to hold the camera.

Certainly it took only a short time for the first wave of German soldiers to settle in. In the early days at Rosengart, up to three soldiers at a time were billeted out to each home. Because they had their own field kitchens, Maria was not required to cook for them. With their army rations, the soldiers had more food to eat than her family did anyway. But she washed their uniforms and underwear. My father cannot remember details of them, but he recalls how properly they behaved. They were polite to Maria, who must have reminded them of their own mothers. These soldiers were busy with training, and stayed

Boys in Rosengart, near the barracks

only for a week, maybe two, before they headed off to their destination, the front. They were always replaced by more eager
young fellows with still fresh faces. However, as the combat
troops came and went, marching off to battlefields, a few soldiers remained stationed at Rosengart, and these young men,
he remembers a little more clearly, but again, without concrete
details such as their names or even what they looked like. Maybe to him, at the time, they just looked like anyone else.

At the end of town there is a barracks in which twelve soldiers
have set up their anti-aircraft guns. Sometimes at night, they
let Peter and his friends shine the search lights, that is, until
the villagers complain about the bright beams invading their
homes and the soldiers tell the boys their fun is over. Nevertheless, the boys often loiter by the tracks. Sometimes they bring
these fellows the fresh eggs they find scattered among the grass,
trading them for candies. In exchange for an egg, one of them
gives Peter the photograph of the boys he had taken a few
months back.

Peter also goes to the collective's stables where the Germans keep the horses, and there he hangs around like a barnyard puppy, like Mops. Talking with the soldiers, he quickly learns to speak high German, switching from the low German his family speaks at home. As Peter shows up one day, a few soldiers are attempting to saddle the white stallion, the beautiful one his father had caught and was later ordered to relinquish. The spirited animal will not let the soldiers near. Peter sniggers.

"What are you laughing at, *Bubi* (boy)? You think you can ride him?" They find the affable, gangly boy amusing.

"Yeah," Peter replies, "I can ride him." He speaks before he thinks.

They offer a dare, "If you do, we'll give you candy."

It takes more than one man to hold the animal, another to put the bit in the horse's mouth. The stallion strains in protest, strands of tendons twisting through his neck. Peter eases his way over, wraps a hand in the tangled mane, places his foot in the cupped hands of a soldier and is hoisted onto the twitching back. A soldier hands Peter the reins and the stallion is let loose! Peter lies flat against the horse's neck, holding tight. Onto the field-road, flared nostrils fiendishly glistening pink, and with coal black eyes, the horse is a white devil, streaking. The boy hangs on as the stallion gallops in the direction of Sakhalin; Peter hopes the animal will wear himself out. They race towards an oncoming horse and wagon, then past. It's Katje, his cousin's wife, her mouth hanging open like a barn door — just his luck that she sees him. He rides up the long hill, the horse charging across the steppe's smooth and gentle slope towards the ancient earthen burial mounds of the Cossacks.

The horse finally slows to a trot, then a tired canter, and Peter reins him in. He holds the reins tight now so the stallion cannot run again, turns him around and rides back to the stable at a slow and steady gait. Surprising the soldiers who look twice at the "kid" who has done what they could not, Peter grins broadly as they hand over the promised candy, but this will be as far as the glory goes.

At home Maria scolds him, "What were you thinking? You could have been hurt. *Tante* Katje said you were white as a sheet when you passed her, the horse running away with you like that!" That meddlesome woman, thinks Peter, rolling his tongue around a melting square of German chocolate, but he knows that in a place like this, nothing gets past your Ma.

❖

The inhabitants resumed their agrarian life under the governance of the Reich's officers. When the German troops arrived at the close of the summer there were sunflowers, potatoes, corn and beets in the fields. Now one of the priorities was to divide the harvest.[16] Every collective under occupation was divided into sections, each section assigned to various groups of villagers. My father remembers there were about five to seven other families in the group with his own. Most of the family units did not have fathers or husbands. "We were exceptionally fortunate to be together during this time," he reminds me.

After so many years of Soviet collectivization, villagers throughout Ukraine anticipated privatization under the occupational government. They believed the Germans would be different. Once again, however, the division of labour was economically driven. Due to the lack of machinery and lack of men, the Germans assigned an adult male to each group to manage the heavy work. The truth is that the women were equally capable of hard labour. It was their way of life. Now, however, if a group had a male assigned to them, he was arbitrarily in charge. Jakob was assigned to a group as an overseer. And the truth is that this was just another form of collectivization.

People living in German *Lebensraum* (living space) were not required to take up arms, but to work for their German occupiers. Along with any war prisoners, boys and men, aged seventeen and older, Ukrainians and ethnic Germans, including the Mennonites, worked at various jobs for the occupying army. While the family worked in the fields, young Jake was sent by the German army to haul ammunition to the front. He was

Jake in Zaporozhye, circa 1941

shipped all the way to Leningrad, gone for months. After Jake
returned from the front, he was sent to Zaporozhye to work at
the railroad station as an *Eisenbahnbeamter*, a civilian job on
the railway, the *Reichsbahn*.

Unlike Jake, some of the inhabitants living under German
authority volunteered for various duties that ranged from administrative work to military units. Many young men who considered themselves ethnic German felt it was their duty to assist
in the struggle against Stalin and Communism, especially those
born between the 1920s and '30s — young people who grew up

under heavy oppression.[17] Even some Mennonites cast aside the principle of non-resistance.

Occasionally Peter walks the twelve kilometres to visit his oldest brother at the railway station. One afternoon, Peter cuts across the steppes over a field road on his way home from the city. Some days he sees German soldiers guarding skinny Red Army POWs as they march them along. Today the trail is deserted, but Peter notices something up ahead. As he draws near, he slows. A body of a Russian soldier. He can tell by the clothing. Peter steps closer. Perhaps this soldier was wounded, unable to keep up, or had he tried to escape? Pulp, like that from a watermelon, splattered about, blackening in the sun, flies buzzing and landing in it — *gleich tot* — dead at once, after a bullet split his skull. Peter gags, his legs fold, and he retches again and again.

It is early in the summer of 1942, and the Germans occupy the entire Ukraine. Heinrich Himmler, the leader of the *Schutzstaffel* (SS), is in charge of the region. The partisans have been weeded out by the strong military presence here. The Germans don't want attacks on the great Dnieper Dam and the large industrial city Zaporozhye. Rural village life in Rosengart unfolds uneventfully as the war carries on elsewhere. Jakob manages the harrowing, much as he had done before the German occupation, but now with strong horses. It is Peter's job to ride the horse, ensuring the rows are straight, while Gerhardt holds the cultivator. Cultivating and ploughing, this is the rhythm of Peter's childhood between 1941 and 1943. Quiet. Mundane.

Because there is a shortage of men, Peter is old enough by age eleven to pair up with thirteen-year-old Isaac Toews. The deep spring ploughing for potatoes and beans is heavy work, too heavy for the boys, so they don't do that, but, bareback and barefoot, wearing only shorts, they work among the beets, sunflowers and corn. After the summer harvest of oats, barley, and wheat, they plough these fields for the next year. The wheat fields will be sown again with a crop of "winter" wheat.

Summer ploughing requires an implement that has a seat on it. Isaac sits and works the plough as Peter rides the horse, or sometimes they trade off. Using this plough is a coveted job because no one has to walk; the other implement requires two horses and someone to walk behind it. First the boys plough, then harrow the lumpy soil until smooth, and afterwards they seed the rows. Peter and Isaac are also responsible for the horses. Early in the morning they load the wagon with feed and set off to work. At lunch, they return from the field to feed the weary animals and sit beneath the wagon to eat their piece of bread in the only available shade from the sun's hot rays beating down.

As in the story from my childhood, the two ride the horses to the Dnieper to wash them, racing there until the animals foam with milky sweat. As the boys draw near the sandy banks, the scent of the river rises in a stream of air, chilled like a refreshing drink. They taste sweetness as they inhale. In the river, cleansed from work, they splash and swim. In the distance they see the Germans troops taking a break from their duties, too. The boys are fascinated as they watch the tanned muscled soldiers resting along the sandy shoreline, or playing in the water, whooping and laughing. What amazes Peter most is the sight of the motor boat zipping along the river, towing a soldier behind the wake on a plank of wood — a water-ski!

The villagers carry on tilling the land. In late summer, when the solar arch is lower over the rolling plain, the brigade tends the watermelon fields, which are divided into twenty sections. Peter works in the patch of striped melons. This variety is not as good as those with the white rinds, sweeter than all the rest — the ones Peter and Isaac long for. They decide on a plan: at night they will load a few of the sweet melons into the pushcart and stash them away. Under the moonlight, each glowing globe of fruit seems better than the last and soon the cart is full, heavy with ripe melons.

"We'd better empty this cart and bring it back," the older melon thief says. A missing pushcart would be noticed. The bush behind Peter's house will make the perfect stash for their cargo, and a meeting place after dark to feast like kings of the watermelon patch. They unload the fruit, return the cart, and go home.

Peter dreams about watermelon in his sleep — his unlimited supply, its sugary juice quenching his thirst, his mouth so full, it slides down his chin.

In the morning, he must forget about the watermelons for the day, since it is the start of the school year. This year he and Helen will be in different classes, and the next-door neighbour, Herr Dyck, a Mennonite man, will be the new teacher of the second and third grades. Under the occupation forces, schools are reopened, up to the fourth grade, and throughout 1942 and 1943 German teachers are installed in all the schools.[18] However, in the cities, some of the schools are cancelled, even grade four, and the young students work to dismantle buildings so the materials can be shipped to Germany.[19] Here in Rosengart, Peter and Helen go back to school.

At school, the teacher gathers the school boys for an announcement. "I have something very serious to discuss with you. As I went for a walk early this morning, I discovered something surprising. Does anyone know what that was?"

The other students have no idea what he means, but Peter and Isaac do.

No one speaks.

"All right then, I'll tell you — *a cache of watermelons*. Who knows anything about this?" Peter and Isaac say nothing. "I've reported the stolen melons to the village mayor," Herr Dyck continues in his droning teacher voice.

The mayor, installed under the occupying army, must address any and all theft in his village. He decides that because the teacher does not belong to a group that farms and, therefore, food is allotted to him from the village, the teacher can keep the watermelons for himself, but he should find out who the culprits are and report them. The teacher instructs the boys to interrogate one another.

"Did you do it? Did you do it?" they ask in round.

Peter avoids the question and to deflect suspicion, he chimes in, "Did *you* do it? Did *you* do it?" Isaac asks the others, too. No one here has stolen the melons. No matter. Herr Dyck will have enough watermelons for weeks, and so he turns the class's attention to reading.

One afternoon, during a class outing in the village, Henry, Peter's friend who lives at the corner of his street, finds a rocket-propelled grenade that has not exploded. Henry picks it up and holds it out to show the boys.

"Don't touch it! It will explode!" exclaims one boy, while the rest of them huddle around Henry, extremely curious and very anxious, hopping from one foot to the other in excitement.

"Naw. I'll show you. Watch," says Henry. He bends down to pick up a rock with his right hand. He crouches, pounds the top. . . . What a deafening noise!

When the boys look, Henry's right hand is a bloody knob; his legs, too, seem torn off because of the holes in his pants *and all the blood*! But his legs look worse than they are, for he springs to his feet and runs. (Later the boys repeat to their parents how Henry was "in shock.") The boys chase after him but can hardly catch up, and when they do, they hold him down as one of them races to find the teacher.

Herr Dyck takes Henry to the German field hospital nearby. Henry's legs are fine but on his right hand he has stumps, partial digits, where his fingers were. When his hand heals and Henry returns to school, he must learn to write left-handed. Father remembers that it was only the part that propelled the grenade which exploded. The grenade was a dud. Otherwise. . . .

The boys often go into the fields around the village, finding piles of ammunition.

This is what my father remembers, "One time we found a

Molotov cocktail — a bottle of fuel with a rag wick in it, held in place by a bottle stopper. You lit these to throw at tanks. We found one, along with a pile of ammunition." It was a Soviet munitions dump, one of the many scattered about. Finding these dumps was a regular after-school activity.

The boys are giddy with excitement as they strike a match and light the rag. One throws the flaming bottle into the pile and they all run away. It explodes into a fireball, and next, it seems as if an entire army is shooting at them, bullets zinging, piercing whistles followed by explosions. The cluster of boys stays hidden until there is silence.

Boys play war games with hand-made pistols, miniatures they fashion from wood and rifle cartridges for the gun barrel. They fill the barrel with pebbles and paper, then gun powder, small deposits left in discarded casings strewn about; match heads work well too. After school the children pick up casings casually as if they are gathering wild blackberries. When enough are accumulated they can stage a battle. War games are more exciting than school.

Herr Dyck is a teacher whom Peter, without any *Sitzfleisch*, (that is, unable to sit still) cannot seem to please. The only possible explanation for this, Peter concludes, has *nothing* to do with him, but with Mennonites. Peter is the *other* kind, the son of a "Brethren" pastor. On one morning before school begins — late autumn chill clinging to his skin and bones — Peter stands near the stove. Here comes Tina, the teacher's pet. She pushes Peter away from the warmth, and losing his balance he stumbles into the coal bin — *crash* — black coal clatters noisily across the hard floor. He jumps up to chase her, the two of them squealing, just as Herr Dyck enters the room.

The teacher's face clouds over. Peter stands on the spot, frozen, as the storm swiftly approaches. Then a thunder clap, a flat palm against the side of his head with a force that knocks him into a desk. The second strike launches Peter into another desk on the opposite side. Peter is dazed for a moment. To clear his head he shakes it. Blinking, he thinks, *This isn't fair . . .* as he lies on the cold floor in silence. To speak would make matters worse. And then, with his chin set, eyes narrowed, he slowly stands up as defiance takes hold. *I'll show him . . . I will not cry!* By now he is too old for tears. Besides, very soon he will understand that fairness has little to do with anything at all.

❖

My father and I are looking at photos. I pick up the one of him taken when he is a schoolboy, in the first autumn during the occupation. Peter is ten years old. His hair, grown out on top, swept over to a side part, is shorn on the sides above his ears. The part is so straight, there is not one stray hair; I imagine he has patted it down with spit. His hair catches the light. The shiny strands on top and the stubble at his temples are bleached from working in the fields under the summer sun. Although the photo is black and white, the boy is a picture of health, flaxen-haired and tanned. In another time and place, this might be a picture of a boy scout at summer camp. This beautiful child with full lips, slightly parted, does not smile, although his eyes, large and light, hold a sparkle. Almost a smile, yet so serious. Or is he tough? Something shiny is clipped to Peter's collar. I ask my father what is on his collar.

"That's an Edelweiss. It was a sign of the German Reich that we children wore on our uniforms during the occupation. Only this," he taps his finger on the photo, "isn't an official uniform shirt."

My father goes on to explain that the occupational forces organized *Hitler Jugend* (Hitler Youth). More accurately, the children at age ten entered *Jungvolk* (for the boys) and *Jung-mädel* (for the girls). At fourteen the boys began *Hitler Jugend,* while the girls entered *Bund Deutscher Mädel* (The League of German Girls). The compulsory youth organization was part of a broader "people's" organization, the *Deutscher Volkssturm,* to keep the population thoroughly under military control. The

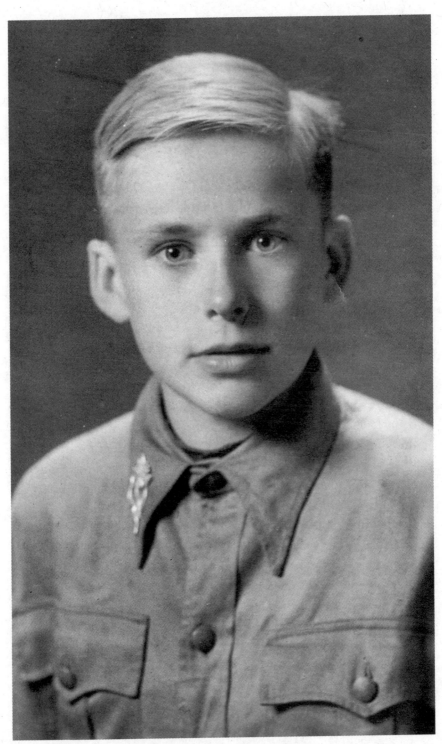

Peter age 10, Rosengart, 1941

Volkssturm and the local *Jung*-clubs had only make-shift uniforms, with collar pips to pin on.[20]

"The leader, a Nazi, wanted to send me to the city — probably Zaporozhye — for training but my parents wouldn't allow this. My mother sewed this shirt; it was grey green, olive coloured," he says matter of factly. My mind is crammed with unsettled thoughts. The officers sought out particular children, those with an Aryan look.

"The German leader was an old World War I veteran from the infantry and he made the boys practise marching." Heaviness, like a sandbag, weighs in my stomach as I imagine tow-haired little boys goose-stepping in rows through the streets of Rosengart. As I sit at my desk, I see them faintly as I gaze out the window of my writing room, phantom children marching in rows past my front lawn.

My father says that the meetings were on Sunday, which bothered his parents. Although they could openly worship for the first time in their family life, within six months into the occupation, it seemed obvious to Jakob and Maria that the Nazis, too, were opposed to Faith for the most part, keeping the children from church on Sunday, just as the Communist regime had done. Now, as before, the weekly youth meetings for the children were compulsory. Nevertheless, Jakob was able to preach again. He preached at the Mennonite church in Schönenburg, an hour's walk from home. The congregation was a mix of Brethren and other believers, 180 members.[21]

While Hitler seemed to permit religious life, this "freedom" was in areas where the people were easy to control. Because of the systematic breakdown of religion in the previous decades, the Soviet Union was such an area.[22] My father tells me of a strange incident that seems to illustrate this point. "The *Hitler Jugend* leader questioned the boys about the preacher, concerned about anyone who might be unfriendly toward the Reich. Someone said that the preacher was drowning people in the river. Not understanding, the leader became concerned that the church was a cult. He asked me if I attended. I said sometimes.

'Where is the church?' he asked. 'In Schönenburg,' I said. I told him my dad was the preacher — he was *baptizing* people."

Peter asked the man if he wanted to come to church. He answered yes, but his only motive was to see if it was subversive. One Sunday morning Peter escorted him to church, and afterwards, the *Hitler Jugend* leader never returned nor asked anything more about a cult.

Another curious thing happened around this time. An old familiar face appeared in Rosengart. The man wearing the German uniform was Gerhardt Fast, someone Jakob had known as a young man in Michaelsburg before the revolution. Fast had gone to Germany; it was not uncommon back then for young single Mennonite men to leave for Germany to study at university during the colonies' better days. They left to become teachers and theologians, or to study medicine and commerce, returning to take up positions within the Mennonite institutions and industries — schools, churches, hospitals, factories and businesses. But after the revolution, there was no reason to return. Or perhaps Fast had been part of the emigrations during the 1920s and had gone to Germany as other Mennonites had done. In any case, now he was back in Ukraine as an officer of the Reich, dressed in a brown uniform with gold trim and decorations. These officers were given the nickname, *Goldener Fasan*, (golden pheasant) by the villagers who thought they resembled fancy birds strutting about.

Herr Fast had come to Rosengart and the surrounding area to collect data about village life, which he would include in the reports on ethnic Germans in Ukraine, fastidious records for the Ministry of Occupied Eastern Territories, headquartered at Dnipropetrovs'k.[23]

My father remembers one particular visit of Herr Fast. As Herr Fast enters her home, Maria's disapproving glance is a reminder to remove the offensive revolver from his leather holster. He places it on the table. The adults go to the room behind the kitchen to visit.

Peter enters the kitchen. After playing with crude pipe guns, the sleek pistol draws him like a magnet. He looks over one shoulder, and the other, thinking he has enough time, Ma and Pa are still conversing with Herr Fast behind the wall. He places his hand on the cool metal and picks up the weapon.

Mary enters the room. Before she can say a word, Peter grins, points the gun. "Bang!" he says.

Mary's wild shrieks alarm the adults who rush in at once. Herr Fast knows it's time for him to leave.

Afterwards, Jakob and Maria scold Peter sharply, *"So eine gefährliche Dummheit!"* (such a dangerous stupidity). Then they send him off while they discuss, not Peter, but Herr Fast. Peter overhears snippets as they wonder aloud why a Mennonite, a friend from the old days, would join the military and return as an officer — *Ein Goldener Fasan.*

❖

The precise village reports, prepared from the questionnaires Herr Fast and other officers distributed in the early 1940s, were lost for many years but finally discovered and brought to the United States where they are housed in the Library of Congress.[24] These reports produced the revised immigration lists of the German colonists who moved to Russia; they contain valuable genealogical information that people of German descent later turned to, as I did when I first began my father's story. As I pore over the photocopy of the *Dorfbericht* (Village Report) compiled by *Kriegsbeamter* (Officer) Gerhardt Fast, I see that it is dated March 21 to June 20, 1942, Rosengart. The stamp indicates the report was sent to Berlin, September 6, 1942. Fast's handwriting, a meticulous cursive script, is as uniform as a computerized font. There are no mistakes, no letters stroked out or words misspelled. His penmanship is indicative of my perception of an officer of the Reich. Precise. Systematic. Looking back, my father says he believes that Herr Fast's visit to their home was to explain to Jakob and Maria that National Socialism — or at least the way Herr Fast saw it — improved life for Germans in Ukraine.

In truth, the Nazis attempted to set up their empire in Ukraine. Heinrich Himmler considered this land to be nothing more than a food source for Germany and colonial living space, *Lebensraum*, to be ruled eventually by an Aryan *Herrenvolk* (master race). This included the eradication or enslavement of the native population, referred to as *Untermenschen* (subhuman).[25] The ethnic German colonists, *Volksdeutsche*, fell into the middle category of a dispensable labour force for the Reich, the land serving also as a buffer zone between the Reich's territory and enemy land. The Mennonites, and others, in Ukraine fit well into this plan. And so, in Rosengart, which means a garden of roses, as they worked, these folks not only experienced a reprieve from Stalinist repression, but the heavy German presence insulated them — for a time — from the battles raging elsewhere.

Then events began to shift. On November 19, 1942, Soviet forces encircled German-occupied Stalingrad. The fighting continued on through the bitter month of January 1943, with Hitler ordering the troops to fight to the last man. The Germans were starving and freezing to death, and not surprisingly, by the first days of February, many had surrendered. Hitler viewed defeat as betrayal; he thought his troops should have shot themselves with their last bullets.[26] In the beginning of 1943, on January 2–3, the German army retreated from the nearby Caucasus.[27] Their retreat from Ukraine would soon follow.

5

◆

The Great Trek
Begins

*Being human is an imposition on human being and
human nature. It requires resistance to temptation,
strength in facing frustration, and refusal to
submit to immediate satisfactions.*

— ABRAHAM HESCHEL

◆ THE RUSSIAN-GERMAN FRONT — UKRAINE, 1943

Again I am talking with my father about life in the Ukraine. He
picks up a picture from our collection and says, "This is the
last picture taken in Ukraine. It must be the summer of 1943,
the summer just before the front shifted closer." My father
remembers that it was taken on a Sunday afternoon beside
their house, but the house is outside of the photograph. Next to
Mary, Peter and Helen in the photograph is a small bush of
Johannesbeeren (red currant). Behind them, the flat blanket of
Ukraine is spread out and, like a loose thread, a road unwinds
on its way to the horizon, past the speck that is the soldiers'

barracks. The sky is stretched so wide over the steppe it lightens like the skin of a full balloon: a nearly white firmament, cloudless. In the distance, the branches of an acacia tree fan out like a sun umbrella. It is hard to believe that life would so soon be interrupted by the changing events of the war.

Elisabeth was born that summer, on July 18, 1943. There are no early photos of the youngest child, born when Maria was forty-eight. Aunt Liz remembers nothing of her early childhood, except the sound of Maria's songs: "Her voice had a quality that I will never forget. A beautiful sound, like no one else's; I've never heard anything like it again."

It was the sound of Maria's alto voice singing barely above a whisper as she clutched her infant daughter to her pulsing heart. "How," Maria must have often wondered, "will my tiny child survive all this?"

What Maria and the others realized was that the Soviets were defeating the Germans. By the middle of September, it was the German army ordering an evacuation of everyone in cities near the Dnieper River. Later that month as the evenings grew colder, in the Chortiza region, the Soviet army was situated in the east, just across the river. Fields of wheat would become killing grounds once more. Before the evacuations of rural areas could occur, however, Hitler ordered the *Volksdeutsche* to harvest the crops for the benefit of Germany and the military. Otherwise the retreat might have occurred as early as spring.[1] The army was preparing to retreat in other ways. Knowing already in August that the Soviets were advancing, the German security police in Kiev began to hide evidence of mass killings. Bodies buried at Baba Yar were exhumed and incinerated.[2]

Once most of the crops were in, the villagers were given the orders to evacuate; a commander appeared in each settlement announcing that inhabitants should pack their food and belongings. All those located closest to the eastern front left first. One village at a time, they joined the long caravan of wagons and horses trekking westward to Poland. The deep ruts carved

Peter with his two sisters, Mary and Helen, Rosengart, 1943

into the dirt road as the refugees left were soon washed away in the heavy autumn rains, the road turning to a river of mud.

That season, the orchards were glutted with apples, but in many places the final apple harvest had to be abandoned. The unpicked fruit would drop from sagging branches to rot on the ground — once carefully grafted and pruned trees crying fruit. After the evacuation, the Nazis destroyed the area east of the Dnieper River, obeying a "scorched earth" order from Hitler, similar to Stalin's in 1941.[3]

Maria's parents, Peter and Katherina Siemens, had already

left Michaelsburg on foot, taking their grandson Daniel whom they had raised. Mienke also left with her own two small sons. Her husband, like many men during the occupation, joined a self-defence league to protect German villages from partisans, and then, as a result, was conscripted to a German military unit in the retreat.[4] Many wives were forced to leave, alone with their children.

Katherina died along the journey but, except in general historical commentary that the dead were buried along the way, there is no record of her burial. Her funeral would have taken the following course. Because the Red Army was close behind, Peter and his children would have shrouded her with a blanket they cannot spare, yet must. They would have hastily placed Katherina in a shallow ditch — the "cemetery" for children and old people — as the caravan of refugees pushed relentlessly onward. Only the falling snow of approaching winter would provide a more reverent burial.

Jakob and Maria never had the chance to say goodbye to Peter and Katherina. Just after Maria's parents left on foot during the first week of October, the retreating German army crossed the Dnieper's frigid currents, still flowing before the ice set in. The Soviets were dangerously near and the settlements on the west side of the river, like Rosengart, were still not evacuated. These villagers were to be sent out on trains.

Peter recalls a bee-like droning that grows louder. But there are no bees! Planes strafe the village, aiming at anything that moves below. Artillery crackles and booms as the Reds fire into Rosengart.

Knowing that they must leave and quickly, Jakob approaches the German troops, offering the family pig and chicken in exchange for transport to the nearest train station so they might join the others who have already left. He worries it will be too late to escape if the family journeys on foot.

"Get in the back of the truck. We have little time," a soldier instructs. Besides potatoes, Maria has prepared food, cured pork, lard for cooking, dried fruit, and *Zwieback*. Hoisting these bundles, everyone scrambles aboard. Maria holds Elisabeth tightly to her bosom, Peter clings to the low sides of the truck bed as it lurches forward, gears grinding, jostling them over the next fifteen kilometres to the train station at Kanserofka. There, the truck brakes to a halt as nearby horses stand hitched to empty wagons. Beyond, a train hisses on the tracks. Hundreds of refugees mill about in the afternoon cold that bites like a stubborn mule.

Kanserofka to Krivoy Rog (Kryvyi Rih)

At Kanserofka, black smoke churns out from a train ready to leave. Farther up the tracks, on the siding, a chain of rusty, open boxcars sits ready for the refugee transport. The men set to work, fashioning make-shift roofs for the boxcars from sheets of metal. Women vigorously pitch straw inside. They will need protection from the relentless winds and rains that will soon turn to white, thick snow flurries.

Their preparations consume the evening. Women boil water for *Prips* over a fire, while children gather wood to feed the flames. A smoky aroma mingles with the evening chill to tingle nostrils. Later, as darkness falls, firelight adds poignancy to the folk songs and Mennonite hymns in a minor key. The music tells of both love of place and the sorrow of departure. Soft light and dark shadow.

Early morning light pours over the steppes. People load wood, food bundles and water into limited spaces. Some have even brought extra clothing and blankets. In the distance, planes hum, their sound muffled by the steady murmur of the crowd. The air carries the engine vibrations, like beating wings, the thrum felt before it's heard. Then the noise of engines as planes swoop low to strafe the fleeing families — planes supplied by the allies, manned by Russian pilots.[5]

The crowd scatters to take cover from the pelting lead. Mothers grab their children and flee to ditches; Peter and others dive beneath the train cars. Shouting, whining engines of loco-motive and aircraft, steam, dust and darting refugees; then it's over.

"Mama? Pa?"

". . . Peter!"

Names and replies oscillate across the train yard.

The loading resumes, seventy-five people in each boxcar. Peter feel better that Isaac and his family will be on the same transport. The first stop will be Krivoy Rog, one hundred kilo-metres west. The transport travels slowly down the line.

By October 15 the Red Army controls the city of Zaporozhye. The hydroelectric dam, rebuilt by German troops, is bombed once again on October 16, this time by the last retreating Ger-man troops.[6] Next, the Russian army takes Dnipropetrovs'k, and so, on a trip which should not take long, everything stops as the Reds cut off the route and surround the train.[7] Time freezes: there is an empty space in memory as the refugees remain trapped and motionless on the tracks. Two weeks? My father recalls only the sounds in the distance. Whistling shots, tap-tap-tapping, explosions nearby, and inside, babies crying. The sun rises and sets with indifference over the boxcars on the bombed and contorted railway line.

Food is not a problem, for the people eat sparingly. But the water barrel empties. As the waste buckets fill up, the air inside the boxcar grows foul. It is hard to breathe and harder still to move about, but at least packed so tightly they stay warm. At night, if the sky is clear, Peter can see stars through the cracks of the make-shift roof. There they are twinkling in Heaven, that place where his parents say there will be no war, or death, or hunger, or sin. In the mornings, the sound of artillery begins again. Some days are quieter.

Only when the artillery shelling is still in the distance does a German soldier open the boxcar for them to stretch their legs or go to the "toilet." If the front has moved, Peter may go outside, but must not wander from the train; there are still partisans nearby. Off to the side of the track, men dig holes in the small hills and put a pipe in the top of the mound, a smoke stack. These are the ovens to bake bread. The women mix together self-rationed flour and salt, oil and eggs. It is late October by now. A skiff of snow carpets the land. People gather it up and scrub their faces. They melt snow over fire to cook potatoes. The air is cold and steel-gray; it smells like more snow is coming.

My father remembers what happened after the guns finally grew silent. "The German line pushed the Soviet line back far enough for a convoy of trucks to transfer us to the station at Krivoy Rog."

Listen. The sound of trucks arriving, one after another. Then German voices. "Come out: It's all right, come out now!" from beyond the flimsy boxcar walls. The sunset's rose light filters into the darkened cars as the doors slide open. Refugees stumble off the train like cabbages rolling out of a bin.

"We understood at once: the Germans had opened the circle, but we had to leave the train. The rails ahead were twisted apart. We climbed into the trucks quickly."

The transfer occurs with great haste, but there are many refugees and the confusion is everywhere. This next scene is surreal as it plays again in my father's head: An old woman in her ragged *platok* (how old was she?) loses her balance. She falls off the back of the truck and is crushed under weight of the next one. "My mother knew the lady."

Screams from the people in the first truck make the driver stop, but only momentarily. He does not have time. The trucks move again; everyone must keep moving. "What could we do?" asks my father rhetorically. He was a child at the time, pulled by the war's unforgiving current.

"We drove through the countryside. I saw a dead soldier hanging out of a burning tank."

They drive in a convoy past gaping holes, the grass charred for miles as smoke spirals upward like prayers of contrition. Soldiers are clearing burning wreckage from the roadway.

Maria cradles baby Elisabeth, face inward. Mary and Helen sit closely, arms linked together, not for warmth in the cold, but for sisterly comfort in their anxiety. Arms wrapped around their knees, a place to sink their chins, Jake and Gerhardt scan their eyes back and forth across the road. Sometimes their glances intersect in wordless speech. Peter remembers Jake hiding in the cellar two years earlier. Before the falling darkness covers them, he sees the bodies of young men scattered everywhere, utterly still. They look like broken dolls among the mangled steel of tanks.

As the trucks arrive at the Krivoy Rog station this night, it is not quiet. The evacuees are engulfed by the sounds of wailing and screaming. Moments earlier, they learned, a freight train had rammed, full speed, into a refugee train.

These refugees had also been fleeing. At a previous railway station, they too had been overtaken by the Soviet army. Half were captured, while the rest managed to escape, to hide in ditches, in fields, and in haystacks. For fifteen days they waited. Even their bones felt saturated from rain, until finally, the Germans drove the Soviets back again and brought them to a station where they boarded the train for Krivoy Rog.[8]

Now this disaster.

"I can still see it," my father says. Tangled steel rail, debris, and bloodied bodies strewn about the station yard with people moaning, skin lacerated — gashes in flesh like crooked red mouths. Some people are covered with angry burns, scalded, on impact, by boiling water that splashed from boxcar stove-tops.[9] Parents, anguished, discover their child is dead. Amid the constant din arise these words: "Russian sympathizers. . . ." "Partisans . . . switched the tracks." "Sabotage!"

The new tide of refugees passed by the dead and wounded. Seven children were never found. Another pastor aboard that unfortunate transport conducted a hurried funeral. Jakob would have prayed. That was all one could do, for the trains were leaving. Even the injured had to climb aboard — although some would die along the way.[10]

Krivoy Rog (Kryvyi Rih), Ukraine, to Litzmannstadt (Lodz), Poland

My father remembers how they squeezed into boxcars once again. This time there was no time to prepare the cars, so they were open at the top, coal cars. It was the end of October, wet and cold. People were no longer clean. "My head tingled; and I still wore the same shirt and pants. We sat and picked lice out of our clothes or combed them out of our hair." I imagine Peter in the tightly packed boxcar, the odour of salty bodies and damp clothes, his small slim fingers picking lice from his stubbly hair, his grimy clothes too short, creased and threadbare. Sometimes the boxcars were simply shunted off to sidings to await being hitched to another train.

The train to Poland was rerouted slightly westward to avoid the frontlines at Dnipropetrovs'k. Father thinks they passed through the corner of Romania. The cars were so crowded that baggage was hung on the outside — only to be stolen along the way. "Everyone was so poor, who could fault someone for stealing bundles hanging from a refugee train?"

The train stopped from time to time for water, an hour maybe. When it did, the boxcars emptied, folks scurrying like mice to line up along the track, men on one side, women on the other, their only privacy possible.

Once more the train stops. Where? Maybe by this time they are in the Polish countryside; the borderlands all look the same. People jump off the cars as usual. Peter, too. Distracted by the wide open fields, he ventures further, and when he is a good distance from the tracks, he unbuttons his pants. Privacy! He drops his pants around his ankles and squats, concealed by the high grass. In that moment the train whistles.

He hops up and down to hurry. Yanking up his pants with one hand, he races toward the train; he would rather lose his pants than miss the already moving train. Panting, and with a final burst of energy, Peter grabs the ladder of the last car and pulls himself up onto the bumper. Sweating, and soon shivering, he sits alone on the last car watching the countryside slip away. For what seems to be hours until the next stop, he thinks only about how cold he is, not about Jakob and Maria, sick with worry.

They arrived in Poland at the end of October 1943. In Litzmannstadt (Lodz) they were placed in a large temporary transfer centre. A sign reads *Entlausung* — delousing station. Everyone must separate into groups and strip down, men over there, women and children under age twelve in there. Each refugee was covered with solutions and powder, their clothes baked. Men's and boys' heads were shaved, women's and girls' braids snipped off if necessary, their physical features noted. The group remained in the camp only for a few days, for the Soviet front was advancing.

❖ DRESDEN

Their next transport reached Sachsen Province, Germany, near the Polish border, in early November 1943. Jakob and Maria and their family relocated to a refugee camp in Freital, a suburb of Dresden, and remained there from early November until early February 1944. At this time, the city and its surrounding districts were crammed full of civilian refugees fleeing from the rapidly advancing Red Army. Mary, then nineteen, remembers the clothing she and others received at the camp to replace what they had worn for the last month. She says, "Some of the clothes had a yellow six-point star." Along the journey she had seen people moving in groups, just as they had been, but wearing such a star — the Star of David.

My father, then twelve, remembers snow, pure-white, falling over the city. How clean it was! Beyond the train station, Dresden was a city of cathedrals and opera houses, perched on the banks of the Elbe River, "the balcony of Europe" Goethe called it. A city of high culture and well-dressed families with lovely homes. Over the Christmas season there were candles glowing in the windows, and wreaths and garlands graced front doors. Imagine seeing this as a worn-out refugee from a Ukrainian village on the steppes; or through the eyes of one ragged little boy. "I had never seen anything like this. It looked so beautiful, and I heard the familiar Christmas carol, *Stille Nacht* (Silent Night). What a sight, the sparkling city of Dresden, a white blanket covering the darkness of Hitler's favourite city.

The Mennonite Historical Society has obtained the official records, filled out in the first relocation centre of refugees into Germany, November 1943, and later filed on January 22, 1944.[11] The SS required these documents, which were sworn statements as to the physical/mental condition of the refugees and their pedigree. Either 100 percent German or less than. On each space under paternity, is written *100% Deutsch*, but these documents reveal that Jakob did not know the name of his paternal grandmother — his father Jacob Letkemann's mother. He has left this space blank. In the space for his paternal grandfather, Jakob wrote, "Jacob Letkemann" — a good guess; that was his father's name, and according to tradition, it might as well have been his grandfather's name. But in fact, Jakob's grandfather was Gerhardt (married to Sarah); Gerhardt, the first Letkemann born in Russia after his parents Heinrich and Elisabeth emigrated from Prussia and settled at the island in the Dnieper River around 1817. I recall the photo I discovered in the box of photos, with my Aunt Liz at her kitchen table, the one in sepia tones, orange with age, of a man who resembles my father, but was his great-grandfather Gerhardt, and I fill in the blanks that Jakob could not.

Jakob and Maria also filled out a form stating the places they have lived up until that point:

Jakob Letkemann — born Olgafeld, Fürstenland Colony, Ukraine.
From birth to 1907 — Olgafeld, Zaporozhye, Ukraine*[12]
1907-1915 — Michaelsburg
1915-1916 — Leningrad*[13] (*Russischer Herr*) (*Sanitäter*/Medic)
1916-1923 — Saratowka, Siberia
1923-1926 — Michaelsburg, Ukraine

1926–1930 — Kleefeld, Siberia

1930–1935 — Michaelsburg, Zaporozhye, Ukraine

1935 — October 20th, 1943 — Rosengart, Zaporozhye, Ukraine

November 10th 1943, until now, Lager (Camp) No. 93, Dresden, Freital, Zaukerode

Maria Letkemann born October 29th, 1895, Kleefeld, Slowgorod Colony, Siberia*[14]

From birth to 1905, Masseiwo, Dniepertros'k, Ukraine

1905–1907 (The name on the form is indecipherable)

1917–1923 Saratowka, Siberia

1923–1926 Michaelsburg, Ukraine

1926–1930 Kleefeld, Siberia

1930–1936 Michaelsburg

1935–1943 Rosengart

November 10, 1943 — Lager 93, Dresden

The document also required the name and address of a relative who was a citizen of the German Reich. Jakob and Maria simply recorded *Onkel* (Uncle) Johann Leidyn, Treuberg, *Ostpreussen* (East Prussia). He was the brother of Maria's mother.

❖ LAGER 93

On the edges of Dresden, the family is settled in their new home: Lager 93. It is a three-storey brick school building transformed into a refugee camp. Someone has taken a group picture. Among the children on their way to school, one can see a small group of teenagers and men going to clean houses or work in factories. They are dressed in winter hats and coats. The ground and the rooftop of the school in the background are white. Bare trees hold out empty gnarled branches. The fence around it is simply made of sticks. The faces are so grainy my father cannot point himself out for certain: he could be the boy with the too-short pants whose shins and shoes stick out. His mother made him a pair from a blue wool coat, so perhaps he's the boy in the stiff pants. Or the boy with the shaved head, hatless. I think so.

Refugees in Freital, Lager 93, near Dresden, 1944

For a month, prior to attending school or jobs, the group was quarantined. There were over four hundred people, those brought by the Germans from other countries, all living in rooms divided by blankets. Each family lived in one curtained-off cubicle. Isaac Toews' family lived at Lager 93 as well as did the Braun family, also from Rosengart, and a young woman from Nieder Chortiza. In the evenings they gathered together to reminisce about home. During such a time, Peter and Isaac shared the story of their stolen watermelons, and in this setting everyone laughed at how the boys had joined in with each other to ask, "Did *you* steal them?"

At night, the sirens shrieked warnings. High wails sent everyone to the bunkers to sit in blackness as planes flew overhead dropping bombs on nearby neighbourhoods, towns and cities.

In the *Lager*, my father slept on an upper bunk, high enough to see over the curtains. He chuckles a little when he says, "I saw what went on in the entire room." Birth, copulation — nothing is hidden from adolescent eyes. Quite an education, I think, as I imagine family life in the fishbowl-like *Lager*.

After a period of quarantine, the teenagers and adults were sent to work. Mary worked in a childcare centre, or what was called a *Kindergarten*. Jakob and Gerhardt were sent to a munitions factory, and Jake worked at a transport company. Together with the other mothers and infants, Maria remained at the camp to take care of Elisabeth, and to tend to kitchen chores and keep "house." Peter and Helen went to school.

My father's school stories reveal the real lessons he learned there. It all begins when he is told he must register for school among the German children. He knows his ABC's in German and can read a little; he has learned this in Ukraine during the occupation where he left off in the second grade. The teacher looks over his gangly frame and decides he must enter grade four. He is one of the two refugee children in the class and he feels self-conscious, not only because he cannot keep up and must copy his lessons from the other students — the teacher is not wise to this and even praises his work — but because he looks foreign. His hair is shaved to his scalp, while the German boys have neat haircuts. His clothes are threadbare. His mother has even made him a pair of pants from a navy wool coat. The pants are hand-sewn, and he should appreciate her labour. Instead, he complains to her about how awful the pants look, "Like stove-pipes!" He doesn't want to wear them, but he has nothing else warm enough. And although Maria tells him to be thankful, she understands how out-of-place he feels. She feels it, too.

It is obvious that Peter is not one of the German children; he is Russian, they say. He has always thought he was German for that's what the Ukrainians called him. The Mennonites even spoke German. Now, in Germany, he is Russian. On the way to school he hears the German children calling out, "*Ruski, Ruski, Ruski!*" But even on the rare occasions when he is recognized as German, he is *Volksdeutsch*, not *Reichsdeutsch* like them. There is a world of difference.

One particular day, on the way home from school, the German boys follow him once again calling out, "*Ruski!*" over and over. Finally, today, it is enough. Peter turns around, faces the taunting classmates, then runs towards them! This surprise tactic causes them to scatter. Peter chases after one boy running towards home crying, "Mama, Mama!" The boy reaches his house and scampers inside, still calling for his mama. And Peter races in right after him, right into the kitchen where he grabs the boy's arm and scares him further by shouting, "I'll show you *Ruski!*" But he promptly realizes where he is, turns and dashes right back out! Scared, too.

An upper-grader, a *Hitler Jugend* (Hitler Youth) leader, makes it a point to harass Peter. "*Ruski, Ruski!*" Peter gives chase, angry as a terrier that doesn't realize the opponent is a bigger dog. Later, when the other students are gone, the teacher calls Peter over to his desk and says in a tone that carries a warning, "Peter, never again beat up on a member of the *Hitler Jugend!*" But a curt —ever so slight— pat on the back as Peter is dismissed conveys that the teacher is impressed. And thereafter the older boys leave Peter alone. He has their respect. One lesson the pacifist preacher's son has learned in school is to fight back.

Finally, Peter makes a friend. This boy is from Berlin. After the fierce bombing of that city began, school children were evacuated to attend school elsewhere. And it was lucky they were evacuated since in March 1944, Berlin will be razed by allied B-57 bombers. Ironically, some are sent to Dresden, which will also be bombed, in fact a month earlier than the final Berlin bombing. Peter's classmates do not accept the new boy either, so the two outcasts have this in common, a valid reason to become comrades.

Math equations and grammar are very difficult, but there are other things Peter becomes quite good at. There is a store in Dresden where the children go to obtain notebooks and pencils when the class makes an outing to the zoo or to see a play. All school supplies are rationed, and in order to get scribblers or necessary supplies, the students require a signature from the *Oberlehrer* (head teacher). Peter manages to perfect the fluid cursive signature. Soon, the storekeeper notices the same children stopping in for supplies. He grows leery. Finally he demands a closer look at the signature on the requisition note. "Are you children certain that your teacher signed this?"

A woman in the store overhears the proprietor. She offers to help. "I know the *Oberlehrer* very well; I can identify his signature." She takes the forged slip from Peter's hand; his stomach flip-flops as she inspects it carefully. She seems to take forever. Finally she says to the storekeeper, "Yes, that's it, all right."

Peter's favourite subject is art. The teacher instructs the students to choose a subject, but when Peter tells him he will sketch the *Führer*, the teacher is alarmed because an inappropriate caricature will pose a problem. He advises Peter not to attempt the drawing. Nonetheless Peter works conscientiously at the drawing with his pencils, shading in shadows, and erasing spaces to create light; it glints from the eyes. A thick moustache under the nose, like a mat under a door, completes the sketch. At the end of the class Peter hands in his work. The teacher inspects it and raises his eyebrows. His expression reads, *this is remarkably accurate.*

Peter attended school for only a few more months, until the area around Dresden grew too dangerous. When the night raids increased, the refugees at Lager 93 were sent on to Yugoslavia, to work as farm labourers. This occurred just days before Dresden was to be fire-bombed by the British. Even though he never saw the complete destruction of Dresden, my father has recalled the days before the attacks and the bombed-out buildings. He remembers that when the German anti-aircraft guns shot down allied planes, the bombers unloaded their arsenal, which then destroyed whatever lay in their path. Such destruction would be only a glimpse into Dresden's impending fate, when on February 13 to 15, in two separate attacks, a swarm of bombers reduced Dresden, a city crowded with civilians and refugees, to rubble and ash. Historians now estimate that the dead range between twenty-five and thirty-five thousand. But the fate of most refugees is unknown. Untold bodies were incinerated in the blazes. This firebombing has since been described as a war crime.[15] It is noteworthy that Allied plans were for the Americans to bomb first, but bad weather had prevented an American attack.[16]

In a journal entry on the day of 9–11 when the World Trade Towers were destroyed, I made the following comment:

> We live close to a small airport; this morning no planes fly, the US President has called for all planes to be grounded, and we, here in our Canadian border town experience his orders. It is eerily still. I notice the silence and the startling blue of the sky. I do not hear birds or even see any fly by. I call my parents. Dad answers, although he is transfixed to CNN and Peter Jennings who I hear in the background along with televised screams and crashes. We don't really talk, but the phone line connects us as Dad watches the towers crumble. Over and over it is shown. He finally says, "It's like Dresden — the bombed-out buildings everywhere."

Despite time or distance, destruction and disaster become inextricably linked in my father's mind.

◈ YUGOSLAVIA, 1944

In 1944, train-loads of refugees, many of whom left Dresden before its destruction, were scattered throughout Yugoslavia. Among them were the Letkemann, Toews and Braun families of Rosengart, as well as Peter's school teacher from Freital, Germany. Aunt Mary has sent me two old monochromatic postcards that she kept from Yugoslavia, now eastern Slovenia. They are of Cilli (Celje), a picturesque town in the vineyard-covered hills, a hamlet that sprang from a settlement founded by the Roman Emperor Claudius in the middle of the first century. The first

Postcard of Cilli, view beyond train station

Cilli, view along the river bank

postcard contains the view just beyond the railroad station of the town nestled on a gentle hillside. In the photo one can see a train in the foreground as it journeys through the rolling farmland and vineyards of the low Stajerska range, on tracks that lead from Cilli's station to Maribor, near the Austrian border. Houses with tile roofs dot the pastures and at the top of a grassy mound is a higher knoll, thickly covered with coniferous forest.

The second postcard is of old buildings along the river bank. Here one sees a wooden bridge over the wide Savinja River. A tree in the foreground leans from the grassy bank over the water's edge casting a great shadow on the lawn behind it. The tree must be centuries old, its bark deeply creased like the skin of a crone, but its branches, as well as those of the trees in the background, are budding with growth. It looks like springtime in Cilli. It is a beautiful place and I can see why Aunt Mary would have kept the postcards.

At this time, Yugoslavia experienced varying types of treatment at the hands of the Germans. Hitler partitioned Yugoslavia soon after the German conquest in April 1941, dividing the northwestern area of Slovenia into German and Italian occupation zones while establishing the puppet states of Croatia and Serbia.[17] Slovenian partisans formed groups to actively resist the Nazi occupation, uniting under the Slovenian National Liberation Front. This group joined Josip Tito's Yugoslav Partisan Army. Such conditions proved perilous for the refugees, who, transported there by the Germans, were associated with them.[18] Some historians posit that the violence against the *Volksdeutsche* in Yugoslavia was more relentless than in any other country.[19]

◈

"In Lemburg, Yugoslavia, I was placed in grade five until summer break when I worked in the fields, hoeing and weeding. Then I went into grade six at Neukirchen a few kilometers away, and had to walk to school until the family moved here. I attended only for a few months in each place because of the war," my father explains.

Because the partisan activity was so strong in Lemburg, Jakob asked for work in a safer place. The family was then sent to Neukirchen to work on an estate. Neukirchen (Novozwerka), which means "New Church," is the next community after Lemburg, four kilometres away, but before Buchenschlag. Each is a village near Cilli. Jakob felt it would be somewhat safer than working on the smaller farms. Peter recalls that he was pleased to find he would be able to go to school. In fact, a photograph of his school class has survived. Eight boys and eight girls are arranged in three rows: fair and dark-haired, all from different backgrounds. In the middle row of girls, one wears a dirndl dress, the others wear printed jumpers. Some of the children wear sandals while others are barefoot on the sandy ground. In the first row, sitting cross-legged, are two boys. And there, in the last row at one end, is Isaac's brother, Abram Toews, one year older than Peter. Peter is at the other end. The two are bookends. Together with little Frieda Toews, who stands in the middle row, they are the only Mennonite children in the class. Peter, the only child not paying attention or looking at the camera, is gazing off to the side, toward Abram, grinning as the two girls standing in front of him giggle in a suspended moment. Peter must have said something funny.

"When we first came to Neukirchen," Peter recalls, "there was a big tree in the centre of town. On May Day the children danced around it with ribbons. Once in a while Isaac and I went to Cilli, about ten kilometres away. That was a good outing."

Peter's life in Neukirchen seems ordered and normal. While the rest of the family works, he and Helen attend school. Their teacher here, Maria Reiner, is from Austria. Peter thinks she is a kind lady. Everyone must speak German at school, but outside the Yugoslavian students converse in their own language. In this school, Peter is "German." *Fräulein* Reiner praises Peter

Peter's class in Neukirchen, Yugoslavia, 1944. Peter is in the back row, on the left.

in front of the class for speaking German, "All of you students should be more like Peter."

To a boy of Peter's age, however, it's more important to be accepted by the class than liked by the teacher, so Peter promptly turns to the students and says in their language, "What does she know?" The Slavic language is easily picked up by a child who speaks Russian.

By now Peter has turned fourteen, and in Neukirchen, along with the teenagers his age, he must enroll in the next phase of the Nazi Youth Program, the *Hitler Jugend*. Peter receives brown leather shoes — he has never before owned a new pair of shoes. They are his exact size and he learns to keep them as shiny as chrome on a new car; polishing shoes is a discipline he will never lose. He receives a summer uniform *and* a winter uniform. Shirt, shorts and socks for summer. For winter, a long-sleeved shirt and dark blue pants. He is proud of his uniform; these are the best clothes he has ever owned.

Once during the week and every Sunday, the children go to training and sing songs, *Deutschland, Deutschland über alles.*

Germany, Germany, above all else. And *Schwarzbraun ist die Hazelnuss, schwarzbraun bin auch ich. Schwarzbraun soll mein Mädel sein, gerade so wie ich,* an old folksong that now carried the ominous idea that a boy should choose a girl of his own "kind." More subtly, not only are these young Slavs, Ukrainians, and *Volksdeutsche* to learn that they belong to different groups, but also that each group is of a lower "class" than the superior *Reichsdeutsche*.

One day, when school is out for summer, Peter and Isaac are picking cherries on the estate. During the lunch break, they climb a tree and sit in its fork; the glistening cherries are like jewels among the leaves. The harvest is so ripe a light summer rain will split the red-black skins. The fruit bursts in their mouths as Peter and Isaac gorge themselves among the branches, cherry blood dripping from their teeth.

"HEY, get out, GET OUT!" It's the foreman and he's raising his whip. Snap! The leather is meant to sting the boys but misses as the angered man keeps hitting the tree. Ripe cherries fall like cookie crumbs each time. Isaac shouts a Slavic word — it sounds like *boodle*. It means stupid. "You big Stoo-pid," Isaac yells down again as the boys jump from their branches and tear off.

Later, when Isaac is home, the foreman comes to reproach Mrs. Toews. He tries to tell her that her son was stealing, omitting the detail of using a whip. He says that Isaac called him "*boodle*." But Isaac's mother speaks mostly low German, and besides, in her anxiety she is flustered by the foreman's shouting. She misunderstands his rapid Slavic speech; to her, *boodle* sounds similar to the low German word for bottle. Ah ha! Just lately she has noticed a bottle missing from her small cache; she does not own much. Oh dear! Isaac has accused the foreman of *stealing!* No wonder the man is so upset. After he leaves, she scolds Isaac fiercely, but he doesn't correct her. Isaac knows he would have gotten the same "earful" if his mother knew that he had called the foreman stupid.

Jakob and Maria also try to maintain discipline and structure in their cramped accommodations. The house is divided in half by a hallway. They occupy the room on the right, the left side is empty, and the estate foreman lives upstairs. It is a Catholic area where spires rise on grassy hills like trees. There are no Protestant churches here, so Jakob conducts a service at home for the family once a week. Jakob and Maria read the Bible openly now and pray with their children.

◆

After a time, however, the danger grew in Neukirchen, particularly from the partisans. Partisans were ordinary citizens by day; they may even have worked side by side with those brought from Russia or Ukraine and other German-occupied countries. But at night they raided villages, kidnapping young people, taking them into the forest to "persuade" them to join their fight against the occupiers. Those who refused were shot, execution style.

On one occasion the German authorities in Neukirchen received advance information from an underground source that there was going to be another raid on the village. They ordered the young refugees to gather at the municipal hall, arm themselves, and defend the town. Eight, including Jake and Gerhardt, reported to the hall. As my father tells this story, he says he can still sense the stillness of that night.

Two a.m.: Peter is awake. It is very quiet except for the dogs barking. The shooting starts. Partisans emerge from the forest to attack the municipal hall down the street; at the house, a grenade is thrown against the front door. It sounds like summer thunder pounding in Peter's eardrums, followed seconds later by a spray of splintering wood, pieces clattering against the tile floor.

Another grenade lands in the empty apartment across the hall but doesn't explode. Men enter their quarters; Jakob steps in front of his family, who are wearing only night clothes, little more than underwear, as the intruders shout, "Tell us who you are!"

Jakob, trying to remain calm, responds in Russian, "This is my wife, these are my children — we are from Russia." Stalin is Tito's ally so they leave the family alone.

Outside there is fierce fighting. Gerhardt is on the roof of the municipal hall, firing. Jake is inside, guarding the front door in case one among them is a partisan waiting to open it to the invaders. Also inside are the town mayor with men and boys from the neighbouring village.

The hall is on fire. Thick, oily smoke roils and stings Gerhardt's eyes as he stomps on the orange tongues and smothers the flames with his jacket. Jake notices one fellow inch towards the door. He doesn't trust him; he pins him back. They scuffle. Jake knuckle-punches the man between the eyes, hard, and the man slumps to the floor.

From inside his house, Peter hears shooting in the street and notices a girl's voice. He hears someone — an older boy — call to the girl to keep firing, then a shot in her direction and her shooting stops.

Four a.m.: Re-enforcements arrive. The partisans retreat.

When the sun rises, Peter goes to the hole that was the front door; there are no bodies in the street but there are stains and pools between the cobble stones. Blood is everywhere. Bullets have pock-marked the face of the house. It's so quiet. Jake, Gerhardt, and another worker from the estate arrive at the house to detonate the grenade in the apartment across the hall. Peter overhears them talking about last night, "Two or three hundred partisans. . . ."

◈

They lived in Neukirchen for almost a year, but after this particular attack it grew too dangerous. Together with the Toews family, the Letkemanns moved on to work at another place, a larger estate named Gestitthof, near the town of Begegrad, renamed Buchenschlag by the Germans. Their friends the Brauns were relocated to the town of Buchenschlag itself. And this is the town where Peter attended school, walking there from the estate on its outskirts. Peter liked his teacher, an older German man who seemed pleasant and helpful; Peter was actually one of his favourites. Otherwise, the experience of attending school was a difficult one.

"Here, I was placed in grade seven. I knew only addition and subtraction, no division or multiplication. And here again, the German kids had to join the *Hitler Jugend*. The Slovenians were in it too, but of course we didn't know if their parents were in the underground resistance. We suspected that the foreman of the estate was a partisan by night. Besides this, his son was always harassing Helen. I fought him to stop it." When my father looks back on his school days there, he says, "It seems I always had to fight my way home after school. There was always rivalry and fighting between the children."

Usually he stayed close by the younger Toews boys. "Once it was Abram who was beaten. There was a whole group of them, but I felt I had to help him. . . . We fought the fellows off, but the next day all those boys came after *me*, and Abram didn't help me. After that beating, I began running home from school every day."

At last, however, there comes a day when he realizes that it will be the last time. He is tired of running home each day and promises himself he will do something about it. Finally the coast is clear. He stops to gather pebbles, shiny small ones that shake out a rhythm in his pocket the rest of the way. He remembers having played soldier with his friends in Russia and has an idea.

Peter collects what he needs, a small piece of pipe — it must be closed at one end — and a piece of wood and two pieces of wire. He whittles, the small blade of his *Hitler Jugend* pocket knife carefully scraping away the bark, like skin from bone. The wood beneath is white and becomes the gun handle. Next, he patiently files a slit into the pipe, near the back end. Wrapping wire around the pipe and handle, he fastens them together. This is a homemade pistol. Now he needs a rubber strap to cover the front end of the pipe, to keep the ammunition in place. Gunpowder? He will have to collect discarded casings. These he finds lying about everywhere. Match heads will also do. What else?

Along with the cache of pebbles in his pockets, the ammunition will be made from old piston rings. Peter places them on a large rock, and with another, pounds them into pellets. He puts bits of paper, rolled into balls, down the pipe barrel, but not all the way, leaving space at the very end for the gun powder. Next he pours piston fragments and pebbles into the pipe barrel. He adds some coarse salt for good measure. He pokes it down with a stick, and fastens the rubber strap over the barrel so the "ammo" stays put.

Matchsticks in his pocket, the "loaded" gun in his rucksack, Peter heads off to school. He's ready for the local boys. All day he waits for school to end and when it does, he dashes around the corner of the building. He's safe for the moment. He takes out his pistol, taps a stream of powder into the slit at the back of the ammo chamber and, holding the pistol at his side, walks toward home, match ready, knowing the pack will soon be closing in behind him.

"Hey you dirty *Kraut*!"

There are five of them trailing close like village dogs eyeing a stray cat ahead . . . and when the cat runs the dogs give chase! Peter sprints a hundred yards until there is enough distance between him and the gang. He stops and turns to face them, holding out his crude weapon. The boys stop, but then erupt with laughter.

"Don't you laugh or you're gonna see what'll happen!" Peter warns.

"Are you going to shoot us with *that?*" they retort, not threatened in the least.

He loosens the rubber strap. "Come closer and see." Not too close, Peter thinks, or they might see his hand shaking from the adrenaline; he really hopes the pistol will fire as it did after so many tries at home.

"Ha! What an ugly looking gun!" The boys take a few more steps.

Peter lifts his foot, striking the match to the sole of his shoe.

Closer . . .

Touches the flame to the slit in the chamber filled with gunpowder.

Closer . . .

BANG!

The pups scatter. It works! Peter walks home in peace, happy to be left alone, so pleased his home-made pistol is a success. He's quite good at devising things. Afterwards the boys at school want to know how Peter made it. Will he show them? It seems the boys are no longer enemies, but are they his friends?

School goes a little better these days. But the partisan activity increases and grows more violent. One evening Peter is returning from a Hitler youth meeting in Cilli. He no longer wears the uniform; that's too dangerous. The sky is already a deep shade of twilight. As he nears Gestitthof, he has two routes to choose from; he can take the short cut along the worn footpath through the estate, or continue on the main road that winds around. It's probably safer out in the open. Peter, however, decides on the shortcut.

As he reaches the gate of the estate, two dusky figures step out from the trees. One shines a beam of light on Peter, "*Halt, Geheimpolizei!*" (Stop, Secret Police). Peter is startled, and is suddenly nervous. The large shadow-man holding the flashlight speaks German and asks Peter, "What's your name?" Peter does not answer; he simply stares at the dark form who asks for his name again, this time in Slovenian, so Peter replies in Slovenian.

"How old are you?"

"Thirteen," he says although he is really fourteen, but a little on the small side, and luckily Peter isn't wearing a uniform!

"And where do you live?"

Peter tells him he lives here, at Gestitthof. He is just on his way home.

"All right, scram. Hurry up!" And Peter hurries home.

Usually, by the time Peter arrives, Jakob is also there following a long day of work, but tonight he is not. Maria and the children wait and wait, anxiety thickening with each hour. At midnight a figure at the door — Jakob has arrived. Peter stands behind the doorway, lights out, and, as Jakob turns the latch to enter the unlit house, exclaims loudly, *"Halt, Geheimpolizei!"*

It was supposed to be a joke.

My father still recalls his own father's reaction, how gravely upset Jakob was at the prank. The reason Jakob had been so late coming home was that he had been detained by the police. "It was my dad's job to transport the female workers to and from the estate, women from various eastern countries, forced to work under the Germans. In the morning he collected the women, and in the evening following work in the fields, he brought them to their places by horse and wagon."

Father continues his explanation, "If I had gone by way of the road, I would have met my dad and could have told him about the police at the gate. But following my encounter, I cut through the estate. When my dad came down the road awhile later, he met up with the same men, who took him, along with the women workers, for questioning. They let the women go, but not my dad. He was questioned for hours, though he maintained that he was Russian. Finally, they took the horse and wagon and let him go."

My father relays this episode of his attempt to be funny. One may often joke, however inappropriate it may seem, in order to diffuse a stressful situation or curb one's own anxiety. I think this story is an illustration, not of teenage awkwardness, but of this aspect of the human psyche. And like Peter's school escapades, this vignette also gestures toward Peter's indomitable will in the face of frightening circumstances. I recall now that when my father first asked me to write his story, he also requested that I include a little humour. I realize that he did not want his story to focus on his obstacles, but on overcoming them — in his own unique way. Whether or not one finds Peter's actions in particular situations comedic, clearly, the absurdity of war-time life stands out.

6

❖

Arriving at
1945

Most of us arrive at 1945 not as agents, leaders,
soldiers. We arrive as hangers-on or as victims,
in crowds, pushed and pulled by events over
which we feel we have no control.

— MODRIS EKSTEINS

❖ GERHARDT

These are the last pictures taken of Gerhardt. This one, probably in early 1944, when he was barely nineteen years old — just
a little older than my son graduating from high school — is
three inches by four inches. It is an *Identitätsphoto* (identity
photo) from Cilli. The solid bones beneath his cheeks stand out.
A faint line divides his chin, like a small firm apricot, where, at
the bottom, the line to the crease of his left ear forms the strong
edge of his jaw. His face is narrow, chiselled; he is thinner than
usual. He wears a dark wool jacket, and I notice its weight, so
thick in contrast to the thin undershirt beneath. A low scooped
neckline exposes the V at the centre of his prominent clavicle

Gerhardt, his "identity photo"

ridge. His thick straight hair is shiny, brushed smoothly back from his forehead, blonde because the whole front is lit up. If this were a high school yearbook, he would be the handsome captain of a sports team with the promise of a bright future and the attention of all the popular girls, but he is a refugee. Gerhardt doesn't smile.

The next photo is the same size. In it, Gerhardt's face is fuller, taken from the opposite angle. From this side, his face is handsome too, still serious. As can be seen, his thick crop of hair is brushed back once more and glows like a crown of light above his forehead. This shot is of him sitting, right hand on leg, left arm crooked with hand at his waist. Gerhardt would have been a teenager when he was drafted into the communications unit of the *Wehrmacht* in late 1944. He wears a uniform like a mechanic's belted jumpsuit. There are no tell-tale insignias or badges. If the photograph were wider I might make out if there is an arm-band over the balled muscle of his left forearm, but it's impossible to tell.

Jakob and Maria prayed fervently that their sons Jake and Gerhardt would not be called to the front. It seemed enough that they were required to serve in the defence of the town as an added duty to their labour. As the war continued, however, the Germans were increasingly drafting young men into the *Wehrmacht*. A general and mandatory call to arms was issued on October 18, 1944.[1] Jakob and Maria acknowledged there was no choice in the matter, and were thankful the boys had not been conscripted earlier. Fortunately, the brothers, although stocky, were not tall. Those who were at least six feet tall were automatically conscripted into the SS. Interestingly enough, the

Gerhardt age 19, Communications Unit, late 1944

most notorious SS unit, the Death's Head squad, feared among civilians and soldiers alike, was a voluntary unit.

On October 20, 1944, Belgrade, the capital of Yugoslavia, fell to the advancing Soviet forces. Gerhardt was sent to Maribor, just beyond the mountains near the Austrian border. He was to train in radio communications, but because he had little education, he found it difficult to learn and adapt. According to my father, a few months later Gerhardt would voluntarily transfer out of communications into an artillery unit; he would fight against the "enemy Russians" whose oppression he had experienced throughout his young life. Gerhardt's reason for joining an artillery unit to fight might have been that he saw it as a way to resist the Communists. Or did Gerhardt simply concede that it was only a matter of time? At the time of his transfer, late in the war, other non-combatant conscripts were also transferred with orders to fight and given rifles.[2]

Jake was trained in the *Gebirgsjäger*, part of the infantry intended for mountainous terrain. He was first sent to Graz, Austria, stationed there for a few months before he was sent to the eastern front near Vienna. Each soldier was given a rifle, probably an old used one from a captured Russian, and given little to no training for armed combat, never mind that armed combat would mean close combat.

As for the boys fourteen and under and older men, they were not forced to fight at this time. Jakob and Maria and their younger children carried on working at the estate in Buchenschlag. Partisans continued to raid the villages at night. On one occasion, just before the night ebbed into dawn, the partisans attacked Gestitthof, robbing it, even taking away some of the young people. They did not come to Jakob and Maria's house, but the next day people were excitedly talking about the raid. They said that the partisans had been asking about the Letkemann boys who had fought at the municipal hall in Neukirchen.

Shortly after, Jakob and Maria received a package from the

German government. My father states, "Jake and Gerhardt each received an iron cross for the defence of the Neukirchen municipal hall, though they would never see these medals."

❖ 1945

By January 9, 1945, German lines on the eastern front had collapsed and a full retreat began. On January 27, the Soviet Army liberated Auschwitz. Sixty years later, on my birthday, I dwell on these events before my time. The newspapers are filled with sixtieth-anniversary commemorative pieces. That the Soviets were the liberators seems like an unexpected plot twist. I have read, in recent historical scholarship, that in one of Stalin's Gulag camps the entrance reads, "Work in the USSR is a matter of Honour and Glory."[3] I think of the gateway at Auschwitz, declaring, ARBEIT MACHT FREI (Work will make you free), and through the sharp lens of hindsight, I reflect on how the Mennonites, *Volksdeutsche*, and Ukrainians once viewed the German occupiers as their liberators from Stalin's purges. . . . The faces of oppressor and liberator blur, are indistinguishable. Suffering comes into focus.

That spring, sometime in March, the *Volkssturm* called up boys from the *Hitler Jugend*. The German army was suffering severe losses and began to conscript younger boys, even as young as fourteen; those eighteen and older were by this time fighting and dying in forests and fields throughout the eastern front. Peter and Isaac walked to Cilli to report for mandatory duty. After registration they would be expected to leave in one week's time — the job for the *Hitler Jugend* boys, to dig the necessary trenches. My father says the commander, an older veteran, decided that he, Peter, slightly built at fourteen — and looking thirteen — was too young, and told him to go home. In the western region things were not utterly desperate, and the officer was reasonable when considering which youngsters to send home. Peter was relieved, mostly because he did not want to dig trenches, but a few weeks more and the officer might have sent

Peter off with a shovel and a rifle. Sixteen-year-old Isaac did go, and returned to Buchenschlag after a short period of digging trenches. However, at the eastern front, where the fighting raged, the *Volkssturm* called up young boys and old men and sent them into battle. This measure was Hitler's last ditch attempt to avoid the inevitable defeat.

About this time, Gerhardt was shipped out from Maribor to East Prussia, and from there to the Russian front. Just before he left, he wrote home. In a short note he told his parents, *Macht nichts was vorgeht, ich traue auf Gott* (Don't worry about what may come, I believe in God). He could offer Jakob and Maria a measure of comfort only regarding his soul, not his life.

By March 28, 1945, little more than one month before the end of the war, the German defence lines crumbled. On the eastern front, on what was only Gerhardt's second day of battle, his artillery placement received a direct hit. The note that Jakob and Maria received from the war department stated their son had been killed in a grenade attack on the battlefield in Ober-schliessen, East Prussia, March 30, 1945. The letter informed Jakob and Maria that Gerhardt had not suffered; it said that he died instantly. Gerhardt Letkemann, December 28, 1925 – March 28, 1945. He had just turned nineteen in December, a few months before. Gerhardt was buried in Steinkirchen, Po-land. Of course, the names of these places soon changed; and as for a grave marker, or even a graveyard, the family still has no idea where Gerhardt lies.

My father says that as a teenager, he could not absorb the news of the telegram, that long afterwards, whenever he saw a young soldier with a stocky build and blonde hair returning from the war, he thought it might be Gerhardt. "But eventually I stopped looking for him," he says.

And there was no news of Jake. No letters home. No telegram from the army.

My father remembers seeing the defeated German troops marching by in Yugoslavia. He heard one of the soldiers say he had thrown away everything, that he didn't want to fight any-more, and he didn't want to be caught with a gun. My father reflects on this a moment, "I think that was a mistake — to be caught without a gun. Partisans ambushed stragglers or un-armed people and killed them." Was it better or worse to carry a gun?

Soon after this, someone, perhaps from the resistance, came to Jakob and Maria's house to interrogate them, to determine whether or not they were "German." In this case, Jakob had to think quickly about what was the "correct" answer and main-tained they were "from Russia."

Meanwhile, Peter had come home to find a bicycle leaning against the front of the house, near the entrance door. Bicycles were scarce these days. Before going in, he could not resist tak-ing it for a spin. Hardly anyone owned a bicycle, certainly not Peter.

When the stranger concluded his questions for Jakob and Maria, he went outside to discover his bicycle missing. A few minutes later, Peter rode into the yard, fenders rattling, to the scene of his parents assuring the stranger that surely the bicycle had not been stolen by anyone they knew. Jakob turned to Peter, his voice sharp and thin, "Peter!" But the stranger said, "Now, now, no harm done; boys will be boys." Once he left, Jakob fin-ished, "What were you *thinking* . . . these are very dangerous times."

By now the German army is in full flight. Through it all, Isaac and Peter roam the fields near the stream, swollen with melting snow, now a rushing torrent. Maria would be alarmed if she knew the boys often wandered about so carelessly, but despite the danger of the fleeing army they cannot resist the lure of the grassy fields in spring, the sunlight glittering silver like scales over the serpentine watercourse.

Slovenia's runoff gushes over rocks in the streambeds. In the distance the boys hear a muffled explosion — a geyser of water, then a downpour. They hear low voices.

The two cross the field and come upon a group of German soldiers on the bank "fishing" with hand-grenades. Having nothing to eat, the unit has been tossing grenades into the river; after they explode, glistening fish rise to the surface. Crouching behind a curtain of tall grass the boys spy on the group for a while, but a soldier keeping watch spots them. "Hey, you! Come here!"

"They made us wade into the stream to collect their fish. It was April, still quite cold. They weren't nice to us, so after gathering up the floating fish, we said we couldn't find anymore. They took what we brought out and then left." Father remembers the scene clearly.

In only their underwear, Isaac and Peter creep back into the frigid water, and breathlessly reach down to the stream bed to pick up the rest, fish whose air sacs had popped from the explosions, and sunken to the bottom.

"We took them home — fish for supper."

❖

On April 30 Hitler committed suicide. He put a pistol in his mouth and pulled the trigger.[4]

"By the end of April, the beginning of May, the remaining German troops in our area had retreated though there were still a few stragglers, and it was clear to us that Germany was capitulating," Father states.

On May 7, there was an unconditional surrender of all German forces and the final documents were signed. The victory was celebrated May 8, known as "Victory in Europe Day." The USSR waited an extra day before beginning formal celebrations.[5]

While the rest of the world celebrated victory, my father recalls that in Yugoslavia there was only chaos: "The partisans returned as soldiers of the Yugoslavian army. This created havoc. There was anarchy. The Yugoslav military, bandits and young rebels were a mixed and disorganized group. They rounded up all German-speaking people including refugees; there were many mass murders in the woods."

At night, the partisans ambushed a German train full of ammunitions and wounded soldiers. The next morning, Jakob took Peter, along with Isaac, to investigate. Boxcars lay like broken toys. Inside, they discovered tins of meat and biscuits. Jakob and the boys took as much as they could carry back to hide for the hard times to come. "To this day some may still be in the attic where we hid it," Father conjectures. "We had even planned to go back to the train."

Why they could not becomes evident in my father's explanation of what followed. "The Germans in the area did not want to surrender to the Yugoslavs; rather, they wanted to surrender to the Americans in Germany, and they were anxious to leave for Germany. In addition, the Croatians had fought for the Germans and were therefore, regarded by the Slovenians and Yugoslavs as enemies, and they also wanted to leave." (A historian explains that the Croats, a Yugoslav people group, did not resist the German invasion in 1941, and as a result the Germans showed them favour.[6]) My father continues, "Not wanting to surrender to the Yugoslavs, the Croats and Germans marched through the area — thousands of them over three days. One night during this exodus, the Yugoslavs detonated a mine among the marchers. Imagine. People, horses, blown up, and scattered. We would have had to step over corpses if we wanted to return to the train; it was impossible."

Peter witnessed the lawlessness. On one occasion he saw what happened to those left as stragglers from retreating groups. Standing about one hundred feet away, he watched as four local fellows grabbed an individual. They beat him with their rifle butts. Sickening thuds, bones cracking, groans. Peter ran off. He didn't want to be beaten, too.

Another day: Peter is walking alongside the railroad tracks when he thinks he hears something in the ditch ahead and stops to listen. Moaning. He walks cautiously to the ditch beside the rail line where he sees soldiers lying there, left behind. They have been there for more than a day, perhaps a few, and are probably dying. "Water" "Water." Peter hears them whispering.

A man walks past as Peter stands there, and says, "Get lost! These Germans and Croats aren't worth your trouble." Peter sprints home.

"Pa, come quick, there are men lying in the ditch by the tracks, left there to die!"

Jakob still has his old tunic from Russia so he puts it on. "Don't follow me, Peter," he orders as he rushes away. He heads for the Slovenian foreman to ask for the horse and buggy.

The foreman is emphatic. "I won't have anything to do with this, Jakob. It's too dangerous to transport them, just leave them there — they're probably dead by now anyway."

"Listen, you are Catholic." Jakob appeals. "Doesn't the Scripture teach us to be merciful? When the man lay by the roadside half dead, the Samaritan stopped and took pity on him. Remember what the expert of the law asked Jesus? He wanted to know how to inherit eternal life. What did Jesus say? He said, 'Go and do likewise.'"

"*Ach,* Jakob," the foreman sighs heavily. "You speak like a priest — though one day your deeds will get you killed."

"Please . . ."

With a wave of his hand, he mutters, "All right. Let's go."

The two men go to the spot where Peter has told them the men lay, and load them, slack as carpet rolls, onto the wagon. They will take them to the hospital in Cilli. Along the way, they are stopped by soldiers who ask them what they are doing.

The foreman remains silent.

Jakob answers, "I'm a Russian simply performing a humane deed." With that, the soldiers let them pass.

It is now May. The war is over but weeks of anarchy follow. From beyond his window as he lies in the darkness, Peter hears faint crying in the night. It comes from the nearby meadows, pitiful sounds somewhere on the far bank of the river. Shots ring out and echo through the trees. Then a terrible hush falls over the night. Only the trees whisper. The forests of Eastern Europe silently speak their secrets to the wind.

In the morning, Isaac finds Peter and tells him that he, too, has heard something. Peter and Isaac walk to the meadow, just ten-minutes from where they are living. They wade across the shallow stream that divides the field, to the far bank, to the stand of white birch and poplar trees, and then into a clearing. The fallen leaves and grass have been disturbed; dirt turned over, still dark and fresh. The rustling of the cool breeze through the trees touches their ears.

The boys poke the loose earth; Peter's stick pushes against something beneath. Both scrape away the soil, then recoil. Shoes . . . girl's shoes on small feet, socks around ankles. . . .

Run! Run away!

Rumours in the village state that a group of *Bund Deutscher Mädel* had been taken. Young girls, raped and shot.

Although the times were dangerous, my father tells me that he continued to go out.

"But Dad . . . *why?*" I ask. "Weren't you afraid something would happen to you?"

My father draws his shoulders up. "There was always danger. It was what I knew. To find out what was going on, I had to investigate."

From Gestitthof, Peter takes a shortcut along a footpath through the woods into Buchenschlag. He sees three young men, about twenty years old, approach. Peter walks on, head bent slightly, eyes off the men. Although he does not want to draw attention to himself, Peter glances up for a split second and notices that the one in the middle has been beaten, his face like putty, reshaped, swollen and bloody. Peter knows the face! The *Hitler Jugend* leader. Peter drops his gaze, but still sees the fellow's hands, tied behind his back. One of his captors presses a gun into the small of it. "They probably marched him into the bush," says my father. "I never saw him again."

My father recalls how it ended for those brought to Yugoslavia as labourers to work on confiscated farms under the Germans. "We didn't live far from the main road and we saw how the people were driven by guards on horseback, made to run until they fell, and were beaten. Others would try to pick up the ones who fell and carry or drag them along. And so one day, members of the Yugoslavian 'army' — Communist partisans — also came to our place. They said, 'Take what you can carry.' We put on our best clothes, packed food, rations from the train; we had a baby buggy and put these things in it along with Liz, who was just two."

But just before it came to this, he said that Jakob and Maria took the iron crosses for Jake and Gerhardt that had been sent to them by the German army for the defence of Neukirchen, and threw them down the outhouse.

Father remembers it this way: "Marshall Josip Tito was leader. Yugoslavia was Communist. And all the German-speaking workers from various countries were rounded up, along with German soldiers, for a march to a prison camp. From there, the civilians would be sent over the mountains to Russian-occupied territory in Austria. There was one horse-drawn cart for possessions. The group had to walk."

Of the half-million people of the workforce originally sent to Yugoslavia by the German army, virtually all of them fled, were expelled or sent to labour camps by Communist partisan forces. An estimated twenty-seven thousand were sent by rail cars back to camps in the Soviet Union.[7] Who really knows how many were killed?

◈ THE MARCH

From Cilli, Jakob, Maria and their children begin the forced march of German refugees, under guard. Their first destination will be Maribor. On the map, the distance from Cilli to Maribor appears to be about forty kilometres, "as the crow flies," but in reality the route winds its way through the green hills of the Starjerska, and then climbs an altitude of almost sixteen-hundred metres in the Pohorje Range, part of the Central Alps, before descending to Maribor along the River Drava. These mountains are dense with pine forests and wildlife. Five years after my father trekked through the region on a mountain path, the first ski lift was built in 1950. In 1945, however, on the forced march, there were only a few remote alpine farms, hunting cabins and pilgrimage churches sprinkled along the way.

Time unravelled like a ball of wool, no longer measured by sunrise and sunset. My father estimates the march took approximately one week. Did it? It could have taken at least that much time if they did not use a main road, and were walking along a mountain path with old and sick people. Few brought any food, nor were they given anything to eat. They had to beg and forage along the way, all the while the guards were terrorizing the bedraggled group. My father took it upon himself to run to the few way-side huts asking for something to eat. "Sometimes people gave me food; other times they spat on me and called me a damn German."

The first part of the trek took them in the direction of Croatia, to a German POW camp in Anderburg (the German name), otherwise known as Sentjura. There were people from Hungary, Bulgaria, Romania and those from Russia. An old Hungarian woman, unable to walk well anymore, was permitted to ride on the horse-drawn cart, but the rest, except Elisbeth in the baby carriage, marched along on foot. There were about thirty-five altogether including the Toews, Brauns, and Fräulein Wall, who had been a teacher in Ukraine. They did not know their destination. The guards were young, the oldest perhaps twenty-one, the others were sixteen or seventeen. "One of them I knew, Stantko from the *Hitler Jugend*, but he pretended he didn't know me and I pretended I didn't know him," says Father.

They have not gone far. Peter is wearing his best set of clothes, which includes his *Hitler Jugend* shirt and a raincoat, and over his shoulder a strap that he has made of leather and fastens to his belt. He needs the strap to hold up his belt, where he attaches a can-opener, a pocket knife, a hand mirror, and a comb — all manner of things boys can use in the woods. These items jangle, making an important sound as he walks. Stantko wants Peter's shoulder strap.

"Give me that shoulder strap."

"Get lost, it's mine," says Peter.

"I'll give you Hitler money," Stantko bargains.

"I don't need Hitler money."

"Well, you used to!" Stantko jeers.

"Well, you used to, too!" Peter won't negotiate any kind of trade, although in this circumstance, Stantko doesn't really have to negotiate.

Jakob overhears the boys, steps up behind his son, places his hand firmly on Peter's shoulder, which means, "Give him that strap." Jakob realizes that the fate of the whole group is now in the hands of these young men and boys, likely members of the Yugoslavian Partisan Army, at liberty to do with them what they please. Without further protest, Peter unfastens the strap from his heavily laden belt, slips it off his shoulder and hands it over, but he is thinking he could have fought Stantko and won.

The POW camp is in the forest, a wire fence marking its circumference, topped with a tier of razored barbs. The long shed is where the civilians sleep. Military prisoners sleep outside. And food is scarce for everyone, let alone for prisoners-of-war. The week-long stay is occupied by nothing but waiting; Stalin had given orders to ship Soviet citizens to Soviet-occupied Austria where they will be sent back to the Soviet Union.

Isaac and Peter usually roam the prison camp, talk to the captured German soldiers who are thinking about when, or if, they can go home. The two boys walk around to the back of the camp near the trees. They see some sort of discarded cylinder, simply misplaced, lost, or forgotten. A flare! They disassemble it and remove the powder. Isaac has matches in his pocket. "Let's light this stuff and see what happens," he suggests. The next thing they remember is a sound like air rushing out of a tire, fizzling, and then *poofff*! A gray-smoke mushroom grows and it seems like the whole camp is under it!

The guards run towards the boys who stand at the base of the cloud of smoke now rising and beginning to clear. Exposed, there is no point in running away. Where would they run to? The guards grab Isaac and Peter by the collar, shoving them roughly toward the administration house — to isolation in the cellar for the rest of the day and throughout that night.

"What idiots!" the boys say about the guards. Soon the night is cold and they begin to realize what it means to be in prison. It is a very long and uncertain night in the dark, dank basement.

Near the ceiling, tiny, dirt-coated windows allow morning light to trickle in and puddle on the floor. The door latch clicks from the outside; Peter and Isaac are relieved to see the guard who opens it.

In the morning all the civilians in the camp were gathered together and divided into groups. Once more the Letkemanns, Toews, Brauns and Fräulein Wall remained together in one group. Again, they set out on foot with the same five young guards, into the mountains heading for Gonabitz, a small town halfway to Maribor. The old Hungarian woman rode in the cart, and the baby, Elisabeth, bounced along in the spring-worn pram. It took a few days on the path to make their way through the first mountain pass. Beyond that, they finally reached a clearing where there was a farm. "In that clearing we stopped and stayed overnight." When I was a child father had told me a small shard of the story, and now he puts all the pieces together.

In the morning the guards select Jakob, Mr. Braun and Mr. Toews, hand them shovels and order the men to dig holes. The group watches, terrified — the holes look like graves. When each man has dug a pit, the oldest guard sets up the machine gun.

Peter huddles together with Jakob, Maria and the girls. At Jakob's quiet instructions, the family kneels to pray. Peter is very close to Jakob, in the curve of his father's boney chest. Then

Jakob puts his lips to Peter's ear and breathes a whisper that only the boy hears, "Peter, when the shooting starts, you *run*. Survive, find Jake. Let him know what has happened to us."

But Peter doesn't want to run, to risk being the only one of his family left; he would rather die here with them, "No." He chokes on the word, and it is the only time he ever says this word to his father.

A squeeze on the trigger, a terrible sound, this round killing only the old woman from Hungary who rode on the cart. She has constantly complained about the guard's mistreatment, reason enough for them to kill her. At the sound of the shot, a lady from the nearby farmhouse frantically runs over to interrupt what might happen to the rest. She urges the guards to be quiet; there are still German SS hiding in the forest. The guards hastily march the refugees onward. By evening the group has travelled down the mountainside to Gonabitz. Just outside the town, they overnight in a farmyard with permission to sleep in the barn.

In the morning, the guards instruct their prisoners to line up while they rummage through each sack of belongings. They order people to undress, then select the articles they want. Peter still wears his stained *Jugend* shirt, and his shoes from the uniform are mud-caked and ruined. They do not want anything to do with that uniform, so he is the lucky one who gets to keep all his clothes. Except for his raincoat. They take that. Next they order everyone to gather in the farmyard. They hold up a watch. "Who took this?" demands the young man in charge.

No one knows whose watch it is. Does it belong to someone in the group? Or does it belong to one of the guards, and they are playing a cruel game. No one confesses.

"Are you going to tell us, or will you all die? *Alles für einen und einer für alle*" (All for one and one for all), the leader sneers, quoting a German military slogan. The others stand in front of the group with rifles cocked. The twenty-one-year-old commander yells, "Fire!" The others squeeze their triggers.

All is quiet. The chambers were empty that time. But now

each soldier has levered a bullet into the chamber of their rifles. People are crying. Next the young guards slide their hands over the women and feel between their legs as if searching for something hidden there.

"If you don't confess, the next time we will shoot you," the leader threatens. This carries on for a terrifying while. Finally, an old lame man, a First World War veteran, steps forward and says he is the one who took the watch. Everyone but the old man is allowed to get dressed.

"Get down on your hands and knees — a hundred push-ups!"

It is agonizing to watch the old man rise and fall, his hands in the dirt, his spindle arms trembling until he collapses after only a few, and the gendarmes kick dirt in his face and eyes, spit on his balding head so saliva drips from his brow and runs down his cheeks. They swear loudly at him, filthy names for a German. The old man lifts his shoulders from the dirt and attempts more, and the whole scene is repeated. The rest of the group stands by watching helplessly as the old man pushes off the ground from his waist up, and as the juvenile guards kick his nearly useless legs with their boots.

The agitated guards tire of this. The man stands, nearly naked, bent, his ribs protruding, knees like knots in brittle branches as they ransack his suitcase, a mock investigation to find the watch. But what is this? A German flag with its black swastika like a poison spider on a blanket. Next, an iron cross. They attach the flag to the old man's back, hang the medal around his neck, and force him to hobble in front of one of the guards on horseback, and to shout "I am a traitor! I am a traitor!" He limps as fast as he can, away from the farmyard, with the horse and rider at his heels. The other guards crow at the sight.

Exhausted and beaten, he can hardly crawl back to where the anxious group is waiting. When one asks him why those things were in his suitcase, he rasps quietly, "The suitcase belonged to my son; I took it by mistake."

The next morning, before the sun rises, the refugees gather

their few belongings. Today the march will be along the road. There is no food, no breakfast before leaving. Elisabeth cries and the woman from the farm slips Maria a jar of fresh milk when the guards are preoccupied. A good woman, Maria thinks.

Sometime later that day, a shiny black car with Russian military personnel slowly passes by. It crawls to a stop; a burly officer climbs out. "What kind of people are these?" he asks the guards, but before they speak, the young teacher from among the group boldly asserts, "We are Russian." There is a house near the roadway and the officer beckons her to come along. The rest wait by the road as she disappears inside.

A short while later the officer and the teacher return to the road. What happened inside one can only guess. He says to the young guards, "I give you strict instructions not to harm this group. If there are any problems, or if any of these people are harmed, you will be shot." Should not the safety of the group be attributed to this courageous young woman, rather than the sympathy of a Russian officer?

Hungry after marching for days along the road, Peter runs ahead to beg. If there is a house close to the roadside, he has time to run and knock on the door to ask for bread or milk, "Please, something for my little sister." Only once does Peter fall behind the group. When this happens, a guard strides up behind him and thrusts the rifle butt into his back. Peter's breath is gone, his back smarts, but he scurries up to the front of the line. From then on he makes sure to stay ahead of the group.

During the march, Maria becomes increasingly ill. Her dress is sweat-soaked but her bones are ice. Mary and Jakob walk one on each side of her, draping her arms over their shoulders, holding up her limp body between them. Peter and Helen take turns pushing Liz along.

Finally the weary and shabby group reaches Maribor on the other side of the mountains. Here is a prison camp where they will stay, and for the first time along this trek they are given something to eat: a slice of bread. The flour has been mixed with sawdust. It tastes awful, but everyone is famished. They gulp it down. In short order, their stomachs convulse: first the stabs of pain, then vomiting.

In Maribor, before the Austrian border, the guards from Cilli leave the group.

Peter has been to Maribor once before, by train from Cilli, to visit Gerhardt during his training here, before he left for the front. Mary has also been here before, so both know the layout of the city. This time, however, is very different. The displaced group must march through the centre of Maribor where people angrily call out, "You damn Germans." They are spit on, their hair and faces, on their clothes as they file past on their way to the train station. Humiliation burns like a fever. It feels like shame, and sometimes, even for years afterward, the refugees will confuse the two.

At the station they are loaded, once again, into boxcars headed for Austria's Russian occupied territory, but everyone knows the final destination is to be Russia. The man directing the people into crowded cars asks Jakob, "Where are you from?"

Jakob answers quietly, "From Russia."

The man replies, "Well, you're lucky today. The people from the prison camp last week were tied, bound with wire, and thrown into the Drava River, husbands, wives and children. At least they'll put you on the train."

It was at this moment, my father tells me, that Jakob gave up believing, as he always had before, that things would change. After all those years in Russia, after all the many times the family might have escaped but did not, this was the moment that Jakob finally relinquished his hope that life in his home place would improve for his family. Although they faced repatriation, in some ways, perhaps in this moment, Jakob had truly "escaped." He was free from false hope.

7
❖

Austria,
1945 to 1947

Try to be buried in ground
that remembers you.

— ANNE MICHAELS

❖ RUSSIAN ZONE

The refugees boarded a boxcar, this one hitched to a train bound
for Graz, approximately fifty kilometres away in Austria's Russian zone. From Maribor, the rails followed the way of the Mur
River, through the hilly countryside of Steiermark (Styria).
Here, Graz was once the crossroads for Germanic, Balkan, and
Mediterranean trade; its crumbling architecture had, before
the bombs, proudly reflected such status. As they arrived at the
Hauptbahnhof (central train station), the weary band could
see Schlossberg (Castle Hill) rising above them. And just beyond
the station lay the city, spread out, with the river, a wide silver
ribbon, running through it.

The sunset was painting the tower remnants and tiled roof-tops a vivid shade of vermillion. But the city centre was laid to ruin, blackened with soot. The new guards deposited the refugees in the bombed section. Here, Jakob, Maria and the others found the only available shelter, in basements beneath the rubble, to live as vagrants amid the acrid stench of ash and decay.

The guards left instructions, curt and severe, "Be here when we return. Anyone missing will be hunted and shot." They did not say when they would be back, just sometime soon, it was assumed. For the following two weeks the group survived by begging and scavenging.

The first day, Jakob takes Peter along to search for canned goods among the rubble. They find a few tins of ham, herring, biscuits. In time, Peter and Isaac pair up and wander to the better neighbourhoods. While one goes to the front door to ask for food and the dweller slams it shut, the other slips around to the back garden where he fills his pockets with early potatoes, carrots or cucumbers.

Peter roams throughout the city on the streetcar, using a system he has devised, hitching a ride on the back step then drop-ping off before the conductor makes his way from front to rear collecting fares. Peter rides throughout Graz like this; only once does the streetcar parasite get caught while dozing off at the back. The conductor pushes him off, and he lands on the cob-blestones like a tumbling gunnysack of bones. Fortunately he is not severely hurt. After this Peter is more vigilant.

On the last day — although no one knows this is the day the guards will return — Peter is out foraging for food. Jakob, too, is scouring alleys and basements along with other homeless peo-ple. With so many missing, the soldier in charge is clearly upset, directing his rage at those who remain: Maria, the other women, the children and the old man. As the soldier spits out profan-ities, Peter appears and steps into the line of refugees. Then Jakob arrives, joins the line-up, and so on . . . until everyone is present and accounted for.

The diatribe follows, "You're worthless! Useless! A bullet is too good for the lot of you — you should have been left to die."

The guards order their unwanted charges to form a line to begin the walk into the main square near the train station. There, in front of the large building that houses the Russian headquarters they stop, wait at the base of the stairs as one guard ascends to the double doors, and disappears. Moments later, a rotund officer peers down from the landing. Jakob and Maria stand with their four children gathered closely. In a guttural pronouncement thick and sticky with Russian inflection, the officer demands to know, "What kind of people are you?"

A lady from Hungary speaks up, "We are from Hungary."

Others answer, "From Romania. . . ."

But most remain silent. Fearing repatriation, no one dares to answer, "We are from Russia." Stalin remains in power.

"What? No Russians here?" The impatient official thrusts his fists above his head. "Then go to the devil — we don't want you!" he shouts.

At this, Jakob urges his family "Run!" Around the building, to the only place they know, they flee toward the ruins. The family hides in a basement for four more days, during which time Peter continues to do what he did before — roam the city, scavenge and beg.

There are others hiding among the rubble, and it is never safe. Russian soldiers prowl nocturnally. Fearing what the soldiers will do to them, Maria forbids the girls to wash — not that there is even water available for that. She instructs them to rub their faces with soot and dirt. Their uncombed hair is like knotted hemp. The girls sleep huddled near Elisabeth, between Jakob and Maria. At night, inside their underground "home," fear hangs thick as fog; outside, soldiers' drunken voices shout in Russian. One night, soldiers, reeking of vodka and sweat, stumble into the dark cellar. They spot a woman and one heaves her over his shoulder. They leave. She is crying. "No, no . . ." Her words of protest are as powerless as bubbles.

Many of the soldiers take whatever they want. They like

watches. My father tells me the following story. "You might see one with three watches on his arm, or half a dozen, always looking for more. People wryly joked about it: a Russian soldier steals a large wall clock, takes it to a jeweler and says, 'I want two watches made from this.'"

What is it about watches? In war, these objects of jewelry grow in value, as if to signify that time is rare and precious. The implicit irony is that, in war, people, temporal beings, become objectified and de-valued, and watches, mere objects of time-keeping, more prized.

During the days following, Jakob searched for a safer place, and when he returned the fourth evening, he had the good news that he had found refuge on an estate, Schloss Rheintal, about twelve kilometres from Graz. But under one condition. There was little food in Austria's Russian occupied territory. Jakob had promised to bring along a supply of foodstuffs. In turn, his family could shelter there, inside little more than a chicken shed, and work on the estate.

The owners were American, their surname was "Fast," and although this was a familiar Mennonite name, they were not. The matriarch was perhaps ninety years old, her two daughters, sixty and fifty-five, and her son, forty-five. The son was a farm machinery dealer in Austria, and when the war broke out the family remained. With stars and stripes in red, blue and white waving from their flagpole, they survived, unharmed through-out the war, and now continued to do business under the occu-pation of their Russian allies.

"It must have been a nice place at one time," my father says. "There was a dam that formed an artificial lake, once full of fish. The soldiers opened the dam and emptied the lake of them, but otherwise they left Mr. Fast alone."

At Schloss Rheintal, Jakob and Maria and their children worked on the farm. Once again, as in Rosengart, now a life-time ago, they herded animals and tended the fields. They did not have ration cards because this would have meant a record of their presence here. Beyond their initial arrangement, they bartered work for food, lest they be discovered.

Each morning, as the sun began its ascent over the Alps, Peter arrived at the barns where the dairy cows underwent their seven o'clock morning milking. As soon as they were milked he led them out to pasture for the day. At times he watched the cows. Other times he worked in the fields. At five, the shadows of the perennial snow-covered peaks chilled the Mur Valley and it was time to bring the cows, pendulous udders swinging, in for their evening milking.

Peter was always hungry, so he cupped his palms and scooped up the grain spilled during threshing. Maria boiled it for porridge. In his spare moments, Peter plucked vegetables from the garden, or climbed into cherry trees, as he used to do years before with Isaac. Perched among the branches, he gorged on fruit, not caring that the hawkish old lady would screech if she caught him in her trees, or that later, his stomach would bloat and he would have to squat in the tall grass. Even while herding cows, Peter constantly shifted his eyes away from the herd for any chance to pocket potatoes or fruit from nearby patches and trees. Today, my father calls it "stealing."

The Toews, the Braun family, and Fräulein Wall, each found places on different farms. Once in a while, the families contacted one another to see who among their displaced group was still in Austria.

The day came when Mr. Toews told Jakob and Maria that he and his family planned to return to Ukraine. Mr. Toews decided to believe the Soviet promise to the Allies of a safe return of all refugees to their homes. My father recalls his last visit with his old friend Isaac. "Isaac was sad, because he didn't really want to go back." Even as refugee boys, they could see that life was different in the towns and cities they had wandered through from what it would ever be in a Russian village. Nonetheless, my father said that Isaac decided to return with his family.

I imagine them trying to say farewell, too old for tears, too awkward for hugs, these two boy-men who have travelled through a war together, unspoken sentences hanging heavily between them like saturated clouds, not yet at the point of rain, but not yet ready to part. Eyes on their feet. A handshake, firm, short, silent. Peter's shoulders sag under the weight of another goodbye as he turns to leave.

Fräulein Wall also decided to return. Separated from her family, she thought perhaps she would find them once again if she went back.

The Braun and Letkemann families remained in Austria's Russian zone. For a while, Jakob and Maria were concerned that word of their whereabouts might have been slipped to the Russian authorities, but the days passed by uneventfully and no soldiers came for them. It was possible that the Toews or Maria Wall had been interrogated after they left, but they never mentioned the others unwilling to return.

Despite official assurances, promises thick and honey-sweet, all those repatriated to Russia and Ukraine were never delivered to their home-place. Sent back in bare boxcars, they had to rely on their own food supplies, if they had any. Many died along the way. Those who survived the return journey were sentenced to forsaken territories. They were branded as traitors for leaving, and sent to coal mines, forests, shipyards, or cotton fields in scorching Kazakhstan. Many were scattered throughout the northern tundra or parts of the Asiatic Soviet Union. Most were swept up in more of Stalin's purges. By 1950, the number of those sentenced to the Gulag exceeded twelve million.[1]

Unknown to Jakob and Maria at the time, Maria's father, Peter Siemens, and her sisters survived the war somewhere in Germany. In addition, Mienke (their foster-daughter) and her young sons were alive. In later years, she contacted Maria. But Maria's father chose to return to his home-place, taking with him his grandson Daniel, accompanied by his other daughters.

Old Peter died on the return journey. His orphan grandson was sent to Kazakhstan with his aunts.

◆

On the afternoon that Peter walks home from Graz after saying goodbye to Isaac, he passes by an army camp set up in a pasture. A sweet aroma wafting from that direction mingles with the scent of meadow grass and fills his nostrils. Off to the side of the road is a field kitchen, loaves of bread baking! Suddenly Peter realizes that his stomach is rumbling.

Calling out in German, as an Austrian boy might, Peter asks the soldier there, "Hey, would you give me some of that bread?" But the soldier does not understand the words, so Peter tries again, hungry for the bread, this time asking in Russian, "Can I have some bread?"

"You speak Russian! Sure, come over here. Where are you from?" A few other soldiers hear the exchange and begin to gather round.

The Russian words just tumble out. It's a bit like a mousetrap snapping shut. The hungry mouse is caught by the tip of his tail, yet there's still a chance to get away if he's quick enough. Peter doesn't want to say he is from Ukraine so he makes up a story.

Peter says to the soldier, "We've just come from Yugoslavia; everything we had was taken, and we were chased out." (So far, this is true.) He continues, "My father was a soldier in the First World War and he fought in Russia — that's where he met my mother, she's Russian. He brought her back to Yugoslavia with him, and Mother taught us children to speak Russian."

"How interesting," says the soldier, handing Peter a loaf of white bread, light, gold and warm. "Where do you live? I'd like to visit your family."

With the bread in his hands, Peter is now firmly trapped by his lie. Or, perhaps one small truth might fix this, so he answers, "Schloss Rheintal, down the road, that way," thinking, *hoping*, the soldier won't come. The thought of soft, white bread cannot ease Peter's unsettled stomach. What has he done? What if the Russians send them back now? His thoughts turn over in his mind. His stomach flips, too.

Peter arrives home. When he hands the bread to his mother, his parents are astonished at the gift, but grateful. "Where did you get this?" they want to know. He explains about the Russian soldier and the yarn he has spun. He adds the part about the soldier wanting to visit and how he has told him where they live. Before they allow themselves to panic, they decide to wait and see. "If he comes, we'll stick to Peter's story," says Jakob.

Not many days passed, and the soldier came to visit. He was grateful for the fellowship. Jakob and Maria were gracious despite how unsafe it must have seemed to them. The soldier visited several times. He was always very friendly, and he always brought them a loaf of bread. He told them the situation was very bad in Russia and Ukraine.

And then, he did not appear again. Presumably, his army unit moved out, and in the uneasy days that followed, no one came to gather up the family.

Rumours circulated at the estate that the Russians were to leave the area and that the British would move in. Earlier on June 5, 1945, the Allies had divided Germany into occupation zones. In July, the Allied powers also divided Austria into four occupation zones. Now, in a transfer of territory these months later, the British took over the Steiermark province (Styria), while Russia accepted part of eastern Germany.

"We were liberated," says Father. "As the Soviets left, you should have seen the boxcars and boxcars — trainloads — of furniture, even toilet seats and sinks off walls. Everything, anything, loaded to take back to the USSR."

He recalls the atmosphere of Graz after the war. Austria had been part of Hitler's *Anschluss* (annexation to Germany) since March 13, 1938, and now the Austrians were simply no longer "German," but Austrian once again. No more the greeting *Heil Hitler*, now it was the usual *Grüss Gott*.

"I was riding in a crowded streetcar. I saw an older man seated close to where I was standing; near me a woman and a British soldier were also standing. When the older man got off, the woman didn't sit in his place. The soldier gestured for her to take a seat, but she shook her head and announced loudly so we all heard, 'A Nazi sat there; I refuse to sit where a Nazi sat.' So the British soldier sat down, wiggled his rear-end side-to-side, as though wiping the seat with it. Then he stood up, bowed and sweeping his arm out to her, exclaimed, *'Entnazifiziert!' (de-Nazified)* — and she sat down."

As soon as the British were in control of the area, Jakob attempted, through the Red Cross, to locate relatives in North America, and to find other Mennonite people in the area. Jakob discovered that Johann Rempel, a man he had baptized in Russia during the German occupation, was living nearby. Mr. Rempel told Jakob that conditions were better in the town of Murau. At this time, the United Nations Relief and Rehabilitations Administration (UNRRA) was at work there, resettling refugees from outside the boundaries of the USSR, where they were presently retained as labourers, or DPs (deported persons) as they were called.[2] Through the UNRRA, refugees received food and aid. Although the entire Styrian province was now under British control, the areas formerly under Russian occupation were in a desperate state, and while the Letkemann family lived in transferred territory, they prepared to move from Graz in the Untersteiermark (lower Styria), to Obersteiermark (upper Styria), to Murau, that had always been in the British zone and where living conditions were better.

❖ BRITISH ZONE

Aunt Mary has kept postcards of this place: Ranten, Obersteiermark. Both are black and white. This first one is a bird's-eye view of Murau in summer time. I know it is summer, because the sunlight whitens the buildings in gleaming contrast with the deep shades of carpet fields and thick woodland. And because along the bottom it says *Sommerfrische Murau, 819m Seehöhe,*

Postcard of Murau, Austria

Steiermark, mit Schloss Obermurau (Summer fresh Murau, 819m above sea level with the Castle Obermurau). Although this view does not reveal the river, the town and the castle are named for the Mur that flows through this valley. Perched on a hilltop in the middle of town is a church, and behind this, a little higher, is the seventeenth-century castle built over the site of the previous one. Murau was founded in the thirteenth century at the crossroads of a trade route along the river where first, the Lichtenstein, and later, the Schwarzenberg families, ruled the valley and built their fairy-tale-like castles.

The second postcard has the following inscribed on the front: *Blick ins Rantental und auf die Niedern Tauern* (a glimpse into the Ranten Valley and across the Lower Tauern Alps). Although in black and white, the image suggests rich hues of green and blue and textures of lush meadows, dense evergreens and sleek rock. Above the valley, the more gentle slopes of this "lower" range — named to differentiate it from the jagged Hohe (high) Tauern — nonetheless rise skyward into points. The treeless peaks are glazed with snow even in summer, shimmering like a tiara. And even on these rooftops of the earth, every place in the Alps is categorized into higher and lower.

As I show Father these postcards, he points out the church on the distant slope. Ranten is tucked away in Obersteiermark four kilometres west of Murau. Jakob and Maria moved here, to live with the other families in the *Pfarrhof* (parsonage of the Catholic Church). The priest, his cook, and the cook's son lived on one side of the parsonage; on the other, the refugees from Russia. The Rempels lived together with two other women named Neufeld, Mrs. Rempel's sister and mother-in-law. Now the Letkemanns moved in. The room was divided with blankets.

Settled in at Ranten, Peter thought he might be able to return to school. He was now fifteen years old, but when he attempted to register he was refused, "NO!" You're a *Piefke* (bloody German). In fact, Austria had been very "German" during the war, and it seemed ironic to Peter that now this village would not permit him to attend school.

The family registered for ration cards in order to receive food; there was no more fear of being discovered or sent back to Russia. In order to receive ration cards, one had to work, and because Peter could not attend school, he, too, was required to work for his rations. Mr. Rempel announced that he had found a job for the boy. The farmers needed labourers.

Although he was prepared to work, my father recalls his disappointment over not returning to school. "Please, no more herding cows. Yet this was the job. I was paid with food: for one week of work, one bottle of milk and some vegetables."

On his first day on the job, Peter finds that the perimeter of the farm yard is fenced but the pastures are open. Narrow fields of alfalfa, wheat, barley and grain stripe the hillsides in gradations from yellows to greens, an endless array of combinations with pastures in between. This farmer has planted his beets beside the patch of grass; Peter has an impossible time keeping the cows on the pasture, running back and forth, perpetually

The Ranten Valley looking across to the Lower Tauern Alps

chasing cows from tastier strips. He simply cannot keep the cows away from the beets.

There are twelve workers, all of them refugees, or German war prisoners. One POW strikes up a conversation with Peter. He's from the north, he says, the Netherlands. When his brother inherited the family farm, he enlisted in the army, but then Germany occupied the Netherlands in 1940 and he was conscripted into the German army. Now with the war over, here he was, a German POW in the English zone, working on a farm. It occurs to Peter that all the prisoners and displaced are deemed "German," though they are from everywhere else but Germany.

The farmer's wife is the cook. To summon the workers scattered across the fields, she clangs the dinner bell, her forearms thick as her thighs. Soon, everyone is gathered around the wooden table in the yard. She has set each place with only a spoon and a coffee mug; in the centre she gruffly shoves a colossal bowl of steaming *Schmarren* (a version of scrambled eggs). Peter is accustomed to praying, so he slightly bows his head.

While he lowers his eyes, everyone else leans into the bowl; churlishly they shovel yellow *Schmarren* into their mouths — this is like eating from a trough! Peter quickly pushes his shoulder into the huddle, but he dips his spoon only once before every morsel is gone. The next day, he is the first one to reach for the bowl.

Week One: Peter runs back and forth to keep the cows on the pasture and out of the patches, but it's hopeless. The farmer observes this, hollering at Peter, "Lazy!" "Stupid!"

All week the cows wander into the alfalfa and the beets. On Saturday, payday, the farmer notices cows in his beets, and angrily breaks a stick off the perimeter fence, waving it wildly as he stomps towards the boy, although he stops short of striking him. At the end of the day when Peter goes to collect payment, he tells the farmer he does not want to be yelled at. The farmer says he won't, and hands Peter a pail of milk that his wife has already skimmed, and a head of old cabbage.

"I hate working for him. He's mean," Peter complains to Maria when he gives her the food. He knows his grumbling will not change anything and, true enough, his mother responds, "We all have to work, just make the best of it and stay out of his way."

"The boss was especially mean on Saturday, likely so I wouldn't ask for my pay," my father tells me.

Week Two: At dawn on Monday, Peter heads out to work, but even before he reaches the barn he hears the farmer's angry voice. The man is in a foul mood already. Peter must let the cows out. Drawing closer, he also hears crying. As he enters the barn, there's the farmer standing over his daughter; the girl, the same age as Peter, cowering, head in the crook of her elbow. The farmer beats the stick down on her shoulders, arms, back. He stops when he sees Peter, and mutters, "Get out of here; take the cows." Without a word, Peter sets to work and the girl scurries away, sniffling. It will be another day of chasing the cows. Another week of degradation.

Saturday, the cows once again wander into the clover patch. The farmer watches from a distance and hurls profanities at Peter, who shoos the cows back to the pasture. The cows leave the sweet clover that flavours their milk, but the farmer won't stop his tirade. From across the field he loudly threatens Peter, "I'll beat you, just you wait!" Frustrated, this time Peter reacts. He runs over to the long row of sticks on the margin of the farmyard and breaks one out of the fence. Stick in hand, he approaches the farmer, calling to him, "If you want to beat me, you come get me."

At the end of the day Peter brings the cows in, but before he leaves for the night he finds the farmer to say, "I quit!"

"Get off my farm and don't you come back!"

"I didn't even get paid for that week," my father recollects.

The Dutchman, observing their heated interaction, says to Peter, "Ah, don't worry, that farmer is a little crazy. We've been hoeing all day; there are still some potato piles on the field that we haven't brought in yet. Just come tonight and take what you can carry — he owes it to you." He tells Peter where he'll leave a burlap sack.

Later when its growing dark Peter prepares to leave the parsonage. As he does, the Rempel's pesky eight-year-old son begs to come along. "Get lost, I have my own plans that don't include you," Peter responds, annoyed.

The priest overhears.

Peter steps out into the purple evening and heads towards the farm. There, by the potato patch, is a burlap sack, just as the Dutchman has said. Peter works diligently collecting the potatoes. Soon the sack is bulging. Peter hoists it over his shoulder for the walk back to the parsonage. The door would remain unlocked until nine o'clock, but when Peter tries the latch, the door doesn't give. After a few more tries, the door creaks ajar, the priest standing behind its frame. What's in your sack?" He takes it from Peter, and asks, "Where did you get these?"

"The farmer. I traded a basket for them," Peter lies. He often helps another refugee, a basket-maker, trade his wares at the surrounding farms for extra food or dry goods. But tonight the priest was watching as Peter left, empty-handed.

"I don't believe you. Where did you get these potatoes?"

"I told you. From trading with the farmer."

Although he lets Peter inside, the priest is not convinced.

Monday afternoon while the others are working at the farm, the police arrive at the parsonage to check out the priest's report of a theft. "Is there a boy here named Peter?"

A little nervous, Peter answers their call, and when they question him he tells them the same story of how he came by the sack of potatoes, the one he told the priest.

"You're lying," they say.

"No, no." He repeats his tale. "I traded baskets, I didn't steal!"

One of the policemen softens. "Look, you can tell us what happened, you're not in big trouble, you're still a minor. Just tell us the truth."

Peter is wary about the "not being in trouble" part and remains silent, so the policeman cuts in, "This is what happened, isn't it?" Then he states exactly what had occurred. The farmer threatened to beat the boy, Peter quit, the farmer didn't pay, and the Dutch POW offered the potatoes. The police had paid a visit to the farm beforehand, questioning the workers there, and the Dutchman had spoken up for Peter. At this point, Peter admits to collecting his "wages."

"You won't be in trouble this time, but you were stealing and there better not be a next time. You'll be dealt with harshly if there is."

My father remembers how embarrassed his parents were that their son had stolen from the farmer and then lied to the priest. "They instructed me to apologize and confess to the man. There was no confessional booth, but the priest led me to his garden behind the parsonage where he put his arm around my shoulder, signed the cross over his chest, and told me he forgave me."

Nonetheless, in Peter an angry ember lingered, and later, the indignation burned on. He thought his confession was private, but as he strolled about the village afterwards, the local children taunted him, *"Kartoffeldieb, Kartoffeldieb!"* (Potato thief, potato thief).

When my father returned to Austria in the late 1970s for the first time since he had left, he and my mother drove through the scenic Ranten Valley, and showing her where he had lived for a time, they pulled their rental car into the *Pfarrhof*. To his surprise the priest still lived there with his cook and, according to the locals in town, their grown illegitimate children lived in the area, too. Smiling, my father greeted him, *"Erkennen Sie mich noch − der Kartoffeldieb?"* (Do you remember me − the potato thief). The old priest raised his brows, a glimmer of recognition in his fading eyes.

◈ THE BASKET-MAKER

My father delivers an old brown, accordion-style folder to me. In it are some of his personal papers, including an identity card dated 23/11/46. This little passbook's cardboard cover is faded brown, timeworn, smooth as cloth, and split in two at the fold. Across the front, in German, English, French and Russian it says, "Identity Card for Foreigners and Stateless Persons." No longer stapled to the seam, the pages inside are yellow, tinged brown at their uneven edges. A round, purple rubber stamp mark declares "Murau." On the lines by each specific heading, my father is described as 164 cm. in height, oval face, gray eyes, blonde hair. His citizenship is "unclassified" and his profession is "Agricultural labourer. Age: 15." The identity photo shows him with clear skin. But there is a faint shadow of "peach fuzz" on his upper lip, his eyebrows are thick dark lines and his face has taken on more angular proportions.

In addition to identity cards, the family also has ration cards. To supplement the food provisions from those obtained with the ration cards, Peter helps old Mr. Goertz, another Mennonite

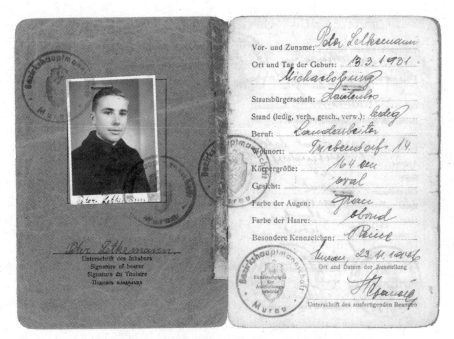

Peter's *Ausweis* (identity) Pass — inside pages

refugee, a basket-maker by trade. He makes all of the baskets, while Peter and Mrs. Goertz take them to market or the surrounding farms to sell or trade, one basket for a pound of butter, a pound of flour and some *Speck* (smoked bacon).

Maria, too, is enterprising. A skillful seamstress, she sews and mends for neighbouring farmwives. She also crafts slippers that she sends along with Peter to trade. He takes the baskets, along with his mother's slippers, and wanders up the mountainside on weekends. Peter has even more items for sale or to trade. He sells the cigarettes from the British care packages, piece by piece. This is black marketeering, so he hides the cigarettes between his baskets, pretending he has only legitimate items for sale when the police come by. Now an entrepreneur, because he no longer works for the farmer, Peter asks the old man to teach him how to make the baskets.

After his lessons from Mr. Goertz, Peter walks along the

banks of the Mur River where the willows grow. He cuts only the straightest young shoots. When he gathers these in spring, the bark peels off easily, exposing white tendons of wood beneath. In the autumn, the bark is tougher, so Peter loosens it by boiling the branches in a large pot. Peeled willow makes lovely white baskets. Sometimes he even dyes the willow different colours. Other times he leaves the bark on and weaves these branches into dark, sturdy work-baskets.

In Austria, people carry everything in baskets. Peter fashions various types in different shapes and sizes. Small round baskets with a handle serve as a lunch pail. Medium-sized baskets are used for marketing, and larger baskets hold laundry. The sturdier baskets are used for potatoes and crisp apples at harvest time, and to carry and hold fire-wood. The largest baskets are used to carry hay.

The tender willows are pliable before they are dried, so Peter can bend them without breaking them. His fingers are stained as green as spring manure. He decides first whether the basket will be round or oblong at the base; to begin, he fashions a "pad" — three sticks, split, all the halves set side-by-side. Then three more sticks, split with all the halves set side-by-side, spaced apart and laid over-top. He uses willow reed, separated into strands, to bind these sticks together. And taking more strips of willow, or "ribs" he calls them, he lays them out, like sun rays, radiating from the pad at the centre. He bends the ribs upward to create the basket's frame, keeping this in place by tying twine around the top. Now he's ready to weave the supple willow through this framework, from the bottom upward, until he reaches the desired height of the basket.

He first weaves to a height of three or four inches. Then he takes a small wedge of wood and a light mallet, and taps the reeds down to compress them. Then he weaves to a height of three more inches and taps down. By now he can untie the twine and weave tightly for a smaller basket, or loosely for a larger one. When the height, or depth, is right, he selects two strong strips, cuts them into appropriate lengths and loops them through the rim. Winding these strands as smooth as rope, he threads them back into the rim for the handle: one at each end.

Because the farmers seldom travel the distance to town from their farms, and their wives hardly ever make the round trip down to Ranten or Katsch, and never to Murau, the robust women are always interested in the baskets Peter brings, and Maria's slippers are practical for the cold plank floors.

Peter can mimic the lilting Austrian dialect, but he is not from these mountains, and when the locals enquire, he tells them about Russia and about the war, well-told tales that cause even the men to pause from their chores and lean against the fencepost to listen. By the time he is finished, they buy or trade, and seal their transaction with a slice of black bread topped with smoked bacon and a swallow of home-made Schnapps that snatches Peter's breath away. Once a month he returns to the same farms, and when the *Bäuerinnen* (farmwives) see him trudge the path to their yard with his stack of baskets they greet him cheerily: "*Jetzt kommt der Korbmacher!*" (Here comes the basket-maker).

I still have one of my father's baskets made of unpeeled strands of willow. It is now sixty years old, darkened with age, though still sturdy. He made this one when he arrived in Canada, one of the last because he found other ways to make a living. Yet this basket brings to mind the boy with silver-blue eyes like sunshine behind the morning alpine mist, who walked the ten kilometre circumference around Murau with his stack of baskets.

At Katsch, Obersteiermark

The following photograph will be one of the last family pictures, a photo that I have not seen before Aunt Mary sent it to me, but I know precisely where it was taken and I can imagine the sound of Jakob and Maria's voices, his tenor mingling with her alto tones in the amber twilight. The two would sit on the doorstep, singing the melancholy hymns of faith in a minor key, a cappella, and from this spot, they dreamt of someday having their very own farm in Canada.

In the photograph, Jakob and Maria are sitting on wooden stools with Elisabeth standing between them, smiling and plump-cheeked. She is almost three. One of her hands rests on Jakob's lap, his thumb and forefinger like a bracelet around her wrist. Her other hand is securely set, palm down, on Maria's lap. Beside Maria, and slightly behind her, stands Helen, her long blonde braids extending below her waist. Next to her is Peter; beside him, Mary. Their clothing was donated through the Mennonite Central Committee and all are wearing mismatched Sunday-best leftovers from the distribution centre in a nearby town. Peter has collected them and brought them home. Peter's flashy shirt is checked with a wide white collar, paired with a clashing striped tie. The family poses on the stoop of Triebendorf 14, their new address in Katsch, four kilometres to the east of Murau, where they have moved in February 1946, after Mrs. Neufeldt's husband returned from the war and the parsonage grew too crowded.I place another picture, in colour, beside this old black and white one; the rounded stoop is the same. I will not include the photo here because it is so modern, but this is what it looks like:

> Four stairs lead from the doorway to the roadway that runs right past the house — typical in Europe, and I wonder if there has ever been a close call stepping out of that house. The plaster is the shade of creamy butter, and worn so thin the stones show through beneath the wood frame windows. Evidence that the house is occupied appears in open windows on the upper floor and potted geraniums at the sills, red ones, like a touch of lipstick, to enliven a pale complexion. As I compare the photos, I notice the same front door in both, wooden, with inlayed panels; it looks like a "Jersey Milk" chocolate bar. Behind the house the mountain inclines sharply; in front, my mother, father, and younger brother stand by the roadside. I am nineteen years old, and they have come to meet me at the conclusion of my time in

Family photo, Triebendorf, 1946 (Jake and Gerhardt are absent)

Europe. My younger brother's football shirt announces the year, 1981. I am holding the camera.

Among the yellowed papers in my father's brown accordion folder, I come across a statement, dated January 11, 1948, declaring that the Family Letkemann has lived at Triebendorf 14 since February 21, 1946. They called it "Aibl," the local name for the property. The four-plex house was located on a smaller cattle estate owned by *Fürst* Schwarzenberg. With his son and godson, the prince lived in Schloss Obermurau, the Schwarzenberg Castle in Murau, during the spring and summer months. Otherwise they lived in South Africa. They also owned a weekend cottage and another estate between this one and Murau. That other estate used machinery, but at Aibl, all the labour was done by hand.

My father once told me that, when he was a teenager, the Fürst offered him a chance to go to South Africa to work, but the family had already made an application to emigrate to Canada. Decades later, when my father was in Vienna with Mother on one of their first European trips, the tour guide spoke of the prince "who had untold holdings throughout the world, though many of these were in Eastern Europe and confiscated." To her amazement, Father enquired about von Schwarzenberg, his son and his godson by name. The *Fürst* died, the son was killed in a plane crash, she said. And the godson? He inherited everything. This makes for an interesting story, but I am stirred more by my father's life.

Jakob and Maria occupy one side of the main floor, while other estate workers live across the hall. The estate manager, Herr Leopold, lives upstairs with his children, Herbert and Gretel. Herr Leopold's niece, Mitzi, lives with them, too. He molests her. The foreman, Zep, lives with his daughter on the main floor. She smokes, dates British soldiers, and leaves her clogs on the planks in the foyer. She thinks it is cute to run and jump into them, but imagine what happens when Peter nails her clogs to the floor.

Peter works in the fields like a man, but his wages are the same as the women receive — the equivalent of twenty-seven cents an hour. At least, he tells himself, he's not herding cows. During the warm spring and summer days, he cuts section after section of high grass with a scythe, gathering it into piles with a rake fashioned from branches, and stacking this into hay mounds that dot the hillside like dozing fairytale trolls. In the winter, he works in the forest, his narrow shoulders and slim forearms burning from the relentless push-pull of the two-man hand saw.

"We worked for ration cards, although I could have made more money black marketeering," Father muses. "But I still went to the farmer's market on Sunday; and I usually made something for my efforts." Among the old papers are the *Lebensmit-telkarten* (ration cards).

Besides selling baskets, Peter starts another enterprise. He has learned how to manufacture cigarettes with the help of a Hungarian refugee working on the estate. Together they grow and harvest tobacco plants, sort the aromatic leaves, sprinkle them with sugared water, then dry them. The Hungarian shows Peter how to roll them. Peter collects empty boxes of the *Englisches Feingeschnitt*, the British brand, from the care packages, and he places his cruder home-grown brand inside. He rolls a cigarette for Zep's daughter, too — tobacco at each end with chicken manure in the middle.

By trading and selling, Peter earns extra money for the family. This is important because the family has decided to try and emigrate to Canada. A Mennonite Central Committee (MCC) worker in Austria instructs Jakob how to apply for immigration. One must have a sponsor in Canada willing to pay for the trip and provide the family with a place to live. To obtain the necessary papers, they must travel by train back and forth to the British Consul in Graz, where they must undergo numerous medical examinations for tuberculosis and glaucoma, and fill out endless forms, and this, too, costs money.

❖ A LETTER FROM AUSTRIA

While Peter sells his wares on Sundays, Jakob spends the afternoons writing. Jakob acts as a representative for the Mennonite Central Committee, compiling a list of those from the Soviet Union living in Austria's occupied zones so that the MCC can assist them. By August 1947, Jakob will have collected over three hundred names.

During this time he finds that his stomach is bothering him; it pinches sharply so he thinks it might be an ulcer. He is fifty-seven years old when he begins to write an account of his life as an itinerant pastor in Siberia and Ukraine under the Communist regime. Jakob also writes to Mennonite publications that circulate in Canada in an effort to contact relatives who might sponsor them to Canada. Eventually his cousin Liese Loewen and her husband Heinrich,who live on Boundary Road in Yarrow British Columbia, along with Jakob's nephew, also named Jakob Letkemann, in Steinbach, Manitoba, have agreed to sponsor them.[3] The departure is set for May, 1948.

Journal entry, July 19, 2000:
It is the day after my father's biopsy. There was a grape-sized lump on his head, cancerous, but contained, and all of it has been removed. We are at the Mennonite Historical Society in Abbotsford, sifting through stacks of old German Mennonite publications, dated 1947, in our effort to find information about his father, Jakob, which until this time, and from the onset of my quest, has been scarce, save for the *Martyrs* book, and that, insufficient. There are three publications of interest to us: *Der Bote*, *Zionsbote*, and *Mennonitische Rundschau*. It is my meticulous father who discovers it in the *Mennonitische Rundschau*, as he scours page after page of German Fraktur, the old Gothic script. As he shows the page to me, there is a fluttering behind my ribcage and my anticipation takes flight. The heading reads, *Brief aus Österreich* (A Letter from Austria). The letter is signed, Jakob Letkemann, Triebendorf, Murau, Österreich!

Jakob addresses his letter to "Dear Brother Klassen" — he refers to C.F. Klassen, a pillar of the Mennonite Community, who had been instrumental while still living in Moscow, assisting Mennonite refugees who emigrated to Canada during the migrations of the 1920s, Jakob and Maria's relatives among them. In 1928, Klassen left Moscow for Canada, but continued his work in assisting the Mennonite people who suffered through the dreadful Russia-wide famine of the 1930s.

After the outbreak of war in 1940, Klassen participated in the formation of the Mennonite Central Relief Committee of Western Canada. In 1947, the towering silver-haired Mennonite leader spearheaded the enormous relief effort to which most Soviet-Mennonite refugees, almost twelve thousand of them, owe their gratitude. Klassen worked to convince American authorities against repatriation to the USSR because many of the displaced persons received German citizenship when the German army resettled them in occupied territories. Of course, German naturalization created other difficulties.[4]

In the *Mennonitische Rundschau* letter to C.F. Klassen, Jakob expresses appreciation for the publication, which provides news from Canada and is a medium for communicating with relatives living there. In closing, Jakob addresses the readership, reminding them of their *Geschwister* (brothers and sisters) facing unbearable circumstances in "Communist Russia," from where God has been banished. After the Soviets defeated Hitler, liberation, once more, brought dictatorship to Ukraine.[5]

My father and I come across a second letter, dated March 26, 1947. We find this one, written by C.F. Klassen, in *Zionsbote*. The heading states, *Wieder zu Hause* (Home Again). It is a brief report from Winnipeg, Manitoba, following Klassen's trip to Germany where the MCC set up a refugee camp, and Klassen's visits to the surrounding areas where clusters of Mennonites were found. This is a condensed translation:

> God provides strength to travel and to do the work. May God bless us in North America and may we extend His grace to help those millions in Europe who are homeless. I bring greetings to our congregations from the workers abroad, from our beloved refugees, and personally as well. Those of you here at home may not realize how vital your assistance is to us. God bless you for your generosity.

At the time these letters were written, during the emigration process, medical check-ups revealed that Jakob did not have an ulcer; he was diagnosed with cancer of the stomach. The nearby towns were inadequately equipped to perform the necessary surgery, so Jakob was sent beyond the mountain passes to a hospital in Salzburg. After his stomach was removed, and another one reconstructed from a portion of the upper intestine, Jakob returned to Katsch.

❖ JAKE

While waiting to emigrate, Jakob and Maria continued looking
for Jake. It had been two years since he left for the war, and
there had been no news. Jakob wrote to friends in Ranten to
see if Jake might be looking for them there. He also wrote to a
friend of Jake's in Yugoslavia to tell her where they lived in case
Jake ever returned, but she wrote back to say she had not heard
from him either. Jakob and Maria then turned to the Red Cross
for help in the search for their missing son. The following
photograph was possibly the last photograph of their son up to
this time.

In this small headshot, Jake is wearing civilian dress. This
might be a photo from his German naturalization in Dresden.
Light shines from one side, light and shadow divided along the
straight line of his sharp slim nose, a prime meridian on the
world that is his face. Pushed off his forehead, dark wavy hair
renders him youthful, but Jake gazes with seasoned eyes under
subtly furrowed brows. His narrow mouth is set.

As for Jake himself, he was captured by Russian troops just as
his unit arrived on the eastern front outside Vienna, ambushed
prior to receiving their military passports and marching orders.
Jake had never even fired his gun; instead, at the time of the
ambush he thrust it into the dirt, barrel down. He never wanted
to fight. Maybe the timing of the ambush was good fortune, for
when he was taken prisoner, he had no identification to state
who he was or where he was from. Throughout the entire interrogation, he wouldn't say that he was from Russia, for that
meant certain death. His lack of identity became his chance
for survival. Jake conjured up a tale. He was an Austrian from
Graz. He knew of an address near the railroad station where
he had worked under the Germans, Graz, Kempler Strasse 17,
and gave it as his own. The house had been bombed; if anyone
followed up they would find nothing.

Jake was loaded onto a transport and brought to Leningrad
(St. Petersburg). As the prisoners marched through the city cen-

tre, he heard a familiar voice shout the odd-sounding *"Yeil Hitler!"* sarcastically addressing the line of POWs filing by. In the earlier days of the war, when Jake hauled ammunition from Zaporozhye to the front, he worked with a Russian who could not pronounce the German salutation, *Heil* (hail). *What were the chances that it was him?* Jake dropped his head and fell in close behind the other German captives, praying to pass by unnoticed. He succeeded.

Jake, his "identity photo"

From Leningrad they marched farther north, along a stretch of land where the Gulf of Finland reaches into Russia like a hand, to a camp near the Finnish border. The malnourished prisoners worked felling trees for watery soup and heavy, tasteless bread. On the verge of starvation or disease, existing in bare wooden barracks, they were prone to exhaustion in the long days and white nights, or hypothermia when the temperature plummeted. During a winter blizzard, in one escape attempt, a group of Jake's fellow inmates fashioned skis from planks and set off for Finland. They succeeded in crossing the border, but from the window of a nearby farmhouse, lamplight glowed like the watchful eyes of an owl. Someone reported them. Recaptured, the POWs were sent back to camp and severely punished.

I learn from my father, the few sparse details that Jake once revealed, only to him, many years afterwards.

Jake survived prison camp by trading his ration of tobacco for a piece of bread, while other men found a measure of solace in the slow drag of a cigarette. During his imprisonment, between late 1944 and 1946, he never spoke Russian. Barely speaking at all, Jake feigned simplemindedness.

Although he maintained he was Austrian, other Austrian

prisoners persistently asked, "Where then?" They could not detect a tell-tale dialect.

Jake remembered the address of the factory near Dresden where he had briefly worked and answered, "I've worked most of my life in Germany." He curtly described the area, and the people he knew there.

The war ended in May 1945, although prisoners were kept long afterwards. Prior to his release, Jake was handed a form with information filled out upon his capture; it was written in Russian. Jake realized he would be questioned, and that his answers must correspond with those on the form, his story given long ago. He also understood that if he were caught reading the form, his charade would be up. Jake placed the form on a window ledge, then pretending to gaze out the window, he glanced at the information he had given two years before.

There was only one prisoner who knew Jake's origins, because he, too, was from Ukraine, and the two had known one another there. But this man gave his word to Jake he would not tell, that he would keep Jake's secret. One last time they were led out for interrogation; afterwards the other prisoner was shot. But he kept his promise.

Before they released the German prisoners, the Russians released the Austrians, transporting them back to Austria by train. When the rail cars finally rumbled across the border into Austria, Jake's fellow survivors turned to him, "All right Jake, now tell us where you're from."

"Russia," he confessed.

"You're not as dumb as you acted," was their response.

From Graz, Jake wrote his friend in Yugoslavia. She wrote back, passing along the news that his family was in Austria; he went to the Red Cross and obtained their current address, 14 Triebendorf, Katsch, Steiermark.

Meanwhile, three months had passed since Jakob's operation, but once again he was not feeling well. My father remembers, "It was I who went to Graz to meet my brother and brought him back to Katsch." Now, sixty years later, my father describes the reunion, "I hadn't seen Jake for so long, and I had grown a little too. I was unsure what to do or say when I would see him. When I met him at the station, I guess I must have looked so bewildered that Jake just looked at me and said, 'Don't you *yammer*.' I tried very hard not to cry. Should I be happy and laugh?'"

The youngest brother is confused by emotions of joy and relief, and sorrow too, that swell like a cresting wave. The sadness of everything, and the gladness of a moment like this. Jake is here! But even now with Jake in front of him after all this time, the thought strikes Peter, "what if Gerhardt could suddenly appear, too."

And Jake, aged by the experience of prison camp, is numbed further by the news that Gerhardt did not survive. The brothers sit beside one another like strangers on the train, one glancing at the landscape while the other gazes ahead at nothing in particular. Peter tries to make small talk on the way back to Katsch where the family waits.

It is a wonderful reunion, but Jake cannot stay with the family. Jakob and Maria are already well advanced in their process of emigration, and they know that Canada will not accept those from the German army. It will be best for Jake to go to the MCC refugee camp in Gronau, Germany. He is to remain there and later join the family in Canada with the help of the MCC.

But before Jake leaves for Germany, he notices that his father has grown thinner. Jakob's once tall frame has shrunk, and fine lines crease his brow as he winces. He dips his bread in weak tea so that it can slip down his throat with less difficulty. He feels a constant pulling, like a rubber band tightening, when he swallows.

❖ HOME

The last family picture is taken in a meadow sprinkled with wildflowers. It cannot be reproduced because the quality is so poor. I will content myself with a description:

Peter is now taller than Jake, and Jake's face is gaunt from his years in prison camp. The brothers wear suits, donated from the relief agency. Mary and Helen wear floral dresses hemmed below the knee, and both plait their hair in Austrian fashion while Liz's light hair is sectioned in ringlets. Maria wears a plain dark dress. I remember her dark dresses in the years that follow — and she sits in a wooden chair squinting into the sun, five of her six children gathered around her. Jakob is absent.

Along with pictorial evidence of this time, there are faded scraps of paper from the file folder that Maria saved and that Aunt Helen preserved. I add these to my collection of time-worn memories, or no memories at all. Aunt Liz has no recollection of this time, so when I show the note to her she comments at how matter-of-fact it reads. And yet, however succinct or brief it is, I am moved because the handwriting in soft faded lead pencil is Jakob's own, and because it is signed, *euer Papa*.

The note starts off, *Tamsweg, Dienstag* (Tuesday) *9, XII.* The year is not given but it would be 1947. I find Tamsweg on the map, a town not far from Murau, en route to Salzburg where the omnibus has stopped, and where Jakob drops the note in the post.

Dear Family,

I am leaving tomorrow, the 10th, for Salzburg on the Omni at 5 a.m. and will arrive there at 11 a.m. The address is Landes-krankenhaus (State Hospital), Salzburg. They will examine me once more there. I will write you after the examination and let you know what my prognosis is.

With all my very best,
Your Papa.

This is the only note from Jakob I find. He remained in the hospital. December passed and with it Christmas. The other papers consist of travel passes and a telegram in the new year, 1948. Just prior to the time Jake left for the MCC refugee camp in Germany, he visited his father at the hospital in Salzburg on January 22, 1948. On March 10, 1948, Maria received a telegram sent by Sister Hedwig from the hospital: the family should come at once. I examine the other passes issued to the children granting permission to travel from Triebendorf to Salzburg, to visit their critically ill father, dated that same day.

These papers carry the scent of long ago, like that found in the pages of a rare old book. These fragile yellowed papers, with their typed words, are the closing pages of Jakob's life — a precious volume.

At Triebendorf, Maria and the children board the next train for Salzburg on the other side of the Tauern Alps. The train edges along the Hohe Tauern range, crawling over spider-web trestles which span near bottomless ravines. It burrows through the mountains, tunnels dark and long as night, to emerge into the light again. The train spirals slowly through the passes. It is still winter in these mountains.

Then suddenly, the train stops. A wall of white covers the tracks ahead. Maria and the children wait as the minutes drop silently, like falling snowflakes, into dark hours. In the morning the rail line is cleared and the train carries on to Salzburg, the town of Mozart. When the family reaches the ward at the hospital, Jakob's bed is empty. The lines of one of Grandmother's poems come to mind:

> We are not given to know the hour,
> He will come like a thief in the night.[6]

My father remembers the man in the ward whose bed was beside Jakob's, and even remembers the words he spoke to the family: "Jakob wanted to see you so badly; he always asked if you had come yet. And then . . . how can it be? When he died, he smiled. I don't understand how a man can die like that — so peacefully."

The death certificate states that Jakob Letkemann, fifty-eight years old, *Landarbeiter* (agricultural worker) Ukraine, Stateless, Address: Murau, Triebendorf 14, died on March 12, 1948 at 9 a.m. Cause of death: heart failure.

I think of my grandfather's smile, the smile I have seen only in pictures, the smile seen by his hospital roommate. Jakob committed to memory passages of Scripture filled with the metaphors and promises of a new life following the old one. ". . . the Lord your God is bringing you into a good land . . . a land with streams and pools of water, with springs flowing from the hills to the valleys . . . a land where bread will not be scarce."[7] To Jakob, so weary from his footsore journey, these words of grace were a comfort.

There is a fresh awareness of a certainty that has always flowed in a rhythm through me as sure as the soft, continuous tempo of my heartbeat. I know that Jakob would have prayed for his wife and family about to leave for Canada, and for us who were unborn.

The following day, Peter turned seventeen. Without his father and brothers, he was the man of the family. He could still almost hear the echo of Jakob's words from months ago, before he left for the hospital, "Take care of your mother."

Father comments that she bore her grief well. He believes his mother might have been familiar with the feeling of living without her husband for extended periods in Russia. And it was a great solace to her that Jake had returned from the war.

Sister Hedwig took Maria aside and inquired if she wanted to spend time in prayer for Jakob's soul. Maria must have seemed abrupt to the nun, for she brushed aside the offer. "That's not necessary," she said. Instead, Maria asked to see Jakob. In her grief, an old fear arose within her that the authorities had falsified his death and Jakob had been taken from her into exile. She wanted to see his body, to know that this was final, to say goodbye. When the undertaker was unwilling to comply, her characteristic willfulness emerged, and finally he conceded, under the condition that the youngest, Liz, not be taken to the room for the viewing. I know Aunt Mary was present, because the memory is hers.

The coffin, a simple wooden box, seemed unusually small for a tall man. What Mary saw was a shock to her. Jakob's neck was scarred from the surgery, broken; his head rested unnaturally on one shoulder. His body was clothed in paper. He had been a penniless refugee.

The funeral was small, attended only by Maria, Mary, Helen, Peter, and Elisabeth, and conducted by a friend that Jakob had made from the Austrian Bible Society. One other very special guest, the highly regarded C.F. Klassen, offered condolences and encouragement. Klassen was once again in Europe working tirelessly among the refugees.

Mr. Klassen handed Peter the money to pay for the grave marker, one hundred marks: the fee for ten years. My father says, "My dad was buried at the State Catholic cemetery with a small wooden cross, and that was about it." Maria kept even this slip of paper, which states when the burial took place, "Tuesday, March 16 at 4 p.m.," and where Jakob was laid to rest, "Gravesite 25-IV-25 — until 1958."

Among the slips of paper there is one more, written by Maria in her delicate script, the words, copied beside it in someone's sure printing, perhaps one of her children's, so that it reads clearly what could not be written in stone, but on a wooden cross, to mark, for ten years, the ground where Jakob was buried.

Hier ruht sanft Bruder Jakob Letkemann. Er ist ein Prediger der Mennoniten. Lutheranische Gemeinde. Römmer 5 Kap. 1- 11.
(Here Brother Jakob Letkemann rests in peace. He [was] a Mennonite Preacher. Lutheran Fellowship. Romans 5: 1-11)

The verses in Romans read as follows:

Therefore, since we have been justified through faith, we have peace with God through our Lord Jesus Christ, through whom we have gained access by faith into his grace in which we now stand. Not only so, but we also rejoice in our sufferings, because we know that suffering produces perseverance, perseverance, character; and character, hope. . . .[8]

Along with the note, the travel passes, the telegram, and the death certificate, is one more document from the Austrian state regarding Jakob Letkemann. In the space designated "Religion" it says *Mennonit* (Mennonite).

I consider the name Mennonite, one that has often been thought of as synonymous with pacifism. But this Mennonite narrative which finds its beginning in an ideology of peace, is one about the experiences of marginalization, survival and war. While non-resistance was a core tenet of the faith for the early Anabaptists ever since the martyrs, the principle of non-resistance has both evolved and eroded over time. At first it meant passive non-resistance, and in recent times, it has often been expressed more proactively as non-violent resistance. For the various groups of Mennonites, adherence to the principle of non-resistance has never been consistent, particularly as they faced acculturation in the society around them, or as they experienced a world in turmoil.[9] There are so many questions when it comes to this foundational aspect of ethno-religious Mennonite identity. What about resistance to violence? What about restraining those who intend injury to others? What about conscription to arms? Jakob and Maria certainly faced all of these circumstances. As I consider these questions, a certainty emerges from this narrative as when sunrays dissipate the fog. Jakob's identity as a Mennonite was, for him, what it meant to be human in a particular way — an outworking of his own spiritual faith through daily acts of peace towards others suffering in a violent world.

My grandfather, Jakob, a pastor, together with his wife Maria, persevered through a life-time of oppression, violence and war. His perseverance formed his character. There is no doubt of this. That his character produced hope, is without question. C.F. Klassen wrote Jakob's obituary dated Wednesday, April 21, 1948, which my father and I have found in *Der Bote*. The closing words were written as encouragement to the family: "Brother Letkemann's *Flüchtlingszeit* (fugitive years) are over. *He is home.*"

It seems strange that this collection of papers detailing the end of his life was so carefully preserved. These historical artifacts are, for the most part, the most concrete information I have had to work with concerning my grandfather, or even of my father's period as a refugee, including dates, places, even the time. Imagine if Jakob's whole life had been so carefully chronicled.

But memories of my father's narrative, probed by my curiosity and coupled with my imagination, have managed to span the gaps and silences, connecting past to present, from a foreign place to this current home. These notes are like folded paper boats floating on a stream of memory, and all the memories flow to a river that gathers them into a story.

❖ POSTSCRIPT

Prior to 1941, among the untold millions of people throughout the Soviet Union who were exiled under Stalin, were tens of thousands known as Mennonites. The exact numbers may never be known. At the time of the German invasion in 1941, there were still approximately one hundred thousand Mennonites living throughout the Soviet Union, most of them in the Ukraine. At this time, the Soviets exiled the majority of Mennonites and other ethnic Germans, together with an estimated three million Ukrainians. Approximately thirty-five thousand Mennonites remained living in Ukraine.

In 1943, in the wake of the German retreat from Ukraine, the Mennonite population joined the flight of refugees. They were mainly used as a labour force in Eastern Europe and Germany, and at the end of the war they faced repatriation to the Soviet Union. Of the thirty-five thousand Mennonites who fled the

Serial Nr. S1 1525   464

Form: MS 1

Preparatory Commission International Refugee Organisation

Certificate for the Purpose of Emigration to Canada

1. The holder of this Certificate is the concern of the P.C.I.R.O.
2. This Certificate is issued by the P.C.I.R.O. in lieu of a national passport to refugees and displaced persons recommended for emigration to Canada. It is issued without prejudice to and in no way affects the holder's nationality. **Citizenship: Russian**
3. This Certificate is **NOT** valid unless it bears the official stamp of the P.C.I.R.O. and a Canadian Visa. In no circumstances is it valid for exit from or entry to Austria (British Zone).

Peter Letkeman.
(signature)

Name	**LETKEMANN**
Forename(s)	**Peter**
Date + Place of Birth	**13.3.1931, Michaelsburg, Russia**
Occupation	
Present Address	**14, Triebendorf, Katsch, Styria, Austria**
* Maiden Name of wife	
Forename(s)	
Name of Husband	
Forename(s)	

* Strike out whichever does not apply.

Description of Holder

Height	4'8"
Hair colour	blonde
Eyes colour	grey
Nose	straight
Shape of face	oval
Special Characteristics	none

Children up to 16 years accompanying holder

(children over 16 years must have separate document)

Name	Forename(s)	Place and Date of Birth	Sex

Space for 2in. photo (of wife if accompanying)

Space for Canadian Visa.

714406 Peter Rossel

DEPT. OF NATIONAL HEALTH AND WELFARE
14
5-AUG 1948
LONDON
CANADA

(signature)

P.C.I.R.O. Stamp (including place, date and signature of issuing officer).

International Refugee
AREA TE...
GRAZ
AUSTRIA

CBO Cameron
5/8/48

CANADA
Immigrant Visa
authority OR.B.4264 7 D.P.
issued at LINZ, AUSTRIA
On 4 - SEP 1948

Valid for presentation at
Canadian Port of Entry within ...... months from date of issue.

CANADIAN IMMIGRATION SERVICE

PASSPORT
DEPARTURE
17 SEP. 1948
2/3
GERMANY (B.Z.)

1336

Ukraine in 1943, an estimated twenty-three thousand disappeared. Twelve thousand Mennonites successfully immigrated to Canada, the United States, or South America.[10] My father was one of these.

After Jakob's death, the family's departure, set for May 1948, was cancelled by the Canadian Immigration Department, and Maria had to reapply, asking the Canadian relatives once again to help her. The relatives assured the Canadian government they would undertake the responsibility to help resettle Jakob's widow and children. The family's departure was rescheduled for September 1948.

Afterword

❖

Life is always on the way to narrative,
but it does not get there until
someone tells this life as a story.

— RICHARD KEARNEY

When I ask my father what he thought or felt as he boarded the Cunard White Star S.S. *Samaria* to leave Europe for Canada, I thought he might say that he had been excited, that the voyage promised to transport him to a new beginning. He was seventeen years old. Instead, he said he couldn't really remember. And upon further contemplation, he said, in fact, that he had no feeling then. I don't take this to mean he was indifferent. Imagine: after years of traumatic and life-altering events, the voyage to Canada was yet another one.

The journey was rough across the Atlantic. He bunked together with other refugee men in the ship's hold (third class), his mother and sisters with the women in second class. Nauseous

Peter on the train

from the engine's fumes, the fresh paint smell of his sleeping quarters, and miserable due to the white tipped swells of infinite grey, Peter sought relief in the cold winds on deck.

When the family boarded the train in Halifax heading west and they reached the prairies, the horizon unravelled endless and bleak, no mountains, not even a hillock. And there were no villages, as on the steppes, only a lone farm from time to time.

They stopped in Manitoba, Saskatchewan, and then in Alberta, visiting with relations who had immigrated years before and working on the farms of these host families. They finally settled in a farming community of Mennonites in Yarrow, British Columbia, and made their home in the unheated garage of relatives.

While living there, they attended a small Mennonite Brethren Church. During that time, the preacher held revival meetings, and when he made an alter call, Peter went forward to express his need for eternal grace. He was baptized in the river a year later.

During that first year in Yarrow, Peter began a string of jobs, from cleaning out chicken houses, cutting wood, picking hops and other crops, to working at the quarry. He generally earned about forty-five cents an hour, and together with Helen and Mary, he managed to repay the travel expenses, the family's immigration debt, within the year. Then Peter went to the city and found a job as a welder in the port of Vancouver. Next, the children helped their mother with a down payment for a thirteen-acre berry farm in Abbotsford. By this time Jake was also able to immigrate. Promising the government not to take desirable employment away from a Canadian citizen, Jake spent his first year tirelessly readying Maria's little farm for crops, and afterwards, he joined Peter in Vancouver to work.

Maria's house was very small, but by this time, only she and Liz lived there; the others came on weekends from their jobs in the city. Still, the house was in need of repair, and so Peter, astutely examining the work various tradesmen had begun, realized he could undertake the project himself. Thus, he taught himself to build, and he constructed an addition. This would be the onset of a life-long career, first in home building, later in real-estate development and holdings. After ten years working as a builder, he met my mother, the middle child of a very large immigrant family from Poland who had survived the war in Europe. Her life, too, is a story.

◈

As I reflect on my own family's 2005 summer trip to Ukraine and Russia, the experience is a little like peering into an heirloom mirror in which I can see the muted images of past lives.

The newly independent Ukraine is struggling economically, socially and culturally, and our brief time there has provided only a cursory insight into the problems its people must face. All through our travels, both in Russia and in Ukraine, our tour guides offered candid views on education, politics, health care, social issues and, of course, history. They spoke openly of the Stalinist regime, calling it "Russia's darkest time."

They also spoke with piercing directness about the war. Throughout Ukraine, the Germans were welcomed as liberators; the general population believed initially that the occupiers would support Ukrainian nationalism — in the same way that the Mennonite people placed their hope in an ameliorative occupational government. Both were wrong. At the World War II Museum in Kiev we learned the location of three concentration camps near the city of Zaporozhye. "Concentration" was the term for civilian camps, but in the museum there is a small, though potent, Holocaust exhibit. In the darkened room, the hush was palpable.

In Kiev's museum, there is also a sobering display of weapons, munitions and a mound of bullet-pierced metal helmets collected from those men and boys, German and Soviet, who fought one another to their death on the steppes. The final exhibit is that of a long wooden table: on one side of it, graceful long-stemmed wine glasses are set in a seemingly endless line; across from each glass is a water canteen or rusted tin cup, dented or with bullet holes clear through them, each one gathered from a dead soldier. It seems to signify Ukraine's desire to come to terms with its difficult history — also to move forward. We filed slowly past.

Along the wall, beside this communion table is a gallery of photographs: families in traditional portrait poses, faces of mothers, faces of children, young sons in uniforms. These were the faces of life in this place, of war and of suffering. Each picture framed a silent narrative. It was as though another's face became our other self.

From Kiev we travelled by train through the countryside to Zaporozhye. We boarded the night train, a summer storm flashing its brilliance out of the blackness, lighting up the countryside, and followed by deafening booms only seconds later. "Just as I remember," my father said. In the early morning light, the familiar sight of the late summer steppes with its tall dry grasses the colour of the sepia, drew him to the windows that lined the sleeping car's hallway. He beckoned us to come and see. The images of the landscape along with the faces of the people we met there continue to linger.

In Zaporozhye we hired a driver, Nikolai, a young pastor, and his wife Anya, recommended to us by local MCC workers in that city. The Mennonites throughout North America have never forgotten Russia or Ukraine and are working throughout the former Soviet Union today, training local pastors and community workers, establishing churches, and providing material aid and services to those in need. It is amazing to see, first hand, how the Mennonite people in Canada, many of whom were once destitute refugees, remember their roots in this way. The Mennonites have an incredibly strong network for material aid.

This network is not only an outworking of their belief in community; it is also an expression of gratitude. One has only to recall how the early Mennonite emigrants to North America sent material help during the famine, and then helped the World War II refugees reach Canada.

However, even with their strong ties to the concept of "peoplehood," the new beginning in Canada was difficult for the Soviet refugees. Out of necessity, the process of acculturation into Canadian society for most of the refugees, such as my father, was swift relative to those from the Mennonite groups of the earlier migrations. The so-called *Kanadier* and *Russländer* initially established their own communities in rural areas, maintaining their way of life and even their German language. In contrast, the refugees from the post-WWII time had been absorbed "into the world," not only under the Soviet system, but during their refugee years when they moved from country to country. Although there was no language barrier between the new refugees and the older established communities, their seemingly secular ways, particularly with respect to pacifism and conscription, and their previous lack of a structured church life, were the grounds of felt alienation. As a result, although the newly arrived refugees lived among Mennonites, they did not always feel "at home."

Moreover, in order to assist the family financially, the older children of immigrant families were required to leave to find work in the city. While this served to hasten their process of acculturation, they experienced discrimination, both within and without the community, although perhaps this increased their determination. If one is honest, memories of the early years in Canada include difficult ones. Nevertheless, despite acculturation, differences and challenges, generosity in all its various forms — volunteerism, material aid and social advocacy — is an overarching and enduring component of the Mennonite fabric of culture and religion. The point also is that, while my Grandmother, a widow, may never have felt at home in Canada, and although the beginning was difficult for my father, because they were given an opportunity to start anew, I am at home.

❖

From the city of Zaporozhye we drove over the bridge where the hydroelectric dam, fought over by both the Soviet troops and the German *Wehrmacht*, spans the river. We continued on for a short distance over rolling fields, these ones bare, after the summer harvest, to arrive at the former collective that was once Rosengart, my father's home, now called Novoslobodka.

Although my parents had come earlier to Ukraine during the first years of *glasnost*, their tour bus had stopped only at the schoolhouse near the village entrance. At the time, my father was not permitted to go further. Without authorization, an impromptu detour from the tour's route was prohibited. Now, along with my family, my father saw it all for the first time since 1943. The village was laid out precisely as he remembered it. At my kitchen counter sometime before our travels, he had drawn a map for me, ink lines forming "dirt roads" on his paper napkin. And in the configuration of his story from memories, islands in history protruding from the river of time, this place has grown familiar, until at last, here we were, side by side on the wide open steppes.

On the uplands, past the corner house where Henry Kasdorf, my father's fingerless school chum once lived, we stopped to speak to the current occupants. Their curious eyes had followed us from our hired van to their lopsided gate in the drooping fence: a great-grandmother, grandparents and a grandchild. We drove further up the road and parked the van. My father's house no longer exists, but he located its original spot, and now another small rustic house, one that already looked old in 2005, had been built on the property, a brown heifer tethered to a post in the weedy yard. A gap-toothed woman wearing a *platok* approached us by the roadside, curious to know why we were interested in her house. As we stood before the front yard of his childhood, young local boys raced barefoot along the now paved road past us, and on that summer afternoon of their youth, I caught a glimpse of my father as a young boy.

As we were leaving the village, at the corner of the bottom road, a man dressed in undershirt, dirty trousers and gumboots noticed us. When father greeted him in Russian, the man invited us to his *dacha*, a garden house that long ago was part of a Mennonite house, and there introduced us to his wife. Both of them looked to be about sixty years old. She had grown up in Novoslobodka. She told us that the Soviets had relocated her mother here in 1946, after the former inhabitants had fled with the German army. Soviet women and children from the devastated cities were relocated to these emptied villages to farm the abandoned collectives. Now this couple lived in an apartment in Zaporozhye close by, but came on weekends to garden. She said, "Those times were so terrible." She told us how the villagers survived by eating the beets planted by the former occupants, and that, in those days, this village had been beautiful. There were flower gardens then, she said; now there are none. But we noticed untidy clusters of pansies, geraniums, and marigolds. From a rainbow of gladiolas growing along the picket fence, she cut a bouquet for my mother.

She then produced for us a striped watermelon and, slicing it on the wooden table in the yard, handed the centre, the sweetest piece, to my father. She hadn't grown it, she said, explaining that the produce was not as it used to be, pointing to the nearby smokestacks sending their plumes of factory emissions our way. And after we said our goodbyes and had driven away, father said to us that the watermelon was not as sweet as he remembers them.

Sometimes the memories are sweeter than the reality was. It's certainly true that we hold to those memories that render the past accessible. The natural course to the past is by way of nostalgic memories — particularly in the experiences of uprootedness, loss and disaster. This is why the watermelons of my own childhood, according to my father, never quite tasted like the ones of his. But perhaps one day, many decades and an ocean away from such experiences and events, a person may reach the point of revealing what past life was *really* like for him or her. Then the stories become a form of self-validation, for it now feels "safe" to speak them — to pass them on, palm open, to one who was not there. In this way the narrative becomes a step in a sequence of lives, of past, present and future generations, providing connections to flesh and blood, place and heritage.

As a listener, however, one must also allow the silences to shape the story. My ancestral story has at times proved almost too difficult to write. With sparse and stark details, Jakob had begun the process before he died. Now together with my father's memories, my voice intertwined with his, the narrative has arrived at its conclusion. With fidelity, care and love, I have presented this story, and in it, I have tasted the sweetness of my present life.

Notes

❖

❖ Preface (pp. XI to XV)

1 Julia Kasdorf, *The Body and the Book: Writing from a Mennonite Life* (Baltimore, The Johns Hopkins University Press, 2001), 177.

2 Paul Ricoeur, from his work, *Time and Narrative*, Vol. 1. Translated by Kathleen McLaughlin and David Pellauer (Chicago: University of Chicago Press, 1990).

3 Anne Michaels, *Fugitive Pieces: A Novel* (Toronto: McClelland & Stewart, 1996), 138.

❖ Introduction: Promised Land (pp. 1 to 12)

1 Acclaimed and award-winning Canadian novelist Sandra Birdsell's *The Russländer: A Novel* (Toronto: McClelland & Stewart, 2001) is a beautifully imagined and truthful account of the experience of the *Russländer*, their community in Russia and its traumatic end.

2 For information, see Frank H. Epp, *Mennonite Exodus: The Rescue and Resettlement of the Russian Mennonites since the Communist Revolution* (Altona, Manitoba: D.W. Friesen, 1962). Published for the Canadian Mennonite Relief and Immigration Council.

3 Henry Schapansky, "The Early Letkemanns," *The Mennonite Historian* Vol. xv, No. 4 (Dec. 1989): 2.

4 This information is gleaned from the unpublished manuscript (1988) by historian Peter Letkemann of Winnipeg. I received a photocopy of this work in a personal letter from Linda Buhler, dated September 7, 2002. "The name is related to the name Lietke, derived from the old high-German world "luit" which is synonymous with "volk." The name first appears in 1555 and is spelled Luetkemann. In the early 1600's a prominent theologian named Joachim Luetkemann lived in

the province of Pomerania, which suggests that the name is of West Prussian and Lutheran origin."

5 Arnold C. Snyder's *Anabaptist History and Theology* (Kitchener: Pandora Press, 1995) provides an extensive overview of Anabaptist history.

6 Thieleman J. van Braght, *Martyrs Mirror: The Story of Seventeen Centuries of Christian Martyrdom, from the Time of Christ to A.D. 1660*. Arnold C. Snyder describes this book is as being "long a spiritual resource in Mennonite and Amish homes."

7 Cornelius J. Dyck, *Introduction to Mennonite History*, 3rd ed. (Pennsylvania: Herald Press, 1993), 47.

8 Henry Schapansky, "The Early Letkemanns," *The Mennonite Historian* Vol. xv, No. 4 (Dec. 1989): 2. Also, Karl Stumpp lists the family of Peter Letkemann and Sarah Goosen in *The Emigration from Germany to Russia in the Years 1763 to 1862* (Lincoln: American Historical Society of Germans in Russia, 1982: 3rd printing, 1993), 15, 187.

9 Peter Letkemann's unpublished manuscript in the chapter entitled "The Descendants of Peter Letkemann."

10 From "The Descendants of Peter Letkemann," see above. See also William Schroeder and Helmut T. Huebert. *Mennonite Historical Atlas* (Winnipeg: Springfield Publishers, 1996), 116.

11 Henry Schapansky, *The Old Colony (Chortiza) of Russia: Early History and the First Settlers in the Context of the Mennonite Migrations* (Manitoba: Country Graphics and Printing, 2001), 82.

12 Karl Stumpp, *The Emigration from Germany to Russia in the Years 1763-1862* (The Historical Society of Germans from Russia, 3rd Printing, 1993), 12-13.

13 Karl Stumpp, *The Emigration from Germany to Russia*, 15.

14 Henry Schapansky's book review of "From Prussia to the Old Colony, Russia, in 1818" by B.H. Unruh *Mennonite Family History* (October 1989): 135. (See also note 15.) Along with his mother Sarah, Heinrich had planned to leave as early as 1803 when the opportunity first arose, but one brother, Peter, died. For this reason they may have cancelled their earlier plans. Mother Sarah was a widow at this time; her husband (also Peter) died in 1796. Heinrich's first wife Agathe had also died February 1816. Heinrich remarried Elisabeth Thiessen of Petershagen on October 16, 1816, and later emigrated with her. The revision list by Mennonite historian Benjamin Unruh is only dated to 1814.

15 Benjamin H. Unruh's emigration list from *Die niederländisch-niederdeutschen Hintergründe der mennonitischen Ostwanderungen im 16, 18, und 19 Jahrhundert* (Self-published, 1955). For many years this

has been the main source of genealogical information, along with Karl Stumpp's book, until Henry Schapansky's more recent work.

16 Henry Schapansky's book review of B.H. Unruh's "From Prussia to the Old Colony, Russia, in 1818," *Mennonite Family History* (October 1989): 134. See also Henry Schapansky, *The Old Colony (Chortiza) of Russia: Early History and the First Settlers in the Context of the Mennonite Migrations*, Appendix 2, Section 1.2.3. and 1.3, 508. The list of 1818 was found by K. Stumpp and forwarded to B.H. Unruh.

17 Peter Letkemann's untitled manuscript. Sarah Martens was the first wife of Gerhardt Letkemann. The author's family is descended from this marriage, specifically, their second son Jacob Gerhardt Letkemann. After Sarah Martens died, Gerhardt Letkemann remarried Sarah Buekert and fathered more children.

Chapter 1 (pp. 15–25)

1 Reference to the transport ship S.S. *Samaria* is also given in Modris Eksteins' *Walking Since Daybreak: A Story of Eastern Europe, World War II, and the Heart of our Century* (Toronto: Key Porter Books, 1999), 94.

2 Frederick Buechner, *Listening to Your Life*, ed. George Connor (New York: HarperSanFransisco), 14.

Chapter 2 (pp. 29–75)

1 Aaron A. Toews, *Mennonitische Märtyrer, Band 2: Der Grosse Leidensweg* (Winnipeg: The Christian Press, 1954), 61–71.

2 Marlene Epp provides reference to Toews' book in her publication, *Women without Men: Mennonite Refugees of the Second World War* (Toronto: University of Toronto Press, 2000), 39–40.

3 Microfiche document *Einwanderungszentralstelle Anträge* (EWZ), 50 E084 0396 obtained by the Mennonite Historical Society, Abbotsford B.C. Files EWZ-50 pertain to the USSR. The information derived from these forms was provided by refugees in 1943–44 during the German naturalization process. Jakob and Maria Letkemann filled out forms in Dresden in 1944. The EWZ microfilms have been indexed by Elli Wise, and a database of Mennonite-specific data from the EWZ files was created by Richard Thiessen. See note 11 of Chapter 5 for more detailed information about these documents.

4 From Maria Letkemann's family Bible, and genealogical information provided by Linda Buhler.
Father: Jacob Letkemann
Mother: Helene Loewen

Son: Gerhard, May 17, 1884, m. Katherina Janzen

Daughter: Maria, May 12, 1886, m. Johan Martens

Son: David, June 22, 1888, m. Helene Leppke, re. m. Anna Enns

Daughter: Helene, ?, m. Epp

Son: Jakob, March 29, 1893, m. Maria Siemens

Son: Peter. ??

Son: Abram. ??

Daughter: Katherina, April 10, 1899, m. Jacob Krueger

Daughter: Sarah, May 20, 1901, m. Peter Krueger

Daughter: Justina, November 6, 1903, m. Kornelius Krueger

The photo was provided by John Letkeman, the son of my father's cousin, also named Jakob Letkemann (grandson of David and Helene). This Jakob Letkemann helped sponsor my father's family to Canada following the war.

5 Photocopy of 1912 baptism records of the Mennonite Brethren Church in Michaelsburg, Fürstenland, lists Jakob Letkemann (mother: Helene Loewen born at Insel Chortiza). From Linda Buhler.

6 A. A. Toews, *Mennonitische Märtyrer*, 61–71. These pages contain the excerpts from Jakob Letkemann.

7 Microfiche document EWZ 50 E084 0396 (Russia) with the last name beginning with "L" – dated January 22, 1944. Mennonite Historical Society, Abbotsford B.C.

8 Karl Stumpp, 28–29. Also, historian Dr. Bruce Guenther has provided information concerning the chronology of events.

9 Dnipropetrovs'k (Dnepropetrovsk), later known as Ekaterinoslav, was the first urban centre where Mennonites settled (five families) in 1804. These Mennonites built at least three large flour mills, one of which is still operating today. It was the second city in Russia to have streetcars.

10 From Maria Letkemann's family Bible.

Father: Peter Siemens, born May 24, 1861

Mother: Katherina Leidyn (Leiding), born November 11, 1863

Son: Peter, February 25, 1889 (*Verband* – exiled)

Son: Johann, March 4, 1891–March 8, 1916

Daughter: Tina, November 12, 1893–November 1931

Daughter: Maria, October 29, 1895

Daughter, Helena, May 6, 1897–March 1919

Son: Daniel, August 15, 1899– ?

Daughter: Anna, November 18, 1901–?

Daughter: Liese, February 22, 1902–?

Son: David, December 22, 1903 (*Verband* – exiled)

11 Microfiche Document EWZ 50 E084 0396, Abbotsford Mennonite Historical Society.

12 Joseph Pearce, *Solzhenitsyn: A Soul in Exile* (Grand Rapids: Baker Books, 1999), 10.

13 J.B. Toews, *Pilgrimage of* Faith: *The Mennonite Brethren Church in Russia and North America, 1860–1990*, 149. Toews' chapter, "In the Shadow of the Russian Revolution" provides a summary of this time.

14 Maria Letkemann, untitled poem, stanza 7, translated from German by Dora Dueck. In German the poems rhyme.

15 Dietrich Neufeld, *Russian Dance of Death*, translated by Al Reimer (Winnipeg: Hyperion Press, 1977), 130. Machnov eventually fled to Romania, Poland, then France and died in Paris in 1934. As a note of interest, tour guides in Ukraine state that Ukrainian history is still in progress and it is not well known about the massacres in the former Mennonite communities. To the newly independent Ukraine, Machnov may be viewed as a "Robin Hood" figure as they seek cultural heroes. Jewish history of the Ukraine also records attacks on Jewish settlements by Machnov and his bandits (e.g. Jewish Holocaust Museum, Paris).

16 Adina Reger and David Plett, *Diese Steine* (Winnipeg: Crossway Publications, 2001), 44. Linda Buhler is the granddaughter of David. See Chapter 2, note 4.

17 Rudy P. and Edith E. Friesen, *Building on the Past: Mennonite Architecture, Landscape and Settlements in Russia/Ukraine* (Winnipeg: Raduga Publications), 433.

18 This happened most notably in the Volga region, the region where Jakob and Maria's colony was situated. Alexandr Solzhenitsyn recorded this in *The Gulag Archipelago, Vol. I* (Book Club Associates, 1974), 342.

19 Gerhard Lohrenz, *Heritage Remembered: A Pictorial Survey of Mennonites in Prussia and Russia* (CMBC Publications, 1974), 259.

20 Marlene Epp, *Women without Men: Mennonite Refugees of the Second World War* (Toronto: University of Toronto Press, 2000), 21.

21 Epp, 21.

22 From the author's personal notes of a lecture given by Marlene Epp, August 5, 2005, reading from *The Diary of Anna Baerg, for years 1916–1926 and 1959*, trans. Clara K. Dyck in 2 vols. (Manitoba, 1977).

23 Roman Serbyn, *The First Man-made Famine in the Soviet Union.* www.ukrweekly.com/oldarchive/1988/458814.shtml (accessed August 4, 2008).

24 Roman Serbyn, website.

25 Jakob Letkemann. Mennonites wrote letters to their relatives and friends in Canada and the United States. C.F. Klassen and B.H. Unruh, among others, surveyed the Mennonite settlements and were instrumental in soliciting and organizing relief aid from America. They met with a delegate from American Mennonite Relief, and formed the beginning of what is now known as the Mennonite Central Committee (MCC).

26 Joseph Pearce, 13.

27 Roman Serbyn, website.

28 Pearce, 13.

29 Francis Haller, "Famine in Russia: The Hidden Horrors of 1921." *Le Temps on the Web*, August 12, 2003. Document printed from the website of the ICRC. www.icrc.org/wev/eng/siteeno.nsf.htm/5RHJY (accessed August 4, 2008).

30 "Famine in the Soviet Union, 1912–22 – Photographs and Postcards" www.artukraine.com/famineart/russie.htm (accessed August 5, 2008).

31 Pearce, 14.

32 Dietrich Neufeld, *Russian Dance of Death*, 131.

33 William Schroeder and Helmut T. Huebert, *Mennonite Historical Atlas, 2nd Edition* (Winnipeg: Springfield Publishers, 1996), 123.

34 Rudy P. and Edith E. Friesen, *Building on the Past*, 435.

35 Helmut T. Huebert, *Events and People: Events in Russian Mennonite History and the People that Made them Happen* (Winnipeg: Springfield Publishers, 1999), 201.

36 Huebert, *Events and People* 193.

37 Huebert, *Events and People*, 201.

38 I have relied on information available to date. However, at the time of this writing, Ruth Dirksen Siemens has published her extensive research concerning the fate of those Mennonite people who wished to emigrate and were denied exit. Banished to the Gulag, their circumstances are revealed in letters to relatives in Canada and preserved. This collection is the largest corpus of letters from the Gulag known to exist anywhere. Her work is entitled *Remember Us: Letters from Stalin's Gulag* (Kitchener: Pandora Press, 2007).

39 Huebert, *Events and People*, 202.

40 Maria Letkemann, untitled poem, stanza 1 of 4. Translation by Greta (Letkemann) Loeppky.

41 Reference to the White Sea Canal is from Jakob Letkemann's account in *Mennonitische Märtyrer*. For more information on the White Sea Canal and the Gulag, see Anne Nussbaum's *Gulag: A History* (New York: Random House, 2004). See also information on the "White

Sea-Baltic Canal" at http://ner.wikipedia.org/wiki/white-sea-baltic-canal (accessed August 4, 2008).

42 Frederick Buechner, *Listening to Your Life*, ed. George Connor (New York: HarperSanFransisco, 1992), 2.

43 The little boy, son of David, is Daniel Siemens of Gummersbach, Germany, my father's cousin. Grandfather Peter Siemens did not approve of Daniel's step-mother (a Russian woman that David married after his first wife died). Concerned that this step-mother would not take care of Daniel, Siemens removed his grandson Daniel from his step-mother, into his and Katherina's care.

44 In *Mennonitische Märtyrer*, Vol. II, 61–71, Jakob repeats an account from his brother-in-law Daniel Siemens who was interrogated and arrested, but not beaten after providing authorities with a "report" of those involved in this "coup": "Whoever resisted writing such things on paper was beaten with an iron weight or the part that is used in wagons, rolled in paper. My colleague was beaten so badly that his whole back was blue. On the third day he died, blood flowing from his nose and mouth. I was not beaten but was sentenced as a political prisoner."

45 Huebert, *Events and People*, 206.

46 *The Holy Bible, New International Version*, Philippians 2:14.

47 Alexandr Solzhenitsyn, "The Ukrainian Famine was not a genocide", *Globe and Mail*. May 31, 2008. www.theglobeandmail.com (accessed March 6, 2008). Solzhenitsyn writes that the accusation of genocide is a politically motivated accusation by "anti-Russian" circles that has "spun off into the government circles of modern day Ukraine" and cannot be proven. Following the article, there has been an outpouring of letters to the *Globe and Mail* in response.

48 See *Globe and Mail*, May 2008–June 2008. See also Maria Danilova, "Ukraine marks 75 years since Soviet man-made famine: President wants the Holodomor deemed genocide," *Desert Sun*, November 24, 2007. Associated Press article, A2.

49 A.A. Toews, excerpts from Jakob Letkemann.

50 A.A. Toews states these are to be found in the *Redakteur*.

51 Maria Letkemann, untitled poem, stanza 2 of 4.

52 Author's notes of a lecture given by Marlene Epp, August 5, 2005, reading from *The Diary of Anna Baerg*.

❖ Chapter 3 (pp. 77–96)

1 Zaporozhye, an industrial city, was formerly an agricultural village named Alexandrov in the 1920s. The Soviets built a large hydroelec-

tric dam here, but before the dam, there were rapids which made the river difficult to cross. The name *Za Poro* means "beyond the rapids"; *Za poro zhye* means "south of the rapids."

2 Friesen, *Building on the Past.*

3 File #22, *Dorfbericht*, German Village Reports (Rosengart) 1941–1942. Mennonite Historical Society.

4 File #22, German Village Reports (Rosengart) 1941–1942. Mennonite Historical Society

5 Friesen, *Building on the Past*, 185.

6 Author's notes from a lecture given by Marlene Epp, August 5, 2005, reading from *The Diary of Anna Baerg.*

7 Information about the arrests is recorded in File #22.

❖ Chapter 4 (pp. 99–125)

1 I.C.B. Dear and M.R.D. Foote eds., *Oxford Encyclopedia of World War II: Ukraine* (London: Oxford University Press, 2001), 434. See also D. Volkogonov, *Stalin: Triumph and Tragedy.* Translated and edited by Harold Shukman (New York: Grove Weidenfeld, 1991).

2 Neil DeMarco, *The World This Century: Working with Evidence* (London, Collins Education, 1991), 263.

3 File #22.

4 See Harry Loewen, ed., *Road to Freedom: Mennonites Escape the Land of Suffering* (Kitchener: Pandora Press, 2000).

5 Karel C. Berkoff, *Harvest of Despair: Life and Death in the Ukraine Under Nazi Rule* (Cambridge and London: The Belknap Press of Harvard University Press, 2004), 17.

6 File #22. See also Epp, 27.

7 Dear and Foote, 1162. Marlene Epp also provides first-hand testimonies in *Women Without Men*, 27–28.

8 Epp, 27.

9 This Jakob Letkemann was a nephew, the oldest son of Jakob's oldest brother Gerhardt. See Chapter 2, note 4 for family genealogy.

10 Epp, 27. See also Dear and Foote, 1162.

11 Dear and Foote, 1162.

12 Berkoff, 30–31.

13 Berkoff, 20.

14 Berkoff, 32–33.

15 Berkoff, 68.

16 Epp, 31.

17 Berkoff, 226–227.

18 File #22.

19 Berkoff, 196.

20 "The German Volkssturm," in *Intelligence Bulletin*, February 1945. See www.lonesentry.com (accessed August 3, 2008).

21 The congregation was a mix of Brethren and Alliance.

22 Berkoff, 35.

23 The village reports made by Officer Fast were for the German government, perhaps under the direction of Dr. Karl Stumpp. Dr. Stumpp worked for the Ministry of Occupied Eastern Territories. He prepared the lists of names of all the German colonists in the Ukraine, including the migration lists of Mennonites from Danzig. According to H. Schapansky, Dr. Stumpp was mostly interested in non-Mennonites and provided the list of Prussian immigration permits to B.H. Unruh. While Unruh's historical work is specific to Mennonites, Stumpp's work concentrates on Germans who settled throughout Russia, including the Volga Germans.

24 File #22.

25 Dear and Foote, 1162.

26 Michael J. Lyons, *World War II: A Short History*, 3rd ed. (New Jersey: Prentice Hall, 1999), 177.

27 Dear and Foote, 1162.

❖ Chapter 5 (pp. 127–155)

1 Harry Loewen, *Road to Freedom*, 32.

2 Berkoff, 302.

3 Dear and Foote, 1162.

4 Epp, 35.

5 My father tells me that the Russian air force was by this time poorly equipped and that the Allies supplied the Soviet Union with planes.

6 Epp, 43.

7 Berkoff, 303.

8 Peter and Elfrieda Dyck, *Up from the Rubble: The Epic Rescue of Thousands of War-Ravaged Mennonites* (Waterloo: Herald Press, 1991), 90.

9 This detail is a second-generation witness account from Paul Born whose mother survived the train collision and told him how people were scalded from boiling water.

10 Peter and Elfrieda Dyck, *Up from the Rubble*, 90.

11 Microfilm Document for Mennonite Refugees with the last name beginning with "L." From EWZ-50, *Einwanderungszentralstelle (EWZ) Anträge* (Immigration centre applications). See the article by Richard Thiessen, *Mennonite Historical Society of BC Newsletter* 8:3 (2002):1,

3 & 4. Thiessen states this is a collection of records consisting of more than 400,000 applications of ethnic Germans living outside Germany during the period 1939-1945. The applications represent only a fraction of the total number of ethnic Germans from the USSR, Poland, the Baltics, Yugoslavia, France and Bulgaria. There were 110,000 files for ethnic Germans from the USSR (EWZ-50). The U.S. 3rd Army seized the EWZ documents in Bavaria, April 1945. They were part of a much larger SS collection: *Einwanderungszentralstelle* Documents: immigration records of ethnic German re-settled during the Third Reich now available for genealogical research.

12 Jakob uses the name current at the time in 1944, although in 1907 this area was designated "South Russia."

13 Prior to the Revolution, and when Jakob served there, Leningrad was St. Petersburg, as it is again today.

14 Maria has written Kleefeld, although in her funeral records it states Masseiwo.

15 *Enwikipedia Online*, "Bombing of Dresden in World War II" (accessed August 4, 2008).

16 *Enwikipedia Online*, "Bombing of Dresden in World War II."

17 Lyons, 131.

18 P. & E. Dyck, 88-90. In an eyewitness account by Jakob Giesbrecht, Mr. Giesbrecht states: "All this territory was, of course, occupied by the Germans. Now a new danger faced us: the partisans. They were armed farmers and intellectuals who fought against the German occupation. Since the Germans had brought us here, and because we all spoke German, they naturally associated us with them rather than thinking of us as refugees. This made it especially dangerous for our young people and for those who worked on large state-owned farms. Consequently more and more of our people left and tried to move to the city. From there they tried to get to Austria. They settled in the area of Murau, between Salzburg and Graz. Those that stayed behind (about 150) were never heard from again." This story involves some of those who "stayed behind." Others of those who "stayed behind" were repatriated to the USSR or perhaps killed along the way.

19 Bernard Wasserstein, "European Refugee Movements after World War II," *BBC History on the Web* (accessed May 18, 2005).

❖ Chapter 6 (pp. 157-175)

1 "The German Volkssturm," in *Intelligence Bulletin*, February 1945. See www.lonesentry.com (accessed August 3, 2008).

2 Others who were conscripted to the communications unit speak about receiving orders of transfer to a combat unit on the front although they were not trained for armed combat. See "Soldier Boy" in Edith E. Friesen's *Journey to Freedom: A Family's Real Life Drama* (Winnipeg: Raduga Press, 2003).

3 Anne Applebaum, *Gulag: A History* (New York: Anchor Books, Random House, 2003). Photograph — no page given.

4 Lyons, 278.

5 Wasserstein, 1 of 7.

6 Lyons, 131.

7 Wasserstein, 3 of 7.

❖ Chapter 7 (pp. 177–213)

1 Robin Milner-Gulland with Nikolai Dejevsky, *Cultural Atlas of Russia and the Soviet Union* (New York: Facts On File Inc., 1989).

2 Dear and Foote, 936.

3 See Chapter 2, note 4 for family genealogy.

4 Herbert and Maureen Klassen, *Ambassador to His People: C.F. Klassen and the Russian Mennonite Refugees* (Winnipeg: Kindred Press, 1990), 124.

5 All About Kiev Online, www.allabout.kiev.ua/kiev-history.shtml, 2006 (accessed August 4, 2008).

6 Maria Letkemann. Stanza from an untitled poem, translated by Dora Dueck.

7 Deuteronomy 8: 7 & 9.

8 *The Holy Bible, New International Version*, Grand Rapids: Zondervon, 1974.

9 Concerning pacifism, peace-making and non-resistance, historian Dr. Bruce Guenther comments that, repeatedly, during times of war, many Mennonites have taken up arms. Even in times of peace, many Mennonites endorse the use of force in order to restrain those who intend injury to others.

10 Harold S. Bender and Henry C. Smith, eds., *Mennonite Encyclopedia: A Comprehensive Work on the Anabaptist Mennonite Movement, Vol. IV, O–Z.*, (Scottsdale: Mennonite Publishing House and Hillsboro: Mennonite Brethren Publishing House, 1959), 392. See also Frank H. Epp, *Mennonite Exodus: The Rescue and Resettlement of the Russian Mennonites Since the Communist Revolution* (Published for Canadian Mennonite Relief and Immigration Council: Altona, Manitoba by D.W. Friesen Printers, 1962).

Select Bibliography

❖

In addition to the sources cited in the text, the works listed below include the sources of the epigraphs appearing in the preface, introduction, chapters, and afterword. Works not directly quoted, but that have substantiated my father's memories, or that have particularly influenced and informed my ideas about narrative and memory are included. Along with scholarly research and essays and memoir, poetry and fiction are also listed here.

Applebaum, Anne. *Gulag: A History*. New York: Anchor Books, Random House, 2003.

Bender, Harold S. and Henry C. Smith, eds. *Mennonite Encyclopedia: A Comprehensive Work on the Anabaptist Mennonite Movement, Vol. IV, O–Z*. Scottsdale: Mennonite Publishing House and Hillsboro: Mennonite Brethren Publishing House, 1959.

Berkoff, Karel C. *Harvest of Despair: Life and Death in the Ukraine under Nazi Rule*. Cambridge and London: The Belknap Press of Harvard University Press, 2004.

Birdsell, Sandra. *The Russländer*. Toronto: McClelland & Stewart, 2001.

Buechner, Frederick. *The Sacred Journey: A Memoir of the Early Days*. New York: HarperSanFransisco, 1982.

——. *Longing for Home: Recollections and Reflections*. New York: Harper Collins, 1996.

——. *Now and Then: A Memoir in Vocation*. New York: HarperSanFransisco, 1991.

——. *Listening to Your Life*, ed. George Connor. New York: HarperSan Fransisco, 1992.

Cornwall, Claudia. *Letters From Vienna: A Daughter Uncovers her Family's Jewish Past*. Vancouver: Douglas McIntyre, 1995.

Dear, I.C.B. and M.R.D. Foot eds. *Oxford Encyclopedia of World War II: Ukraine*. London: Oxford University Press, 2001.

DeMarco, Neil. *The World This Century: Working with Evidence*. London, Collins Education, 1991.

Dyck, Cornelius J. *Introduction to Mennonite History, 3rd ed.* Pennsylvania: Herald Press, 1993.

Dyck, Peter and Elfrieda. *Up from the Rubble: The Epic Rescue of Thousands of War-Ravaged Mennonites*. Waterloo: Herald Press, 1991.

Eksteins, Modris. *Walking Since Daybreak: The Story of Eastern Europe, World War II and the Heart of our Century*. Toronto: Key Porter Books, 2000.

Epp, Frank H. *Mennonite Exodus: The Rescue and Resettlement of the Russian Mennonites since the Communist Revolution*, Altona, Manitoba D.W. Friesen. 1962. Published for Canadian Mennonite Relief and Immigration Council.

Epp, Marlene. *Women without Men: Mennonite Refugees of the Second World War*. Toronto: University of Toronto Press, 2000.

Frankl, Viktor E. *Man's Search for Meaning*. New York: Pocket Books, Simon and Schuster, 1984.

Friesen, Rudy P. and Edith E. *Building on the Past: Mennonite Architecture, Landscape and Settlements in Russia/Ukraine*. Winnipeg: Raduga Publications.

Heschel, Abraham J. *Who is Man?* Stanford: Stanford University Press, 1965; 2005.

Hoffmann, Eva. *Lost in Translation*. New York: Penguin Books, 1989.

Huebert, Helmut T. *Events and People: Events in Russian Mennonite History and the People that Made them Happen*. Winnipeg: Springfield Publishers, 1999.

Kasdorf, Julia. *The Body and the Book: Writing from a Mennonite Life*. Baltimore, Johns Hopkins University Press, 2001.

Kearney, Richard. *On Stories*. New York: Routledge, 2002.

Klassen, Herbert and Maureen. *Ambassador to His People: C.F. Klassen and the Russian Mennonite Refugees*. Winnipeg: Kindred Press, 1990.

Kozhina, Elena. *Through the Burning Steppe: A Wartime Memoir 1942–1943*. New York: Penguin Putnam, 2000.

Kulyk Keefer, Janice. *Honey and Ashes: A Story of Family*. Toronto: Harper Collins, 1998.

Letkemann, Peter. "The Descendants of Peter Letkemann," chapter excerpt, *unpublished manuscript*, Winnipeg, 1988.

Loewen Harry, ed. *Road to Freedom: Mennonites Escape the Land of Suffering*. Kitchener: Pandora Press, 2000.

Lohrenz, Gerhard. *Heritage Remembered: A Pictorial Survey of Mennonites in Prussia and Russia*. CMBC Publications, 1974.

Lyons, Michael J. *World War II: A Short History*, 3rd ed. New Jersey: Prentice Hall, 1999.

Mays, John Bentley. *Power in the Blood: An Odyssey of Discovery in the American South*. Toronto: Penguin Books Canada, 1998.

Michaels, Anne. *Fugitive Pieces: A Novel*. Toronto: McClelland & Stewart, 1999.

Milner-Gulland, Robin with Nikolai Dejevsky. *Cultural Atlas of Russia and the Soviet Union*. New York: Facts On File Inc., 1989.

Milosz, Czeslaw. "A Poem for the End of the Century" *Provinces: Poems 1987-1991*. Translated by the author and Robert Hass. New York: Ecco Press, 1991.

Neufeld, Dietrich. *Russian Dance of Death*. Translated by Al Reimer. Winnipeg: Hyperion Press, 1977.

Pearce, Joseph. *Solzhenitsyn: A Soul in Exile*. Grand Rapids: Baker Books, 1999.

Reger, Adina and David Plett. *Diese Steine*. Winnipeg: Crossway Publications, 2001.

Ricoeur, Paul. *Memory, History, Forgetting*. Translated by Kathleen Blamey and David Pellauer. Chicago: University of Chicago Press, 1990.

——. *Time and Narrative Vol. I*. Translated by Kathleen McLaughlin and David Pellauer. Chicago: University of Chicago Press, 1990.

Schapansky, Henry. "The Early Letkemanns," *The Mennonite Historian* Vol. XV No. 4 (Dec. 1989).

——. Book Review of *Die niederländisch-niederdeutschen Hintergründe der mennonitischen Ostwanderungen im 16., 18. und 19. Jharhundert* in *Mennonite Family History*, October 1989.

——. *The Old Colony (Chortiza) of Russia: Early History and the First Settlers in the Context of the Mennonite Migrations*. Manitoba: Country Graphics and Printing, 2001.

Schroeder, William and Helmut T. Huebert. *Mennonite Historical Atlas*. Winnipeg: Springfield Publishers, 1996.

Solzhenitsyn, Alexandr. *The Gulag Archipelago, Vol. I* Book Club Associates, 1974.

Sontag, Susan. "The Artist as Exemplary Sufferer" *Against Interpretation and Other Essays*. New York: Farrar Straus and Giroux, 1966.

Snyder, Arnold C. *Anabaptist History and Theology*. Kitchener: Pandora Press, 1995.

Steiner, George. *Language and Silence: Essays on Language, Literature and the Inhuman*. New York: Atheneum, 1967.

Stumpp, Karl. *The Emigration from Germany to Russia in the Years 1763 to 1862*. Lincoln: American Historical Society of Germans in Russia, 1982: 3rd printing, 1993.

Toews, Aaron A., *Mennonitische Märtyrer, Band 2: Der Grosse Leidensweg*. Winnipeg: The Christian Press, 1954.

Toews, J.B. *Pilgrimage of Faith: The Russian Mennonite Brethren Church in Russia and North America 1860-1990*. Winnipeg: Kindred Press, 1993.

Unruh, Benjamin H. *Die niederländisch-niederdeutschen Hintergründe der mennonitischen Ostwanderungen im 16., 18. und 19. Jahrhundert*. Selbstverlag (self published): Karlsruhe, 1955.

van Braght, Thieleman J. *Marytrs Mirror: The Story of Seventeen Centuries of Christian Martyrdom from the Time of Christ to A.D. 1660*. Also titled *Martyrs Mirror of the Defenseless Christians who Baptized only upon Confession of Faith and Who Suffered and Died for the Testimony of Jesus, Their Savior, From the Time of Christ to the Year A.D. 1660*. Translated from the original Dutch by Joseph F. Sohm. 24th printing. Scottsdale PA and Waterloo Ont: Herald Press, 2002.

Volkogonov, D. *Stalin: Triumph and Tragedy*. Translated and edited by Harold Shukman. New York: Grove Weidenfeld, 1991.

Wiesel, Elie. *All Rivers Run to the Sea: A Memoir*. New York: Schocken Books, 1994.

——. *One Generation After*. New York: Random House, 1970.

——. *From the Kingdom of Memory*. New York: Schocken Books, 1990.

Wiebe, Rudy. *Sweeter Than All the World*. Toronto: Alfred Knopf, 2001.

Woolf, Virginia. *Moments of Being: A Collection of Autobiographical Writing*. Ed. Julie Schulkind. New York: Harcourt, 1985.

Index

ABOUT THE AUTHOR

❖

Connie Braun was born and raised in the Fraser Valley, in the community of Clearbrook, now Abbotsford. Of Mennonite heritage, Braun is part of the second generation of a family that survived Stalinist Communism, and was forced to flee Soviet Ukraine. Because of the traumatic nature of her family's experience in Europe and the will to begin anew, their story remained largely unknown and unrecorded. With a growing interest in the importance of story as a means to create understanding between generations of the "old world" and the "new," and between those whose experiences have vastly differed, Braun has focused in her academic work on the narrative voice within marginalized immigrant writing. Of particular interest to Braun is how writing may function as second-generation witness to those who experienced history's disasters and ensuing displacement. Her creative work has appeared in *Half in the Sun: Anthology of Mennonite Writing*, and in the Mennonite literary magazine, *Rhubarb*. She has also published papers in academic journals, as well as short stories, poems and reviews in various publications. Braun now lives in Vancouver with her husband and children.

Marquis Book Printing Inc.

Québec, Canada
2008